DIPLOMAT TO THE GALAXY

Confessions of a UFO Dingbat

Written by

Glenda S. Pliler

Dedication

For global awakening

THE EDGE, there is no honest way to explain it
because the only people who really know where it
is are the ones who have gone over.

— *Hunter S. Thompson*

CONTENTS

PREFACE

In *Henderson the Rain King*, Saul Bellow wrote that "truth comes in blows." That was how I learned that extraterrestrials exist, by having my worldview rattled and jolted into reluctant expansion. Changes came in graceless, resistive steps, with occasional quantum leaps up a gravitational wormhole or down a conspiratorial rabbit hole. I wasn't the kind of dingbat who ordinarily looked for stuff like this but I didn't have a choice. The mystery came to me. At first, I resented having to deal with it. Now, after years of being stymied and stonewalled by conflicting opinions and theories and having sorted through mounds of misinformation, rumors, and denials, here I am, writing this memoir. It's been a strange story. I've been faithful to the facts but sometimes I've had to tinker with how I told it in order to make a readable book. Likewise, I changed most of the names to protect innocent and guilty alike.

Old-timers tell me my story is their story too. They usually focus on technical facts rather than addressing the issue of how it *feels* to awaken in a time when the majority ignore, deny, or even ridicule the existence of extraterrestrials. Like them, I began by thinking that anyone who believed in such stuff had to be mentally imbalanced. When I saw a UFO for the first time, I dismissed it as a non sequitur. I didn't even recall it until this book was nearly finished. I'd been packing my car to leave Fairfield, Iowa, in 1997 when a gleam of light got my attention. I looked up to see the sun reflecting from a fat disk so high up that no details were visible. Wondering if the crazies who believed in such things might have been right, I'd felt a sudden thrill of horror.

But the gleam didn't do anything. It just hung there. I watched it do nothing until my neck hurt. Even though it appeared metallic, I finally dismissed it as a trick of the light, went back to packing and forgot it. That's what I do. If I can't solve questions, I go into denial. Now I wonder if dismissing it was like the early researcher who, attempting to get hydrogen to absolute zero, stopped his experiment when the substance began to boil. Not knowing the boiling was a purification stage, he quit the experiment. Had he just stayed the course one degree further, he would have discovered superfluid. Was it like that for me? Had I waited just a bit longer, would I have seen that light fly off, thus leaving no doubt that spacecraft exist? It would have made things so much easier for me to have known all along. Looking back, I think that light in the sky was a portend. I didn't know it then, but that was the day this story began.

Chapter

1

AHA!

Aha! Don't you just love eurekas, peak moments, and epiphanies when pieces fall together and, suddenly, you get it? But this was not an aha! It was an oh no. It was a heart-stopping, bone-chilling, breath-sucking oh no. While I was preparing lunch on a bitterly cold day in the spring of 2005, the old mystery surfaced. I didn't pay it any attention. I'd given up trying to solve it so it had become no more than the chitchat the mind finds to entertain itself with as it wanders from thing to thing like a child left unattended. But then... oh dear God. With no warning buzzer, no screech from a jump across record grooves, no posted sign to warn me that I was nearing a precipice—memories collided and my mind popped open like a soda can. All the parts and pieces snapped into place and I could almost see Tom shaking his head as if to say, "I told you so." Why, why do all these crazy things keep happening to me? Had I come full circle and still failed to understand this mystery? Or was this the answer I'd been looking for all along and I just didn't want to believe it?

***

Back in 1997, I expected that leaving Fairfield was simply the next step in well-thought-out plan. Fairfield was home to Maharishi International University (MIU) and to thousands of people who practice Transcendental Meditation (TM). I graduated from there with a bachelor's in Western philosophy, and then a master's. Between times, I'd worked on staff and on projects for world peace. More recently I'd been working on a Ph.D. in psychology and I'd been doing so well. TM increases intelligence and overall abilities so by age 52, I'd overcome enough handicaps that I was poised for late-life success. I'd landed a contract to write a book using the same research needed for my dissertation. If the book did well, it would pay for my schooling and launch me into a career as a respectable expert. Cool, huh? I was so proud of myself. Neither of my parents had even graduated from high school.

The problem was that I needed money. To get it, I intended to sell my former home in Joplin, Missouri. But, as John Lennon said, "Life is what happens while you are making other plans." While waiting for the sale, I fell off a neighbor's horse, fracturing my spine and messing up my hip. It left me unable to sit upright for more than an hour and my productive, service-oriented life crashed to a dead halt. I had to drop out of the Ph.D. program and pass the book deal on to another writer. Over the next two years, unable to work and with dwindling savings, I plummeted into despair. In a cross between a whine and a prayer, I'd limp up and down my tiny trailer asking over and over, *What should I do now? What should I do now?* One day I heard an angelic voice in my head say, "Well, what do you *want* to do?"

Hearing that voice wasn't schizophrenic. After years of practicing TM, sometimes a gently guiding voice was how answers came. Even so, I couldn't have been more startled. My gratification in life had come from seeking enlightenment and working for world peace while dreaming of greater contributions as an author and authority. Outside of those goals, a personal *want* seemed frivolously unimportant.

It took about two weeks after hearing the voice to realize that my bones had been sending me clues all along, in the guise of memories of sun and sand. Back in the hippie days, I'd traveled around Florida in a VW van with my dog, Daffy. A year later I did Navy boot camp in Orlando, followed by training school in the Florida Keys. Yes, I know that "hippie" and "boot camp" hardly belong in the same paragraph but I've always been an odd mix of stubborn and flexible. When I can be nudged off my fixed position long enough to see things through a different lens, I'll follow the next set of "vibes." The hippie trip led to an experience of enlightenment, and the enlightenment experience made me realize that I needed to go back to college. To get funds for college, I joined the Navy, specifying a non-combat position. Like that, the way a surfer shifts with changes in the tides, I shifted with the times.

But shifts where we can't see any steps ahead of us, like when you can no longer work, that's hard. When the memories first came of how the air smelled in Florida, of how warm sand felt between my toes, I thought they were just random. Those memories would come and I'd think, "ooh, that was nice." I finally realized those memories were memos. They were how my aching bones were telling me I needed to get away from the cold, to go get some of that healing warmth.

I didn't know what someone formerly dedicated to world peace would find to do in the middle of Florida, but in November of 1999, I moved to Avon Park, a little town about ten miles north of Sebring. It was just the next logical step.

***

To my surprise, where the old life had been full of purpose and meaning, the new life was rich with unexpected pleasures. I found a cottage rundown enough to be affordable on Lake Lotela—800 acres of a lake so clean you could see shells eight feet below the surface. I found a used jet ski at a garage sale and found myself awakening into a life more gratifying than I had thought possible. I fell in love with sunrises and sunsets, balmy breezes and year-round greenery, fits of afternoon rains that cooled the heat and washed the air, fresh avocados from my own tree, and, most pleasurable of all, frequent swims in the curative waters of the lake.

The biggest problem I had, other than pain and poverty, was that I was intellectually bored. Humorist Dave Barry, noting that Florida ranked 47th in intelligence, called it *Flori*-duh. I asked the octogenarian at the desk of the local library where I might find mental stimulation and she suggested I check out Reverend Andy at Unity Church in Sebring. At the mention of church, I hid a frown. I didn't like dogma. I knew that Unity's perspective was more suitable for me but my ex-husband had formal training in Unity teachings. He'd called it, "entry-level metaphysics" and I was well past entry level. Ever since I'd had a direct encounter with enlightenment three decades earlier, I'd been a seeker of wisdom. With the degrees from MIU, extensive meditation retreats, and insatiable reading in both ancient and modern knowledge, I was educated enough that later that year I would teach *Metaphysics* part-time at the local college. It was just natural to assume that I was more educated than the average reverend.

Still, my choices were so limited that when another person praised Reverend Andy, I decided to give it a try.

***

What happened was funny. Who would have dreamed that in a relatively obscure part of Florida, an area whose only claim to fame was oranges, car racing, and burglary, that in a concrete block church on the edge of town, one might find a spiritually advanced minister and such a wonderful group of people as had gathered around him?

While I stood in the entry looking at cheap carpet in an unremarkable interior, an ambiance hit me so powerfully that I felt mildly stunned. I didn't recognize at first that what it was, was love. There was so much of it in that little church that it was palpable. Then I discovered I adored Reverend Andy. He married inspiration and scholarship so well that I was never bored. Hoping for even more stimulation, I joined the adult class that met before Sunday services. Do you see anything in those decisions that suggest it would lead to anything weird? I didn't.

The first morning I stepped down into the add-on classroom that had been built between the sanctuary and the sidewalk, eight or nine people sat around four pushed-together folding tables. A woman dressed in a silk caftan said in a warm tone, "Come have coffee and donuts." This was Joanne. Of all the characters I came to love at Unity of Sebring, I would especially love this woman. Like most of Unity's characters, she'll remain in the background except for key moments but these people were to become the joy of my life. I would say to her that someday I'd have to write a book to tell the world how great she and my dear Unity friends were.

"Just stick to the truth," she said. "Don't make us seem too saintly."

We both laughed but for different reasons. Her laughter affectionately chided me for possibly thinking too highly of them while I was laughing at the irony that the ordinary people who attended this class—retirees, educators, homemakers, secretaries, shopkeepers— were angels unaware. They did indeed have faults. JoAnne was a former alcoholic. Juta's temper was as snappish as a spoiled dog. Mr. Butler, a church board member, was notorious for obstinacy. A few had exotic interests such as the guide who organized expeditions to Bimini, the area Cayce believed Atlantis to rest. Most were ordinary citizens who were there because traditional Christianity had left them unfulfilled. Bertrand Russell might have been referring to them when he said, "What is wanted is not the will to believe, but the wish to find out, which is the exact opposite." Rather than promote some orthodoxy, some fixed way of believing to which they try to convert others, these people were here to discover truth inside themselves. They filled me with inspiration and admiration as I saw them wrestle with new concepts. Mozart wrote, "Neither a lofty degree of intelligence nor imagination nor both together are the making of genius. Love, love, love, that is the soul of genius." I was the best educated in the group but these geniuses were to become my teachers in matters of the heart. I loved and respected all of them with something that bordered on adoration.

All of them, that is, except Tom.

***

"...And this is Tom Banks," Mr. Butler said, making the rounds of introductions. It still strikes me as odd that I, who detested dogmas, and Tom, who seemed so incompatible among that sweet, sincere group, were both there at the same time. But isn't life like that, full of miracles and curses that we do not appreciate until it is too late? How often do we take for granted common marvels such as the patterns of bright and shade that filter through our blinds and ferns and philodendrons, flung on the wall by light that has, in a mere eight minutes, traversed 93 million miles? Likewise, when we experience remarkable timing, we typically don't respond as if we are in the presence of signs and portents; we merely call it coincidence. Was it marvel or coincidence that Tom and I, who were so opposite in so many ways, intersected at Unity of Sebring?

At his introduction, Tom stood up and half-bowed, waving his hand with a flourish as if he had an imaginary plumed hat. In a tone that might have won him a role as the unctuous Uriah Heap in a Dicken's drama, he smiled and said, "Thomas Hershel Banks at your service, Ma'am."

I wasn't proud of my reaction. Years earlier, during precious minutes in a higher state of consciousness, I'd seen that hidden underneath our layers of stress, confusion, and distortions, we are all Divine. That experience had given direction and meaning to life. I became committed to treating others with as much respect as if their divinity was out in the open for all to see. Gandhi expressed this philosophy when he said, "If you don't find God in the next person you meet, it is a waste of time looking for him further."

However, I did not find God in Tomas Hershel Banks. My dislike was instantaneous and intense. Dislike went deeper than his looks but his looks didn't help. I wouldn't say he was as repulsive as Jabba the Hutt, but close. I tried to remind myself that on the other side of the blubber and greasy pleasantries, there existed the beauty and wonder of living Divinity but on his five-foot-six frame, rolls of fat made him look, at first glance, so much like a misshapen, overinflated Michelin Tire Man that it was hard to not laugh. Looking again, seeing how the largest portion of his fat slithered under his belt to spread around his hips like a tutu around a hippo, it was hard to not feel revolted. His hazel eyes were vague and his once-red hair was thin and yellowish, worn in a comb-over. Later he would say to me, "I've always been attractive." Maybe he'd always been in denial, too, I don't know.

Have you heard the saying, that to assume makes an "*ass* out of *u* and *me*"? I made two erroneous assumptions that Sunday. I came consciously expecting that compared to Reverend Andy I might be disappointed in this group when what happened was that they were to become dearer to me than family.

The second assumption was that if I ignored Tom he would fade into the background. His looks suggested fading but he had no intention of disappearing. In the Sundays to come, he would attack me as if I was the very devil… or as if he was.

Chapter

THE COSMIC SPIDER WEAVES A WEB

or texts, the class used whatever books they found inspirational, such as Myrtle Fillmore's book, *How to Let God Help You*, or Neale Donald Walsh's *Conversations with God*. Having few dogmatic restrictions allowed us the freedom to accept or reject ideas while we sought practical applications for our personal lives. The topics were in my areas of passion and expertise so I participated with keen interest. But when I spoke up, Tom—who had only three months of college and appeared to be particularly ill-informed—raked me mercilessly. He reminded me of Isaac Asimov's quote about attitudes shaped by "the false notion that my ignorance is just as good as your knowledge." Clearly, Tom thought his ignorance was every bit as good as my knowledge for no matter what I said, he attacked it with unabashed self-certainty.

"What makes you so sure you know the answer to that?" he'd challenge. Sometimes he wouldn't even bother arguing. He just snorted, "That's ridiculous!"

He was especially cantankerous if I referred to anything related to Maharishi Mahesh Yogi. Maharishi was the man who brought TM to the world and began research on it in 1970, thus beginning the modern meditation trend. Having directly experienced enlightenment, even if only briefly, I was particularly enthusiastic about the lucidity of Maharishi's teachings. But Tom didn't get it. He treated it as if I was selling religion instead of speaking educationally about what amounted to a major medical discovery regarding human consciousness.

For instance, one Sunday someone asked for clarification of what consciousness was.

"Consciousness is how awake our mind-body system is," I said. I explained that, until Maharishi, the study of consciousness had been called metaphysics, meaning 'beyond physics.' Previous descriptions had been so conflicting, scientific researchers couldn't make sense of them. But Maharishi took the mystery out of metaphysics by using Western style explanations, thus providing a foundation so that formal research could begin. "Now we have neurophysiological studies and other evidence that can identify higher states of consciousness."

"What do you mean, 'higher states'?" Mr. Butler asked.

"You're familiar with the term 'mystical experiences,' right?" Plato, Buddha, St. John of the Cross, Hafiz, Thomas Merton, Mother Theresa, and many others from all over the world, had written about them. The problem was that, besides the vast differences, their explanations sounded like religious or intellectual constructs and were often dismissed as imaginary or idealistic. Maharishi solved the riddles, explaining that the reasons for these seeming differences were because the individuals were reporting from different states of consciousness, each of which require different levels of human development. Once such states were defined, the various writings suddenly became clear. This is what science does, it makes sense of things. Because of Maharishi's explanations and the research that began in 1970, we can now talk intelligibly about mysticism as a scientific reality, including identifying what stage of consciousness the mystic was in.

"All of us are familiar with the common states: waking, sleeping, and dreaming," I said. "But Maharishi identified four higher states available to human experience. The fourth state—unknown to science before Maharishi identified it—is called transcendental consciousness. In that state, we aren't conscious of anything except consciousness itself. That's probably what Buddhists call *nothingness*. Then, in the fifth state—"

The others were listening with interest but Tom interrupted. "Why are you always quoting Maharishi? Don't you ever think for yourself?"

Taken aback, I blinked. Even when others disagreed, they did so with courtesy. But not Tom. Tom's responses were nearly always insults. Trying to respond with respect and patience, I said, "Tom, I quote Maharishi as appropriately as I quote Einstein or Aristotle or Jung or Schrodinger. It doesn't mean I can't think for myself; I just point out that minds greater than mine already said it."

"If you thought for yourself you wouldn't have to quote anyone else," he said. I didn't know how to respond. I didn't want to be defensive and tell him that independence had been one of my lifelong characteristics, nor did I think it would be helpful to point out how disrespectful it would be to take credit for others' discoveries. All I could say was, "I quote Maharishi because he's a world authority on consciousness."

"At least you say he is," Tom snapped, woefully ignorant of the facts one way or the other.

Week after week, that's how it was. No matter what I said or who I quoted to back up the concepts, Tom found something to criticize.

Joanne tried to reason with him, politely saying, "When she speaks, she has something useful to say, don't you think?"

But, no, he didn't think so. He just shrugged.

***

Just as Tom's insults were predictable, so were my attempts to overcome my negative feelings toward him. It was like the classic Buddhist story of the monk who kept rescuing the scorpion from death in the river. Every time the monk saved him, the little beast stung him. Another monk asked why he persisted. The first monk said, "It's his nature to sting and my nature to be compassionate." I was committed to responding kindly no matter how badly Tom behaved. In turn, the more I responded kindly, the more he seemed determined to be insulting.

***

I am aware that gossip about happenings in church don't appear to have anything to do with UFOs but be patient. Before we can get into orbit, there needs to be a launch.

One Sunday morning a woman named Anita, said, "I've read that science and religion are opposites and I've also read that they are just different ways of looking at the same thing. Does anyone know the truth?"

When no one spoke up, I told her what I knew, how, in the 1600s, Descartes declared that mind and matter were separate. "Since then, it's been generally believed that Divinity is something *out there*, in some purely mental, moral, or supernatural realm, separated from the physical world and the common person. This is called dualism. Religion based on dualism encourages people to believe that God is a being who lives somewhere in the sky, with humans being set-apart sinners who walk on a merely material Earth."

Quantum physics refutes that approach. It recognizes that nothing can be separate from wholeness. Matter is just dense energy and energy turns out to be the product of consciousness. "This gives us a new way to understand what Christ meant when he said, *the Kingdom of Heaven is within.*" If we go deep enough either from the outside via science or from the inside via meditation and purification, we go down through all the layers of creation until we get to the finest level of materiality—the Planck scale. There we find matter and spirit arising in layers out of a single unmanifest field of consciousness. Objective physics calls this the unified field. If we experience it subjectively, it's called enlightenment. "It's not either/or like Descartes claimed, but multiple levels the way quantum physics says."

A flicker of curiosity lit Anita's eyes, suggesting she was in what Piaget called "the teachable moment."

I was opening my mouth to explain how God fit into this picture when Tom spoke up. "Are you trying to sell Transcendental Meditation?"

I hadn't even mentioned TM. "No. What made you ask?"

"You used the word 'transcend.'"

I reminded myself to be patient. "Tom, the dictionary defines transcendence as 'going beyond.' I'm talking about a natural pro…"

He didn't give me time to finish before he said, "Then why are you promoting it?"

Did he really fail to understand or was he being deliberately obtuse? Such disconnects happened so often I could never be certain. I felt I must be polite and treat his question as if it was sincere. "I do promote transcendence. By whatever means one uses to get there, transcendence is how we reach our inner source. Another name for it might be growth, awakening, or gaining new degrees of personal ability. Transcendence is good for everyone."

Tom scoffed, "There isn't anything good for everyone."

It's not good for everyone to become smarter, happier, healthier, less stressed, and more awake? As someone who spent years overcoming a bad temper, I'd learned to defuse anger before it reached the out-of-control stage. With Tom, however, I found myself frequently crossing the line from self-controlled tolerance to wishing I could yank his comb-over.

That's how it was, Sunday after Sunday. Tom twisted my meanings and asked inane questions that seemed to have no goal other than to distort or discount whatever I said. Often, his challenges were only vaguely related to the subject with each one followed by another silly question until we'd made so many left turns that we were off the freeway and into the wild with no relationship to the original question. Later I'd learn that there's a psychological name for such behavior; it's called railroading—knocking the focus off track. Had I known that concept then I might have handled it better but in those days my sincerity made me the perfect stooge—I fell for it every time.

But if I was never prepared for Tom's attacks, what could have possibly prepared me to think he might have romantic interests in me?

Chapter

3

LEFT TURN INTO ONCOMING TRAFFIC

Sunday morning class was over and we were in the classroom waiting for the main service to begin. Planning to throw my paper cup into the trash can under the tall coffee counter, I found Tom inclined on an elbow. In a voice as breathy as saying, "Want some candy little girl?" he leaned toward me and asked, "How about dinner and a movie?"

I blinked with what was surely a deer-in-the-headlights gawk, then tore my gaze from his washed-out eyes hoping to see someone who could save me. Mr. Butler and his girlfriend, Betty, were still in conversation with Joanne, too occupied to notice my social emergency. The rest had gone into the sanctuary, essentially isolating me with Jabba the Hutt.

Tom, having romantic interests in me? How was this possible? Didn't he detest me even more than I disliked him? Less than an hour ago, like every Sunday morning, hadn't he insulted me yet again? The class had been discussing how Charles and Myrtle Fillmore founded Unity because they believed universal laws had cured her tuberculosis.

"What does universal mean?" Betty asked. Betty knew almost nothing about spirituality yet asked wonderful questions.

This was my kind of conversation so after the class bantered around some personal definitions I spoke up. "It refers to the laws of nature—that which is true for all observers. In science, what is most generalized is—"

Almost as if he'd been lurking for just such an opening, Tom chastised, "Making generalizations is labeling."

For a couple of seconds, I struggled to make sense of what he said, then realized he thought generalized meant stereotyping.

I managed to be courteous. "It doesn't mean 'labeling,' Tom, I said. "Science says that theories that apply to the largest number of people or cells or atoms or whatever are the most universal and are therefore the most likely to be correct. I was trying to explain—"

"Just because you say it doesn't make it true," he said.

I tried to be compassionate rather than get defensive. "You're right Tom; just because I say something doesn't make it true. But it isn't my idea—it's a principle from the philosophy of science. Philosophy of science dates to Aristotle and is still a highly respected discipline today."

He threw up his hands as if I was hopeless. "Whatever."

Now, less than an hour after the attack, he was inviting me to dinner and a movie? Did he think I'd be interested in him romantically? Yes, there it was on his face—the open, confident look of the guy who assumes his attention is flattering.

I opened my mouth to take the easy way out—to lie—to say, "Thanks, I'm busy." I try to not lie, but where he was concerned, would it have been lying if I planned to be busy the rest of my life?

Many people lie because they believe that others are objects, fixed entities like red or blue, boxes or circles, fish or fowl. They either like them or they don't. The people they like, they're nice to. The people they don't like but don't loathe, they pretend to be nice to, and the people they loathe they treat with cold disdain or open sarcasm and feel free to lie to them dismissively because they consider them idiots. But the divine vision had shown me that if we can get deep enough inside anyone's head and heart, he or she is as godly as Jesus or Buddha or Mohamed. Some call this inner divinity, God in embryo, yet-to-be-fulfilled potential. Until it is sufficiently purified and expanded, this greatness is buried under layers of ignorance. Consciousness folds itself over and over again countless times until it no longer recognizes itself; that way, Divinity gets to experience not only the saintly good people but also the thief, the murderer, the prostitute—or the Tom— and thereby experience all actions and all feelings, all consequences of actions and feelings, and all wonder of the subsequent awakenings. It's the great cosmic drama. That is why I tried to treat everyone as a Holy One in disguise because, at our depths, that is precisely who we are.

Sanskrit summarizes this attitude in one word: *Namaste*. You've probably seen Eastern people acknowledge each other with palms flat together and held upright at the level of the heart or forehead. It means "the divine in me greets the divine in you." I've seen this respectful attitude make grand changes. It had happened with Kathy, for instance. A semi-regular at our Sunday classes, she had been treating me coldly as if she had put me into the box of people she detested. When I happened to run into her in the storage room where she was looking for songbooks and I was looking for napkins, I took advantage of the privacy to say, "Kathy, I hope you don't find it offensive that I bring this up but I get the feeling you don't like me. If there's something I can do to make things better, I'd like to try."

The common assumption is that we should be nice on the outside and keep our negative feelings to ourselves except when we gossip behind others' backs or until we finally explode with bottled-up scorn, anger, or resentment. Her eyebrows shot up, and her cheeks flamed but she rose to the occasion. "Since you mention it, there is something that bugs me; I think you're a know-it-all."

I said, "That's an ouch, but yes, I can see that I probably do seem that way. I'm afraid I get so enthusiastic about ideas that I forget to be considerate. Thanks for letting me know how you feel."

Proverbs affirm that "a soft answer turneth away wrath." Not only did my answer put out her fire, but she also valued the spirit of openness so much that we became friends. This is what happens when people feel understood and respected, it opens the doors to real intimacy.

Tom, on the other hand, had such deep layers of defenses and denials that sincere communication simply wasn't possible. I wanted to be honest with him but I couldn't very well say, "Tom, it's not my intention to hurt your feelings but I think I should tell you; I find it hard to like you." He just wouldn't get it. Instead of seeing an honest confession like that as an opportunity to mutually move toward deeper genuineness and understanding, he'd either make a joke out of it or he'd take it as a personal attack. So, if I couldn't lie and I couldn't be honest, how could I respond to his invitation?

At that moment, I wasn't thinking of my two-part aphorism that says, A) All problems have solutions, and B) If you can't find the solution, it means the question needs to be improved. In high-speed analysis of how to handle this situation, an idea popped into my head that met the criteria. Rather than do the obvious and avoid him, maybe what I should do is get to know him better. As I had with Kathy and others, by getting better acquainted with the inner person, might I find something in him to soften my dislike? Some common accord? After all, what was so awful about a meal and a movie—especially if he was paying for it? Hadn't he and I many times sat at the same table with various others in our after-church lunches? If I made it clear that I wasn't interested in romance… That thought gave me a sudden chill. Surely, he wasn't thinking… I instantly closed my mind to that awful mental picture while realizing that I must set clear boundaries.

"Thanks for asking," I said, not quite looking him in the eyes. "If you want to go as church friends, that would be fine. But you do understand that I'm not dating these days, don't you?" I'd spoken often enough about how my ex's abrupt abandonment for another woman had eroded my trust so I thought he could understand. But he didn't appear to even be aware of the obvious, that I might not like him because of his brazen attacks on me.

"I get it," he said, waggling his eyebrows. "You think I'm too short and…" He ended it there. I didn't like that. It felt like an attempt to guilt-trip, to squeeze out a denial that I found his weight gross.

Amma, the "hugging saint," flashed into mind. Amma has hugged upwards of 30 million people, blessing them, giving each a moment of feeling genuinely cared for. She didn't just embrace the clean, nicely dressed, pretty ones but also the unwashed, the disabled, the distorted, the stinky sweaty ones… and the repulsively obese. She knew that inside all these unwashed bodies were divine souls. Wasn't it the least I could do to accept Tom as a dinner partner?

But being genuine was also part of being spiritual. Just as it would be unkind to blurt out that I didn't like his blubber, it would be another form of dishonesty to buy into his manipulation, to gloss it over by saying, "Oh, no, of course not, you look just fine." In the rapid weighing of options, the best I could do was to smile and say, "Don't take it personally. Where do you have in mind to eat?"

***

That was how it began, mine and Tom's weird, dysfunctional "friendship." I'd hoped getting to know him better would lead to kinder feelings and deeper understanding but all that happened was that our arguments in church expanded into arguments in restaurants, at his house or mine, on the lake in my paddleboat, in his gift shop as he sorted greeting cards, or standing in line at the movie box office. Neither of us was given to the avoidance of hot topics; we launched boldly where polite couples dare not go, to politics, religion, communication or lack thereof, and quite often, TM, which Tom (who never listened to my explanations) labeled a cult. Sometimes we—at least I—even reached the door-slamming stage. The intensity of my dislike trapped me into feeling morally obligated to overcome it, to reach the universal love and compassion I'd dedicated my life to achieving with all humans. I would have settled for at least enough evenness that inane arguments, anti-meditation jabs, and his passionate but pathetically uneducated political views no longer disturbed my emotional equilibrium.

But it was an infinity loop — *Groundhog Day* without the happy ending. The more I knew him, the more I found to dislike; the more I disliked him, the more obligated I felt to overcome it. I felt like the robot in the sci-fi book Dune. Circling a stranded human, the robot was caught between two of its prime directives—to 1) protect humans, and 2) allow no harm to itself. It was imperative to rescue a human but to attempt the rescue would put the robot in danger. All it could do was to circle about fifty feet away, unable to move closer yet unable to abandon him. Like the robot, I found myself trapped, unable to succeed yet unable to get out.

When it's obvious that two people are so incompatible, walking away is the smart thing to do. Unfortunately, our belonging to the same close-knit Sunday class made interaction all but unavoidable. During the week I might become so frustrated that I determined to call off our sicko association. But then, on Sunday, in the presence of my beloved friends setting examples as sincere seekers of Truth, I was reminded that my job was to be compassionate and loving. What could I do but recommit to the goal? What tightened the handcuffs was that, alternating with our heated arguments, Tom would sometimes show bright promise to values I lived by.

"I really like your idea of a *Namaste* relationship," he said. *Namaste* relationship was the name I'd given to the idea that anyone who was committed enough could work through the illusions, denials, poor communication, and other faults all unenlightened people have— errors that distort reality and cause problems—to rise to the level of Divine love. It's a platonic reflection of the ancient tantric concept that those who develop the requisite skills could experience the living Shiva (masculine principle) and Shakti (feminine principle) come to life within themselves. In contrast, to see the negative in others is an indication that one's vision is functioning at a lower and more flawed level of consciousness. By this standard, seeing the negative in Tom meant that it was I who needed to improve, who needed to learn acceptance, further driving my need to overcome.

Do you see the trap? Fortunately, a person's worst faults often become their greatest virtue. Even though I was still easily irritated I had it under control because, once I conquered wrath, compassion became my best feature. TM and therapy had taught me that, instead of using critical sarcasm, insults, and ad hominem scorn common in my family of origin, I could defuse and heal problems. For instance, instead of calling the cops to "solve" the problem of the neighborhood teens who played their music so loud it rattled my windows, I approached them with respect, communication skills, and sympathy for their needs. I trusted in their abilities to change and grow. Likewise, I had faith that Tom had the potential to change and grow. But I was astonished when he expressed interest in namaste relationships. Did he really want to learn to be fair, reasonable, and understanding? "Let's read about those ideas and discuss them," he said. I beamed, feeling a near-love that he showed interest in one of my favorite topics.

But it didn't work like that.

One evening, sitting together on my sunny yellow sofa, I read aloud a passage about working through issues.

"What does that mean, work through issues?" Tom asked, frowning.

"It means that we need to bring differences into the open and then work them out," I said. "That's the way to resolution."

"I don't think differences should be aired," he said. "Why focus on the negative?"

Was it possible that he was oblivious to how freely and insultingly he aired his differences with me?

"Tom, it doesn't mean that we focus on negativity; it means that we communicate our honest feelings and perspectives in respectful ways to find solutions; that way, we develop a deeper understanding for each other."

He waved his hand dismissively. "I think we should just play nice," he said. "Why get into disagreements in the first place?"

As I tried to reason through to the man who disagreed with practically everything I said, my voice sounded strained. "Because, Tom, there's no way to avoid disagreements. Disagreements naturally arise in relationships."

"I always try to make myself agreeable," he responded, his confident tone leaving no doubt he believed what he was saying.

Hoping that I could reach him using "I" statements and speaking in terms of feelings and needs, I said, "Tom, if we are to communicate successfully, I need more authenticity, more depth, not superficial acceptance."

He shrugged. "Aren't we supposed to be accepting, no matter what?"

That was when I realized that his idea of *namaste* relationships was not working through the challenges to reach harmony, only blind acceptance. But that way was impossible. Acceptance was great in the global sense of accepting the whole person, but merely one-dimensional in the details, a matter of repressing feelings rather than evolving through them. With his method, it took maybe two or three exchanges before I was gritting my teeth. By five or six, I was shouting, "Tom Banks, this is so frustrating! Go home!"

Then, typically, Tom would call the next day and (if he referred to it at all) would say (with no hint of actual apology), "It's too bad we quarreled. Want to have lunch?" Usually, it was me, regretful that I had failed in my spiritual mission, who apologized. "I'm sorry I lost my temper. Hopefully, I can do better next time."

How could I be such an idiot? I've heard relationships like this described as demon lovers, where one can neither escape nor win peace. A psychologist would have diagnosed it as a dysfunctional co-dependency. A lot of marriages are like that, frustrating and unsatisfying with the conditions being unsolvable at the status quo level but still too much a habit to let go. In the case of me and Tom, it was like a belt sander that had the sandpaper worn smooth on one side. When we hit the smooth side I'd think, Wow! I've succeeded in overcoming my dislikes and Tom is finally learning communication skills; this could work! But then it would hit the grit again and new arguments would burst out. Later, just when I was ready to acknowledge that it was hopeless and the better part of wisdom would be to end it, it would hit the smooth section that left me back in the hopeful stage.

I was trapped.

I assumed our relationship served as a stand-in until one or both of us found a significant other. To leave ourselves open to this latter possibility, we agreed we wouldn't tell our Unity friends about our seeing each other. After my saintly claim that I always tried to be honest, I suspect the hypocritical reason for agreeing to this deception was because I would have been mortified if others knew I saw Tom socially. As often as he criticized me both in public and in private, I assumed he felt the same way.

Looking back, I've wondered what planet I was from that I assumed so much.

Chapter

4

HALF WHAT?

W hat could have prepared me for what happened next? It was maybe a couple of months after we began seeing each other. We were having a late weekday lunch at Ruby Tuesdays in Sebring. Most of the customers had already left, the dust motes in the afternoon sunlight settling into a gradual drift while we sat sipping the last of our coffee.

I have no idea what we were talking about before Tom dropped the bomb. This kind of memory loss, known as traumatic amnesia, commonly happens to accident victims in that they can't recall what happened just before the crash. Whatever the topic, I'd said something that apparently provided him with a segue.

"What do you mean, I 'don't understand the truth?'" I asked, failing to grok how he, the uneducated, not-quite-bright guy could challenge me on the issue of truth. "The truth about what?"

"The truth about who you are," he said.

Searching for patience, I stared at him. "Tom, I can't believe you said that. I've been meditating for nearly 30 years; I've had the most enlightening education available anywhere in the world, and I spent three years in intense therapy. Wouldn't you think by now I have a pretty good understanding about who I am?"

He shrugged. "You don't know everything."

I challenged back. "I know myself better than you know yourself."

He stopped twirling the toothpick and stared at me intently as if he was considering what he was going to say next. "I'm really not supposed to tell you, but I think you need to know."

"Need to know what?"

In movies, they give you warning. The music hypes up, the drone of planes or the thwacking of helicopters gets more intense, the ticking of the clock attached to the bomb gets louder, the red-alert sirens go off, lights flash, or people scramble for cover shouting "Incoming! Incoming!" But all I had was Florida blue sky, the hum of conversation between staff as they refilled the salad bar, and muffled laughter coming from the other dining room. What possible preparation could there have been for what he said next?

"That you're an alien."

In a booth at Ruby Tuesdays on a sunny Florida afternoon, an over-inflated Michelin Tire Man had just told me I was an alien.

"An alien," I parroted. Somehow, I knew he didn't mean a non-American alien who'd sneaked across the border, but a space alien.

He pushed his coffee cup aside and shifted in his seat to lean intimately—or conspiratorially, I couldn't tell which—to say, "Yes. You're half Deneb and half Eloysian."

I stared at him, confounded. Cars whizzed by outside on Highway 27 coming and going from Miami; inside, the bus boy was sweeping the entry and the hostess was tidying menus. Ordinary life with ordinary expectations filled the world as far as the eye could see but the space inside our red booth had suddenly become the *Twilight Zone*.

"We need your help," Tom said. "There's a war. The Eloysians are peaceful but the Deneb do really bad things to them. You're half-and-half so you can understand both sides." He leaned back, looked into my eyes, and in a perfectly normal voice, said, "You can get them to stop."

Incongruity is the basis for jokes, and what could be more incongruous than a short, fat, bald man telling a middle-aged woman with a limp that she was a half-breed space alien who needed to stop an interplanetary war? Laughter—more like high-pitched staccato squealing—bolted out of me. The sound wasn't like shared laughter when you've just heard a good joke but whoops so spontaneously contemptuous that it made me cringe. Normal people don't say things like that! While I struggled to get myself under control, the sane part of my mind scanned his face looking for explanatory clues.

I was raised with practical jokers and tall-tale tellers. I was savvy that jokesters usually have subtle merriment in their eyes, little crinkles in the corners, faint quivers around the mouth, or at the very least, an indecipherable veiled look like the ones worn by comedians who keep straight faces while the audience is going crazy with hilarity.

But I saw no meaningful tells on Tom's face. He looked directly at me, seemingly guileless. Was he so completely out of his mind that it was beyond my capacity to spot? I didn't think so. Most of us can identify people like that. I remember one guy, a grizzled, booze-reeking street bum who'd sat down next to me on a bus. I was in the navy at the time. The military transport I was supposed to catch in Virginia had been overloaded so I was traveling to New York to catch a commercial flight back to Iceland, where I was stationed. This old man unfolded a US area code map that he'd ripped out of a telephone book. Pointing to it, he said he had been in every one of the continental states except two,

Delaware and New Jersey. His reason for being on the bus was to visit those final two states before he died. I admired his determination but it didn't take long to recognize that he was a paranoid schizophrenic. A few miles down the road, he told me, "The FBI is watching me."

"How do you know that?" I asked, trying to break through the smell of stale sweat and alcohol to see him as a divine expression of God who was simply lost in samsara.

"Because I can feel them," he said, tapping his head. "They have TV cameras watching me everywhere I go."

"TV cameras?" I had heard about people like him, but this was my first encounter with someone certifiable.

"Yeah. They watch me from the FBI station in California," he said. "I can't do anything they don't see."

Not knowing what else to say, I just nodded. After a while he fell asleep or passed out, snoring all the way through his last two continental states.

A few years later, I met another man who appeared to be narcissistic with delusions of grandeur. He didn't quite claim to be Christ, but he openly stated that he was among the chosen, placed on Earth to save mankind. "Anyone who doesn't follow me is a fool," he'd said. Maybe I was a fool but I didn't follow him. I got into my car and left.

Tom didn't appear as extreme as those guys. He looked normal, as deadpan as if he'd only been talking about his business. He stared at me and said, "I know, it sounds crazy."

"It certainly does sound crazy." I snickered. "What a joke!"

"It isn't a joke," he insisted. "We need you."

Sandwiched between uncontrollable laughter and gasps for air, the best I could do was to say, "Yeah, I'm a diplomat to the galaxy, right? Just waiting to give the orders to save the day, right?"

Still deadpan, he nodded.

Fresh laughter burst out. "Oh, Tom, that's quite a tale." I wiped my tear-stained cheeks with a napkin.

"I knew you wouldn't believe me," he said.

"Of course, I don't believe you. You surely don't expect me to believe a story like that, do you?"

He didn't respond.

What polite thing can one say in such bizarre circumstances? I reached for my purse and said, "I think it's time to get back home."

Tom laid his hand on my arm. "We need you to make that possible."

Creeped out I stared at him. "Come on, Tom, this isn't funny."

"It wasn't intended to be funny."

"Then what is it supposed to be? What kind of game are you playing?"

"I'm not playing games. I'm only telling it like it is."

I made myself take a deep breath. I sipped some water and tried to think what a respectful, *namaste* response would be. Even if he was totally crazy, it was important—even more important—to be compassionate. This man might be delusional. I almost had a Ph.D. in psychology—how could I have missed the signs?

"If you're serious," I said, "you're going to have to give me details I can understand."

He patted his fingers over his comb-over as if he wanted to make sure everything was battened down for the next onslaught, and took a breath. "What I told you is the truth. War's been going on for decades between two races of extraterrestrials. The Deneb are worse than Klingons. They swoop down on Eloysian villages and destroy everything in their path. We're peaceful but the Denebs are…."

"We?'" My solar plexus and the muscles in my face jerked repeatedly with the threat of another violent fit of laughter. "What do you mean, 'we'?"

His eyebrows shot up as if he was startled. I swear, it looked utterly innocent. "I didn't mean to say that," he said, looking away as if now he didn't know what to do next. "Well, I can't lie now that I've said it. I wasn't supposed to tell you this either, but I admit it—I'm an Eloysian."

If we'd had an audience, this could have been a script for a TV sitcom. Tom would have been the straight man and I would be like Lucy, on *I Love Lucy*, wide-eyed with comical surprise at the ridiculous incongruity. The audience is in on the joke but Lucy is a redhead without a clue. At that moment I'd have paid money to have a script in order to have a clue.

"So let me guess," I said, still alternating between moments of belly-jerk laughter and increasing uneasiness over being unable to make sense of it. "You and I are supposed to team up to fight the Deneb?"

He shrugged. "Something like that," he said. "I haven't been told yet."

I rolled my eyes. Pure B movie. "Come on, Tom. This is absurd. It's not funny." I grabbed my purse again and began scooting out of the booth. "Let's go; I want to get home in time to take a dip in the lake."

"Wait," he said, holding up his hand.

I don't know why but I halted. Did he look vaguely distressed or was that my imagination? "All right. Five minutes; no more, agreed?" I laid my cellphone on the table, tapping the clock on its face. "Then you'll take me home, right?"

He nodded. "I really shouldn't have told you. I thought that if I did it might speed things up and that perhaps I could help you." I couldn't believe his arrogance when he'd said that earlier, much less now. "Just keep an open mind," he finished.

As far as I could tell, my mind was not open at all. I knew that my belief that everyone was ultimately divine sometimes left me naïve, but I wasn't irrational. I didn't buy any of this.

He wiped his forehead with his napkin, took the last sip of his coffee, and began again. "We need you."

I looked around to see if anyone was watching me make a fool of myself by treating this with any seriousness. I leaned forward and said, in an equally conspiratorial tone, "Tom, be reasonable. Why would beings from another planet need anyone on Earth, and why, of all people, would you—they—need me?"

"Because," he said, "it's like I told you. You're half and half."

I couldn't help it. I exploded into another peal of galloping giggles. "Just try to tell my parents that. You think they found me in a crashed spaceship—you know, like Superman—and just forgot to tell me about it?"

Tom made a face almost like I was the one who'd said something stupid. "It's not like that. It isn't that you were born on another planet. Aliens have been mating with Earthlings for a long time. Your genes are half and half—half good, half bad. That's why you're so important, because you're the only one who understands both sides."

Hairs stood up on the back of my neck. What he just said had come closer to home than he could possibly know…or at least I didn't think he could possibly know. Half good, half bad. Black and white. Good and evil. In therapy, I had been told that one of my symptoms was *splitting*, in which one swings from one side to another making life appear either all-good or all-bad. Most people never experience such extremes. After the work integrating those opposites in therapy,

I'd even pondered the possibility I might understand the far ends of light and darkness better than almost anyone. It left me with an exceptionally broad understanding of life.

"If it's in the DNA, then why aren't you talking to my brothers instead of me, men still young enough to be fighters?"

"Because they didn't get the spark."

"Spark? What spark?"

"Haven't you noticed that you aren't like anyone else? Didn't your mother tell you that you're odd?"

Had I told him Mom had said that about me? I didn't think so. Under most circumstances, I avoided confessing to being odd.

"Don't people think you're weird? Where have you ever fit in?"

This had to be a joke, a slick, masterful joke by someone I hadn't believed capable of even a moderate practical joke, much less a preposterous one. Indeed, I'd always been oddball, a weirdo, a person of extremes, a peculiar mix of saint and sinner.

Twenty years earlier, Jim, my therapist, had handed me three pages of typed results from an MMPI test. Thinking that three pages of conclusions couldn't be good, uncertain if I wanted to know more, I was reading slowly. I had only gotten to the second paragraph when I started challenging. "It says here that I am *high on the eight scale*. What does that mean?"

"We have to see the numbers in the context of the whole person," he said. "For some, it would be an indication of schizophrenia but in your case, it's likely an indication of unusual thought processes, perhaps some difficulty concentrating, perhaps social alienation. Probably the best way to summarize it is to say the eight scale it is a measure of unconventionality."

"Unconventionality? What does that mean?"

"Humm, do you know who Gary Larson is, the *Far Side* cartoonist?"

I nodded.

"He's probably pretty high on the eight scale."

He grinned as if with a shared secret, and I got it. Before settling into more serious stuff, he and I typically shared a couple of minutes at the beginning of each session with somewhat unusual but well-matched wits—jokes, puns, and rejoinders. His grin now harked back to that, taking the sting out of being officially decreed to be an oddball.

"How do you know it isn't schizophrenia? I asked.

"Schizophrenia is a thought disorder and we don't see any evidence that you have a thought disorder."

"So, I'm not crazy?"

"No, not crazy. You're not the type to go crazy."

In case you wonder later, remember that—unconventional, yes, but not the type to go crazy.

The reality is unless you live in a war zone or other conditions where one is plagued with the misery of high drama, life consists for the most part of creeping forward on the small, small steps of the ordinary. Research agrees with Tolstoy's view that happy people tend to be more alike while oddballs tend to be, well, odd, out of step. I wanted to be normal and I'd been willing to work for it in therapy. To my disappointment, when I'd worked my way to the other side, I found I was still odd. Just healthier and more balanced. "Unconventional," Jim grinned.

For a fleeting moment in the booth at Ruby Tuesday's, I felt a wistfulness. Wouldn't it be wonderful if Tom's story was true and I might discover that instead of being merely weird, I was someone special? I flushed with pride, or ego, I didn't know which, to think that I might be needed. Instantly I recognized how illusory that was. Me buying his story, even if only briefly, was the last straw. Maybe Tom was nuts but I wasn't going to tolerate such nonsense in myself.

"That's it, Tom. Take me home," I said. "I've had enough of this."

He shrugged. "Suit yourself," he said, drawing out the words as if I'd just lost the prize. Typically, it was me with the temper. Why did he sound cross? The basis of anger is almost always fear. If he was afraid of something, what was it?

I didn't care. I just wanted to get home, away from this madman.

Chapter

5

A BLOT OF MUSTARD

C onversation on the drive to Avon Park consisted mostly of stilted, half-hearted comments about this year's orange crop and the weather that was clouding up for the usual afternoon spurt of rain. My mind bounced off one wall and then another trying to find a landing place for what had just happened. Any legitimate answer would do—that Tom was lying, that he was nuts, even that he was telling the truth. It wasn't that I believed him; indeed, who would believe a tale like that? The real question was, why had he told it? The ridiculous story, his straight face, his solemn demeanor—the whole thing was far enough outside the bounds of the explainable that it stirred cognitive dissonance. In my driveway, before I got out of the car, I asked, "Tom, why did you tell me about this… this story?"

He didn't look at me. He looked straight out the windshield. "I made a mistake telling you. If you want to know more, you'll just have to find out for yourself."

I blinked. How was I supposed to find out more if he wasn't the one to tell me?

Uncomfortable, I got out and walked away, hearing a too-fast crunch on the gravel as he sped away. Strange. It wasn't at all like him to act out irritably like that. Inside the cottage, I slipped out of my sundress and into my bathing suit. I wanted to get into the lake to shake off the weird feelings.

At the shore, I glanced around looking for the beady eyes and dotted snout of the alligator. Seeing none, I slid gratefully into the water. Besides the jet ski, my favorite way to enjoy the lake was to straddle a barely-inflated float and then laze around upright but relaxed. Today was different; to release the tension, I paddled briskly. By the time I'd gotten far enough that my cottage looked like an adorable dollhouse, I was breathing hard from the exertion but feeling less discombobulated. Momentarily, rain surrounded me with zillions of crowned droplets, bringing a wave of pleasure. When it ended, I adjusted the float so I could lean back to stare up at the bits of blue sky that already were peeking through the clouds, and to let the easy waves rock me back toward shore.

I didn't want to think about Tom. I wanted to think about pleasant things such as how much I loved my Unity family, how cute my cottage was, and how lucky I was to live on this wonderful lake. But (as anyone who has experienced a serious conundrum can tell you) the mind wasn't going to let me ignore it. Of course, I didn't believe him. I'd have to be an idiot to believe a story like that. But, why had he told it? That was the big question. Somewhere I'd read that an estimated two percent of the population suffers from the need to know the why for everything. I was one of them. I called it Rubik's Cube syndrome—the compulsion to solve intellectual puzzles. Out of an MIU graduating class that collectively scored twenty-two percentiles higher than the national average on competency tests, I scored third highest in analytical ability and problem-solving. If it was a machine,

I'd have to take it apart and see what made it tick. If it were a discipline like philosophy or psychology or even some mundane thing like how firecrackers worked—I had to read or research or take classes until I understood it. My mother said she never understood why, when I was a child, the first thing I did when I got a new doll was to take off all its clothes. But I never understood why she couldn't see that the doll was the fundamental reality, not the clothes.

I needed to understand people too, to discover who they were beyond their social faces. Friends and coworkers often said they felt as though I peered into their souls. I'd had clear experiences of what is commonly called extrasensory perception but "getting" people came at least in part from a knack for seeing the inner workings—the mechanics—of human nature. Until today, I'd assumed that understanding Tom was relatively straightforward. I knew he was insensitive, underdeveloped in character, and opinionated despite knowing little, if anything, about his subject matter. He'd told me his mother had a terrible temper so it was to his credit that he rarely displayed temper. (I'd wondered, was he drawn to me because my quickness to temper reminded him of her?) He appeared to have business skills, or at least he did at one time. He'd begun selling art items on a boardwalk in the tenth grade and claimed he'd once made significant money in a gift shop over on the coast. But here in the highlands his store barely made enough money to pay living expenses. My impression was that he was staid, unimaginative, uncreative. I'd never seen indication that he was given to storytelling and nothing suggested that he was interested in reading for pleasure. "Orders and invoices are all I read," he'd told me. A thick pair of glasses next to his computer made it logical to assume that he didn't see well at reading distance.

So, where did a man like that come up with a story about space aliens and interplanetary wars? And where did he find the audacity to tell it? He wasn't above a mean style of teasing, such as ridiculing Transcendental Meditation and mocking me about being vegetarian, but there's a difference between crude jabs and the ability to pull off a full-scale practical joke of the magnitude today's story required. I didn't think he had that in him. Also, until now I assumed he could be trusted to tell the truth as much as he understood it. So, why this departure from his norm? What could he possibly hope to gain?

The logical answer was that Tom had a mental problem I hadn't been smart enough to catch. He was obviously neurotic, but who of us doesn't have at least some neurotic behaviors, myself included? Even though I'd overcome an uncontrolled temper, I was still too easily irritable, and I still get over-anxious at times. And sometimes I'm guilty of using denial. The difference was, if we are unconscious of our underlying motivations then we are still controlled by them. Years of consciousness expansion and a good therapist had made me aware enough that I was generally able to manage my failings without harming anyone. But many things lay hidden under Tom's ever-smiling exterior. What prompted him to tell this story as if he believed it? Was he so completely out of his mind that it was beyond my capacity to spot? Beyond his persistent belief that if he kept sinking credit card money into his store that it would eventually become profitable—and now this alien tale—I'd seen no evidence that he was delusional.

The con artist angle seemed the most likely.

I've had run-ins with two professional swindlers. In both cases, I'd managed to extricate myself before I lost money but I'd seen how they operated, how they played on emotions and credulity. If Tom was playing a con, why? I had nothing of financial value. There were other reasons to fraud people, of course, including simply for the fun of playing with their heads. This might be feasible, for he often seemed to want to take "Ms. Smarts," as he sometimes called me, down a peg or two. But if so, what was the payoff? Did he think I would like him any better if he made a fool of me?

***

Finally, the breeze and the water eased the tension. I let my head fall back onto the float-pillow and watched the clouds. Beautiful. Almost transcendental. A gull flew by, two smaller birds, another gull. I sighed happily, grateful for my beloved lake. Another bird. The waves rocked me gently. A cloud floated by… then the silver underbelly of a spaceship.

I thrashed violently into an upright position, more panicked than if I'd just spotted the alligator. Even before getting upright, I chastised myself for being so silly. Of course, there had been no ship. I didn't even believe in such things. Apparently, at some pre-conscious point of awareness, my mind had percolated up the question, What if aliens actually existed? Apparently, out of no more than that, I'd imagined a spaceship and had been hit with a rush of fear so intense that, even with no one watching, it left me embarrassed.

Grimacing, I sent thought daggers at Tom. I'd faced enough fears in life to know that the most common source of them is ignorance or distortion of reality. The classic example is that we run from what we believe to be a snake, only to find it is a rope. Panic about an imaginary spaceship had to be like that, an illusion, because aliens don't exist. I should have chuckled at myself and forgotten it. Instead, I began paddling for shore, telling myself that I was tired.

Back home, I showered, meditated, and fixed some supper, resisting thoughts about Tom and ignoring the uncomfortable feelings in my solar plexus. After eating, I flipped through the downloads recorded on my satellite DVR…and yes, there was something that would work, a Discovery Channel documentary about how the brain processes information. It didn't explain why Tom had told me such a wild story or why I got so panicked in the water but it was good enough to numb down my silly anxiousness. I wouldn't give Tom any more thought until morning.

***

Morning came at 2:37.

That's what happens if we don't fully digest concerns before we go to bed—we wake up to chew the cud of it in the wee hours. The moment I was conscious enough to realize what had awakened me, I chuckled, half from humor, half from disgust. I was too rational to believe in aliens and I didn't know any respectable person who did. So why had it awakened me?

The dark of night is always a bad time to try to process anything but I rolled onto my back, hoping to rid myself of it in time to get more sleep. What was it that needed my attention?

"You don't know everything about yourself," Tom had said. *"I'm really not supposed to tell you but I think you need to know."*

"Need to know what?"

"That you're an alien."

An alien. Humph. Tom was obviously playing a stupid joke and some unexamined part of my mind—some undigested "blot of mustard, a crumb of cheese, a fragment of underdone potato"—as Scrooge had called his ghost, had latched onto me. Laughing didn't make it go away so, rather than struggle to dismiss it, I needed to let it surface so I could examine it. In the light of reality, I could pull it out by the roots. No problem. I begin with the straightforward question: was it possible that I was an alien? Even in the dark with no one to see, I felt my face tingle with embarrassment to have framed such a silly question. No matter. The premise was childish but I understood that our minds contain many irrationalities that transmit unconsciously until the light of logical inquiry makes them disappear. Something inside me had reacted to the idea of aliens; to get rid of it I apparently needed to look at it.

One percent of parents don't tell their children they've been adopted. Could I possibly be an adopted alien and no one told me?

I scanned through childhood memories without finding anything that raised so much as a ripple of doubt. I'd been delivered at my great-grandparents' farmhouse in southwest Missouri by the family physician, old Dr. Cappeti, in the presence of my grandmother and my mother's best friend, Joanne Clinkenbeard, all confirmable facts pointing to my having made a normal, human birth-canal entrance into the world. Other indications that I belonged to this family included that I had facial features like my mother's. She and I had even been mistaken for sisters. I could certainly point out some weird folks in the family tree, especially on my dad's side, but what family doesn't say that about at least one relative, "I swear, that man is so strange you'd think he was from another planet." But nothing suggested secrets—no knowing looks across the table, no sentences stopped midway when I entered the room, no forbidding the asking of certain questions. Mom had indeed always called me an oddball and I certainly felt like one, but that proved nothing—the world is full of oddballs. It just wasn't the kind of odd where one finds boxes in the attic containing mystery items like Supergirl capes or birth certificates in strange scripts. It took less than a couple of minutes of scanning memories and analyzing facts to feel satisfied that I passed the test—I was human.

The next question was, could it be possible, as Tom said, that I had alien DNA? Even before the question was fully articulated, my neck hairs bristled. Questions suddenly splintered my mind into a dozen different directions. If only one of these questions was true, my paradigm of reality was going to be in trouble. If I wanted to get any sleep, however, I had to ask, did aliens exist? If they existed, had they mingled with humans? If they'd mingled with humans, how had they done it without it being part of the general body of world knowledge? Merely framing the questions rattled assumptions and left me aware that finding the truth would not be as easy as fact-checking in *Encyclopedia Britannica*.

Of course, encyclopedias are passé now in favor of online wikis but I used to pour over them. "Gosh, isn't that a strange-looking creature?"

one might say while looking at pictures of a duck-billed platypus. It's a scrambled eggs creature—an amphibian mammal with the face of an otter, the bill of a duck, and the tail of a beaver. It swims, lays eggs, and is poisonous. But however weird it is, if it was in the encyclopedia, then one has some reassurance that it's a legitimate, accepted reality. It left one so reassured that, even before finishing the article, one might get distracted and end up reading, say, interesting minutia like a recent discovery by Karl Glazebrook and Ivan Baldry that the universe is not a greenish white, as formerly believed, but a slightly beige white now officially named Cosmic Latte.

When scientists speak of searching for life on other planets, they generally mean life the size of amoebas, and in the year 2000, I knew of no legitimate source listing any life form beyond Earth. The concept of aliens was lumped with fairies, ghosts, vampires, the walking dead, Bigfoot, and the Loch Ness Monster, scornfully dismissed as creatures of the uneducated, the superstitious, or those with overactive imaginations. At least we dismissed them as nonsense until the unknown comes to us in some intimate way, when something rustles in the dark or slithers away so fast we aren't sure we saw it…or some fat jerk with a comb-over tells us that we are one.

The next morning, we laugh at our fears. If we confess them at all it is in the spirit of making fun of our own gullibility, a tale to be told over cocktails at a party. "Let me tell you a good one. I woke up a couple of nights ago gasping for breath with this feeling that something was sitting on my chest. I looked up and I swear I saw red eyes. It only lasted a minute and then…" And when you explain it as a combination of sleep paralysis and nightmare, everyone chuckles and thinks you're a colorful storyteller with a good head on your shoulders.

But what if it isn't a joke? What if the most rational explanation about extraterrestrials is that they do exist? Despite pink organic sheets, I felt my skin crawl.

Space aliens?

No.

I didn't believe in space aliens.

But why, as something I didn't believe in, was it so unnerving that the thought of it awakened me? Where was all this intensity coming from over something equal to a fairy tale?

As the sky began turning gray, the squirrel cage in my mind still had not discovered any answers but the squeak of it had finally put me back to sleep.

Chapter

6

ENLIGHTENMENT

B y the time morning poured through the window, the immediacy
of the puzzles about Tom and the imaginary spaceship had
shrunk into new questions: Why had I been so silly? Was I
getting senile that I let such an unimportant thing keep me awake?
The obvious answer had to be that Tom had just been making a joke.
I should drop all that nonsense to shower, meditate, and pull weeds in
the garden as much as my body would allow and not think any more
about it.

When Tom, in his capacity as chairperson for the church's
hospitality services, called me a couple of days later to ask what I
planned to bring Sunday for the potluck, I politely said nothing about
his madness at Ruby Tuesday's. I even tried to ignore the irritation I
felt at his typical artificial cheeriness. Take care of this church business
and get this man off the phone as soon as possible, I thought.

"Good thing you reminded me," I said. "Would a Waldorf salad do?"

"Sounds good. I'm bringing a ham in case you want to try some."

He knew I'd been a vegetarian for nearly 30 years. "Tom, making wisecracks about eating meat leaves me feeling disrespected," I snapped.

"I just suggested it," he said, his voice lilting with feigned innocence. "But if you don't want to eat good food then I'll just ask you to do something else for me."

"What?" I asked, resentful that he had ignored acknowledging my need to be respected.

"I told Dolores I'd drive her to church while her son has her car but I'm needed to set up tables for the potluck. Would you mind picking her up on your way?"

I felt myself soften. Whatever shortcomings (no pun intended) Tom might have, he was conscientious about helping. I couldn't be certain if he was sincere or if he helped only to appear likable. Whatever his motive, I appreciated the work he did for the benefit of others. I even felt a tiny bit sorry for disliking him.

"Sure," I said.

"By the way, have you been thinking about what I told you?"

"About what?" I asked, afraid that what he was going to say next would be exactly what he did say.

"About what we talked about, you know—Eloysia and Deneb."

"Oh, Tom, don't be ridiculous. I'll see you Sunday."

The conversation left me cross. His alien story was just another mean rag, like teasing me about eating meat, right?

But, once again, the more negative I felt towards him, the more intensely I felt the responsibility to overcome it.

***

My drive to overcome negative feelings came about because of a paradigm-busting spiritual experience that happened in the early 70s when I'd stumbled into a higher state of consciousness. It had been the greatest experience of my life. Using the Sanskrit word meaning **great**, I called it my *Maha* experience—without knowing that such even existed, I'd suddenly transcended into a higher state of consciousness. Before it happened to me, if anyone else claimed it happened to them, I'm sure I would have thought they just made it up. You may not believe me either, especially as it happened when I was working in a place least likely to make sense—in a lounge. I was stone-cold sober, waiting for the next customer to come in.

I suppose the best way to describe myself before I stumbled into enlightenment is to say I was a dingbat hippie. I don't mean that I was shallow; I think it's safe to say there was more substance to me than that. I'd been a seeker since I was a young child. Even before I began college I'd explored and rejected religion, psychology, philosophy, and other disciplines, even science, as containing the full truths about life. All disciplines had bits and pieces of truth, yes; but none grasped the whole picture. I finally started college full time at age 24 hoping it would give me the tools to pull me and my sons out of poverty. I naively assumed it would be like the ancient schools of philosophy where one went to learn wisdom, mastery of life, and other tools to become a better human being. Ha. At the beginning of my junior year, I faced the crushing truth that college wasn't anything more than a string of disconnected facts. Worse, much worse, I personally had no hope of success in it. I was smart enough to make top grades in courses that called for essays but didn't do well if they called for memorization and focused study—classes like zoology, history, statistics, and other fundamentals. I spiraled into despair, gave up, dropped out, sent my kids to live with relatives, and set out on the road in a Volkswagen van. "Hippie fling," my aunt snipped, not knowing that I planned to drive over a cliff somewhere. No one, least of all me, would have predicted that journey would turn out to be a vision quest.

Over the next six weeks, a series of rapid awakenings built up into the big one. At the beginning of the trip, waiting at the last stoplight in Joplin just before the I-44 on-ramp, I decided that before I killed myself, I needed to figure out where I'd gone wrong. What did others know that I didn't? To find out, I would become open, no opinions, no judgments, looking at life as if I'd been born that very day. This attitude played a major part in setting up the conditions to find myself, however briefly, in the shoes of Jesus, Buddha, and other enlightened saints. It was an accident of conditions, that's the best explanation I have for why it happened.

Like other hippies, my friends and I laughed at rednecks and generally scoffed at anyone who wasn't excellent. But when I stopped judging, something extraordinary happened—I began to see that there was something wonderful inside everyone. This perception wasn't yet the full magnificence of enlightenment but it went in that direction. Instead of feeling disdain for the dowdy woman at the checkout line, I saw a simplicity about her that most likely translated into love and patience with her husband and children. The old man whom I would earlier have judged as mean was, I now saw, simply in too much pain to be nicer and the whining kid was not misbehaved so much as lost, crying out for guidance in a world where none was forthcoming. I found friendliness and forthright honesty in the faces of rednecks who let me camp overnight on their farm.

One day, eating a sandwich in a parking lot of a mom-and-pop country grocery where I'd bought the makings, I saw a redneck guy drive up in a battered white pickup, enter the store then return with a six-pack of beer. Seeing an angst about him, I found myself reminded of the line from the Desiderata that read, "Listen to others, even the dull and ignorant, for they too have their story." Later, when I read Thomas Merton's story about awakening at the corner of Fourth and Walnut in Louisville, I remembered this instant in my own life. "Then it was as if I suddenly saw the secret beauty of their hearts... the core of their reality...." Before the trip, I would have dismissed the guy as someone of no consequence. But now I found my heart pierced with compassion. I suddenly realized that, beyond all labels, the only difference between him and me was our life experiences—upbringing, education, and such. But where before I would have thought such things made one superior or inferior, I now saw those were only the dressings, the superficial aspects. There was an "I" inside him, inside everyone, as dear and intimate to him as mine was to me, and equally valuable. Just like me, his body would hurt if damaged and his heart would hurt if he was disrespected or rejected. Indeed, as he climbed into his truck, I felt his pain as if it were my own.

After that, my world ceased to separate itself into fixed categories like rednecks and hippies, high class and low class, smart and stupid, educated and ignorant, good and bad, winner and loser, superior and inferior. I understood that we were not a collection of fixed entities to be praised as perfect or rejected as flawed. We were far more precious than that.

Had it not been that I sometimes had "psychic" experiences, I'd have been a hard-core scientist-type. But since science couldn't explain how I knew things beyond the senses I had to try to figure everything out for myself. My psychic abilities weren't good enough to hang up a "Fortune Teller" shingle or predict winning numbers. Mostly it was intuitive insights into people and a recognizable sense of "no, don't do that." It also included distinguishing when people were lying, not because I was suspicious but because I heard or felt a *thunk* in their voices. Only occasionally could I could predict the future. The most dramatic experience happened during the last month of high school when I "knew" I would not graduate or marry my fiancé. The feeling was so strong that I consulted the school office to inquire if my credits were in order. Technically I did graduate but emotionally I didn't—my fiancé was killed in a car accident on the way to the ceremony.

I know now that intuition is a normal human ability. Most of us have experiences of it but don't call it that. We say things like, "I knew I shouldn't have married him," or "I don't know why but I just had a feeling about those stocks." Intuition is an inner knowing but one so dormant that most of us ignore it the subtle guides. Having a life and children to protect, I hadn't felt that I could put faith in it. On the road, however, with nothing left to lose, I dropped the cautions to put it to the test, feeling my way through the "vibes."

The most important time was when I came to a crossroads and asked, "Should I continue south to Miami?" The answer was a darkly intense "no." Then I asked, "Should I go to St. Pete?" Usually, a yes answer was no answer at all. In this case, I got a warm feeling. So, St. Pete, it was. And St. Pete was where I had the *Maha* experience.

On the road, more "ESP" came, stronger and clearer. I began to "read" people more deeply and I began to see patterns in nature I'd been blind to before. Some would call these insights aha! or peak experiences—when all the parts fall together into wholeness. Understanding comes, not as a linear, thought-by-thought process, but all at once, with a strong sense of recognition, "Ah, so that's how it works."

Full omniscience happened the last week of 1973, in a lounge called *The Office*. I'd left Joplin with $140 and, even though I mostly ate food I fixed myself and slept in the van on backroads, it was during the gas crises so by the time I found the job as a cocktail server, I was so broke that I had to borrow a dollar to pay for my license. The band was playing *Proud Mary* and other of the favorite songs of the times but it was too early for dancing, probably around 8:30. Around nine the place would fill up and after that I would travel non-stop between tables and the server station until after midnight. For now, everyone was taken care of and my job was to be the servant who also waits. In the lounge area, a handful of guests leaned together over red jar candles, trying to make conversation above the loud music. I remember feeling a sense of satisfaction that comes from service, even if only from serving drinks. I turned my head from the band to check the crowd when—with no fanfare, no warning, no intellectual or emotional build-up, no magic touch from elves or fairy godmothers or gurus—the common barroom came aglow with softly glittering divine light.

We assume that only the very pure become enlightened. The classic formulas require one to be free of attachment, desire, and fear. I was certainly not pure but as a hippie with no goals or direction, having been too foolish to have made wiser choices, conditions allowed me, if only temporarily, to be fully present in the moment. Having abandoned the sources of worries, stresses, and responsibilities, I had no past and no future. I was simply present with an unintentional state of mind that unlocked the door to Divinity. One moment it was the same world everyone lives in and in the next breath, I found myself seeing reality's glittering underbelly, ever-present but typically unseen. It goes unperceived by the common mind yet is always there, waiting for us to recognize it. In any other circumstance, doubt is reasonable but this state leaves no doubts. It is Absolute Truth. I saw no robed figures, no beings with lightning bolts; no gold thrones, no kings or masters, nothing supernatural, only the highest perception possible: pure reality, pure consciousness, pure intelligence, perfect orderliness—the very foundation of life swimming in an ocean of love. I felt expanded, as if I now stood on Mount Olympus, able to see the full panorama of creation all around me, the big picture simultaneously with fine detail. Did my mouth drop open? Probably not, for while it was astonishing, it was also natural, totally obvious to anyone who could see it. It was as if I was seeing the very atoms at the basis of life. People, tables and chairs, support columns, everything glittered with sacred light while I, at one with love, truth, beauty, and wonder, was infused with profound bliss. Bliss felt like a combination of love and utter contentment, a joy beyond description. What I was seeing, I realized, was the underlying source of all religions. This was what the greats had tried to explain, what Jesus had called "the kingdom of heaven" and what Buddha had called nirvana. In the hands of mortals, however, the knowledge and understanding of it had become garbled and distorted to the point of being unrecognizable. Heaven was not something that happened after death; it was right here, all around us, something that lived inside us, ever waiting for us to open our minds and hearts to it, inclusive of everything and everyone, with no one left out. It wasn't that some things were holy and some things profane—the reality was that everything in the universe was divine. *Where* **God existed was not a place out there or** beyond here, but inside us, in consciousness itself, just waiting for us to awaken to it. And, when awakened, consciousness knows everything: it is omniscient. I was omniscient. What I saw was self-validating pure truth. This was what Jesus meant when he said, "The kingdom of heaven is within you."

Three weeks earlier, a hitchhiker and I watched the launch of a satellite at Cape Kennedy. Huge orange clouds billowed into the night sky and the very air vibrated. The sand shook under our feet so intensely that our blood trembled with its power.

But that was nothing compared to this. Seeing this, I felt like the man in the Flammarion engraving. It shows a man punching through into enlightenment, his hand outstretched in awe and astonishment at the immensity of the world that lies beyond the ordinary.

Anything I wanted to know was instantly presented to me. Mentally, I asked, "Why don't we always see this?" I was shown an image of a man barely visible under layers of embedded stress. Embedded stress is any wear, strain, and mistakes that are greater than what the mind and body can erase with a night's sleep. Even small unresolved strains or overloads of fatigue and anxiety, any breaking of the laws of nature, leaves imprints that add up to distort the mind-body's ability to function and perceive perfectly, so it clouds our perception. Then, as Plato says, we see shadows or, as the Bible says, "through a glass, darkly."

To see purely, the nervous system must not only be free of obstacles, but it must also be well developed—upgraded, so to speak, so that it can "read" the higher energies of the universe. Indeed, I saw that this was the ultimate purpose of life, to purify and develop sufficiently that we could live permanently in this state, where we could live in the home of all knowledge, all joy, all fulfillment, in the "peace that passeth all understanding." And, I saw, this was the birthright, the essential reality, for all humans.

In that blessed state I learned much, much more, but the part that relates to this story is that understanding that no matter how wicked or weak we might appear to be on the surface, at our core each of us is directly connected to the Divine. Our inner core is sacred.

Being only a silly hippie who had somehow slipped through the cosmic guard gates, I wasn't developed enough to sustain enlightenment. After maybe ten minutes, I felt myself shrink back down into my tiny, sensory-world ego.

Memories waver over time; opinions can be second-guessed; I felt confused about many things that happened before and after. But what transpired in that short time has stood as unwaveringly as a boulder in the river of my life, its certainty as fixed as a cosmic North Star. Its legitimacy was validated by Maharishi's teachings and by ancient records like the Vedas. Having seen, one cannot forget. It left a deep compassion for the "I" within everyone, that core part of us, that which is utterly sincere, utterly sensitive, which loves and longs for love, that which expands with the true joys of life and grieves with the failures and betrayals. No matter how wicked or weak we might appear to be on the surface, we have a direct connection between us and divinity. Each of us falls somewhere on that continuum of returning to our most pure state. One cannot see this without being driven to honor that aspect of everyone with tender respect and patient understanding.

Before the Maha experience, I'd been a lost soul. Afterward, I was like Hugh Conway in the movie, *Shangri La*, ever searching for the lost paradise. However, even ten minutes in the library of the cosmos is a long time. It gave me understanding, knowledge, and direction. I was able to recognize TM when I found it, then Maharishi, then MIU. These developed my mind and character so I succeeded at therapy and continued to become a wiser, more deserving person.

But my negative feelings for Tom felt like a roadblock. I kept looking for ways to get through or around it but it kept leaving me feeling stymied.

Chapter

LUNCH WITH AN ELOYSIAN

A few days later, Tom invited me to lunch at a downtown Italian restaurant. Just before biting into a breadstick, he asked, "Have you thought any more about our discussion last week?"

"What discussion?" I asked, again hoping he wouldn't say *that* discussion. When my Rubik's Cube drive couldn't solve a puzzle, it did the next best thing: it went into denial the way a computer locks up when it is overloaded with conflicting data. I'd made myself forget it and didn't want to be reminded.

Tom looked around as if to see if anyone was listening. "The discussion about our needing you," he said.

Pausing my fork halfway to my mouth, I stared at him, scanning his face for clues. He was half-grinning but on Tom, a half-grin meant anything from a tease to a cover-up for genuine feelings to his version of polite warmth.

I glanced around too, afraid of ridicule if anyone overheard us. "Tom, how can you bring that up?" I said, "Can't we just enjoy our lunch?"

"How could you forget it?" he asked in a stage whisper. "I told you; people are dying."

I looked down at my eggplant Parmesan. Until now I'd had thoughts about inviting him to join me in a swim at the lake. When we were at the lake, we didn't argue much at all.

But it *was* that conversation. I put my fork down, unsettled. "Tom, why are you talking about this… alien stuff?"

He leaned back in his chair, wiped his mouth with his napkin to remove a streak of spaghetti sauce from his chin, then leaned toward me again to speak in hushed tones.

"I told you. There are the Eloysians and the Deneb. The Deneb are raiders and the Eloysians are defenseless against them."

I waited for more explanation. None came. Looking for clues, I studied his face but it was as impassive as a banker calculating loan figures. I struggled to guess what my response should be if I was in the compassionate, all-forgiving space I'd had during my enlightenment experience. But when an ordinary person—at least a sort-of ordinary person—tells you you're needed to help stop an interplanetary war, what is one supposed to say in polite response? I floundered for words. "How is it…that you…uh…know about this sort of thing?"

"I told you. I'm one of them. I have contacts."

"Contacts," I repeated.

He nodded.

I searched his face for telltale tensions indicating a practical joke, too-rapid eye movements showing that he was lying, or jerks, or rolling of the eyes that would suggest he was delusional. I found none of those. All I saw was an obese man with a comb-over forking spaghetti and meatballs into his mouth and staring back at me as innocently as if he'd been talking about nothing more unusual than the Sebring 500 car race.

Self-conscious to be asking a rational question about an irrational topic, I asked, "If there is a war, then why don't you fight back?"

"Because it's against our beliefs. We haven't fought wars for hundreds of years."

He sounded utterly sincere. But it also sounded out of character. When the Sunday class had been discussing the question about how loving people could rise to higher principles of thought and feeling towards those who had driven airplanes into the twin towers, wasn't this the same man who had called Muslims "towel heads" and said, "we should blow them out of the water to set them straight"? Socially, he was helpful, ever ready to offer his home for a church party or to move chairs at the church. But scratch the surface and you found harsh political leanings and warmongering attitudes. I'd even heard him bash the saintly Reverend Andy as a "pompous ass." And wasn't he the same man who, even now that we were "friends," had continued to publicly abuse me on Sunday mornings?

However, only a few weeks earlier I'd been reading a book on cults and had stumbled onto a reference to a group, followers of a man named Rael. Rael claimed he had met with beings from another planet who told him that where the Old Testament says that man was created in the image of God, the word for God, *Elohim*, meant gods, plural, *shining ones*, or *those who came down from the sky*. He claimed that the Elohim had created Earthlings via tinkering with ape DNA to make us in the Elohim image. This would make today's Earthlings the descendants of this extraterrestrial master race. That was too much for me to swallow whole (especially as I didn't believe in aliens) but, liking ideas that blow the doors off ordinary ways of thinking, I played with it. Was it possible that Bible "history" might be open to such radically different interpretations? If interplanetary beings had created humankind, then it is almost certain our ancient forefathers would have viewed them as gods. A modern parallel would be the cargo cults that arose in the south pacific in World War II when Natives encountered modern soldiers who built runways for war efforts and dropped off free food and gifts to the natives. When the war ended, the gift-givers disappeared without explanation. Hoping to induce the "gods" to return, the Natives built life-sized straw planes and new runways in the jungle, carved headsets and other military paraphernalia from wood, and performed ceremonies. Some of these cults still exist today, a living model of how religions get formed.

I'd put the book down to consider. Was it possible to read the Old Testament as a history in which advanced beings created us? I made a quick mental scan of science, sociology, mythology, history, and the Old Testament to see if it might jive. To my surprise, looking at it through that lens, it still made sense. If anything, it made better sense. As someone who'd had the direct cosmic insight to see that nothing existed anywhere except natural law, the destruction of the Tower of Babble, blasting Sodom and Gomorra into singed dust, and bringing down the walls of Jericho would be more intelligible if it had been done with advanced weaponry by an advanced race rather than miracles and pointed fingers by a supernatural god. What made it even more appealing was that the same experience had informed me that God was not arrogant or warlike, not full of vengeance, but the joys of Absolute Truth, Love, Intelligence, Balance, and Order. However, since Rael's theory lacked any real proof, it was all just another philosophy. After a few minutes mental entertainment, I'd dismissed him and his theory.

But when Tom called himself an *Eloysian*, I was startled by the similarity of sounds in the name. Could Eloysia be the name of the home planet for the Elohim? I thought it unlikely. If the Elohim existed, it was logical to think that they must be a very advanced, very intelligent, very enlightened race and Tom didn't appear to be any of that. He knew nothing about the concept of transcendence, ridiculed me for my knowledge of it, and had militant attitudes, the kind that forwards inflammatory political emails before fact-checking them. I brought this up. "If you're from Eloysia," I said, "I haven't noticed you being peaceful."

He shrugged. "That's because I'm on Earth."

I nearly choked, coughing into my napkin. When I could speak again, I asked, "What does being on Earth have to do with it?"

"Compared to Eloysia, Earth is crude," he said. "The energies are different when we're on this side. Not as clear. It is harder to be ourselves here."

I blinked. Before I could think how to respond, the waitress brought the desserts, a Key lime pie for me and a chocolate mousse for Tom. Tom took a last bite of his meatball then pushed his plate aside to begin on his mousse.

The energies are different when we're on this side, he'd said. I'd read something similar about theories of incarnation, where it's believed that the soul comes into the world with certain goals and contracts but once it is in the denser physicality of the body, it may get so caught up in the five-sense experience that the original intentions may get forgotten. Could it be true that in Earth's atmosphere of violence and mass ignorance Tom had experienced something like a fall from grace? I doubted it. It seemed unlikely that if the Eloysians were truly good they could fall as far from the tree as Tom appeared to be. I decided to play along to see if any inconsistencies might emerge so I could catch him in what I presumed had to be a fabrication.

"So, what is it you…the Eloysians…want me to do?"

"Oh, you'll be contacted about that later," he said, spooning whipped cream and chocolate shavings into his mouth then talking around it. "You aren't ready to understand yet. It will take time to adjust."

I tried to ignore the chills playing around my spine. Any mention of aliens as a potential reality stretched me outside my comfort zone, and him talking about needing time to adjust sounded entirely too reasonable. "Why not tell me now?"

"I just told you. You aren't ready yet."

"But…"

Even if it was true that some Intelligence somewhere had determined that I wasn't ready to hear the whole story, my Rubik's Cube curiosity was firing up to understand why I was being told at all.

"Have you told anyone else about this?" I asked, hoping others might have some insight into this strange side of Tom. They would surely say, "Oh, posh. He tells the wildest stories!"

But Tom looked concerned. His brow furrowed, his eyes narrowed and I saw a flicker of a frown.

"Don't tell anyone about this. It could get both of us into a lot of trouble. You haven't told anyone, have you?"

This was an interesting twist. "Trouble? How?"

"Have you told anyone?"

"No," I said. "This is too crazy to tell anyone."

"Well, don't talk. Keep it to yourself."

"Why keep it to myself?"

"If the Deneb knew where to find us, it could have serious consequences," he said, his voice low.

I stared at him. Another B movie script?

"But, how can they find out?" I asked. "Are they here, on Earth?"

"Of course, they're here."

"Are the Eloysians here, too?"

"I'm here, aren't I?" he said in a tone that was smug or sarcastic, I couldn't tell which. Still, I asked, "Others besides you?"

"Lots of them."

"What do you mean, 'lots'? Ten? A hundred? Millions?"

"I don't know," he said. "Sometimes even I can't recognize them."

"Come on, Tom, stop this silliness. You really don't expect me to believe this, do you?"

His tone shifted from B Movie anxious to mock indignation. "Have I ever told you anything wrong? Why don't you believe me?"

"Because it's too preposterous to be believable."

"Whether you believe me or not, don't be telling anyone else about this. I'm serious. It's dangerous."

I didn't know what to say. I had no plans to talk. I'd be too embarrassed to admit I'd even listened to silliness like this. More importantly, I wouldn't talk because it would be unkind to spread gossip about how crazy this man was.

But was he crazy? Did he really believe his story, or was he just toying with me? I tried to keep my tone polite, hoping for something—anything—that would explain why this was happening. "If the Deneb are here, where are they?"

He shrugged. "Everywhere."

"Then why don't we see them?" I asked.

"Because they look just like us. I look human, don't I?"

I couldn't help it; I rolled my eyes in the insulting way you do when you hear something preposterous. "That's comic book stuff, Tom."

With a big grin, he picked up his fork, reached over to his leftover plate to stab a half-eaten meatball, then waved it back and forth in front of me, the vegetarian. "It's as clear as this."

I ignored his childish tease, took a bite of pie, and tried to think of a test question.

In the philosophy of science, one way reality is tested is by asking, have other observers seen, experienced, or verified it? Something like what he was describing—an interplanetary war with aliens who were here on Earth, couldn't exist in a vacuum. "So how do you explain why there is nothing in the news about this?"

He snorted. "There's plenty of news about it. But only those in the know understand what they're reading."

"You mean like a code?"

"No. I mean there is so much misinformation out there, so much distortion that only those who know the truth can understand the facts. You know, reports of UFOs and all that. The mainstream media hypnotizes the public to believe anything."

I didn't know what to say. Tom's take sounded like the script from *Men in Black* who got their insider information from tabloid news.

"Also," he continued, "people react just like you, they don't believe it even when they see it. That's another reason we need your help."

"This makes no sense, Tom. Why would *they* need me?"

"I told you why—you're the one who can understand both sides."

That stirred up a nano-second of pride. Wouldn't it be wonderful to do some real good in life? To have the power to bring peace to these anguished cultures that Tom talked about, the ravaged Eloysians, the twisted Deneb? If Tom was a con artist, this would be the time for the close, just when I was seeing a bit of glamor in his pitch. He could hit me with the punch line ("Ha! Gotcha! You fell for that hook, line, and sinker!") or the contract ("Give me a check for a thousand dollars, and I'll get you a ticket on a spaceship.") or some lewd demand ("All you have to do is stay all night at my house, and the Eloysians will land."). But he didn't do any of that. He only licked the last of the mousse off the back of his spoon and said, "That's enough. I've told you too much already."

Huh? Now I was hooked. I didn't believe the story but the conundrum was beginning to crave closure. There is nothing like "No more" to heat up Rubik's Cube syndrome. "But if you've told me this much, why not tell me the rest of the story instead of just making hints?"

"Because you were supposed to find out for yourself," he said, raising his coffee cup.

I felt a flash of resentment. "Then why did you tell me anything at all?"

"I thought it might speed things up."

"You've already told me this much, why not tell me all of it? Like, if you're are an Eloysian, then how did you get here?"

"I got here the same way you did; I was born here."

"Then what makes you think you're an Eloysian?"

He looked at me with a suave sort of confidence. "I just know."

"How do you kn…"

"Enough. Enough questions."

"Enough?" I felt like the still-hot woman whose lover has just ejaculated and, in an obvious near-doze, murmurs, "Was that good for you too, baby?"

"What's wrong with asking questions about something you say involves me?"

"If you want to know any more you'll have to find out for yourself."

"That's what you said last time. But how am I supposed to find out when you're the only person I know who's ever talked about anything like this?"

"You're Miss Smarts; you'll figure it out. "Are you ready to go home? I have to get back to work."

"Tom, I want to sort this out," I said, almost whining.

He smiled. "If I know you, you will." He raised his arm to flag the waitress and then turned back to me. "If you don't want the rest of your pie, I'll take it."

Chapter

8

PIE IN THE SKY

How I go about understanding people is partly intuition and partly the way good poker players or hyper-alert abused children do, by reading "tells" or "reveals" –minute changes in eyes, faces, and body language, tone of voice, and dozens of other cues that any sensitive person can use to read what's going on inside someone else. Lying was one of the first things I learned to detect. Liars also usually have some lack of directness about the eyes—or too much of it—or do too much blinking, or they make too many glances around. Combined with other clues, you know it when you see it. More importantly, I clued in to tone. Where there is integrity—by this I mean where there is a one-to-one relationship between the inner person and their spoken words—the voice sounds solid and one hears what some call the "ring" of truth. In contrast, liars' voices have dull *thunk* tones. In Tom's case, I heard a lot of *thunks* because he appeared to be considerably unconscious and therefore did a lot of lying to himself. But when he was telling his story, the thing that really made my mental computer crash was that I sometimes heard the strangest, most inexplicable ring of truth.

The term *ring of truth* has been around for ages because, except for the most hardened of us, it's a nearly universal experience. Henry Winkler, who played Fonzie on Happy Days, said it so well it is worth quoting. "Your mind knows only some things. Your inner voice, your instinct, knows everything. If you listen to what you know instinctively, it will always lead you down the right path." I knew from my enlightenment experience that it is possible to intuitively recognize truth, but why was I hearing a vague but persistent ring of it in something as preposterous as a muddled man's story about space aliens?

***

Buddhists say that whatever gets a grip on our attention is an attachment. St. John of the Cross likened attachment to tethering a bird to the ground, referring those things we get fixated on so our consciousness gets stuck, unable to rise beyond it. TM automatically erased such bondage but I still tried to avoid unnecessary attachments, especially anything frivolous. Still, this alien issue somehow got its teeth into me. Two things about it bugged me. One was why Tom told me such a preposterous story. The other was that ring of truth. When my attention wasn't taken up by church or volunteer events, then while doing ordinary things like floating in the lake, fixing the screen on the veranda, or driving to the chiropractor's, questions plagued me. No, it wasn't that I believed him. That would have been silly. But why was I hearing this vague but persistent ring in a story that couldn't possibly be true?

***

If it was a friendly day when Tom and I met, our conversations tended to relate to church and mutual friends, to his business, to my progress in rebuilding my cottage, or to movies we'd seen. You know, chit-chat. If it was not a friendly day, then we argued about politics, TM, vegetarianism, or, paradoxically, about what made up peaceful conversations.

But once the alien issue had arisen, the focus increasingly became me pestering Tom for details. "If there's any truth to your story, then why don't you explain more about it."

"If I told you, it wouldn't make sense."

"Tom!" I snapped, impatient with his vagary. "If I'm required to let things come naturally, then why did you interfere with the natural process to tell me in the first place?"

"Because I thought it would help you open your mind."

"Open my mind to what?" I said, struggling to be respectful to his divine inner being rather than leaping across the table and thwacking him on the forehead with my teaspoon.

"You'll see," he said. "When it's time, it will make sense. Are you ready to go home?"

"Why don't you answer my questions?" I demanded.

His tone was mildly annoyed. "I've said too much already."

I threw up my hands.

For someone who meditated twice a day, who lived a clean, healthy life, and who cultivated a sincere philosophy of love and compassion for all God's creatures, this man pushed all my buttons.

A few days later, we had just finished eating a vegetarian Mexican casserole on my veranda and, of course, I couldn't let it rest. "Come on, Tom," I begged. "Just tell me what this is all about."

"I can't," he said.

"Why can't you?"

"I've told you. I've said too much already."

"You haven't told me anything of substance."

"I can't tell you any more than what I've already said."

"So how am I supposed to find out if you don't tell me?"

"Don't you know how to do research?"

"Of course, I know how to do research," I said, insulted that he had even asked. I'd been curious about how the world worked since I was a two-year-old analyzing whether it was the moon or the clouds that moved. Instantly, I could see that it was the clouds that moved across the moon. Simultaneously, the movement came from the same direction as the wind. To verify my conclusion, I reversed the perception, to suppose that the moon moved and the clouds were stationary. But once you see the right way, you can't unsee it. For a two-year old, that was a relatively sophisticated analysis. Later, after TM raised my IQ and ability to focus so I could return to college, I aced statistics. Likewise, I'd done well in advanced research methodology during the Ph.D. program. I'd even won an award for a study I devised about predicting death in a hospital situation. In daily life, I frequently concocted informal studies to test specific issues.

But where space aliens were concerned, I didn't want to do research. I didn't care. I knew that life was tenacious even on Earth, finding cracks in every sidewalk to grow. It was found even in extreme environments such as -89.2 C in Antarctica, such as under more than seven metric tons of pressure in total blackness at the bottom of the ocean, and even in 1003 C volcanic heat. So why wouldn't it be logical for life to grow elsewhere? It seemed logical to suppose that somewhere, in some galaxy long ago and far, far away, other life forms probably did exist. With billions of planets in the visible universe alone, wouldn't it be outrageously egotistical to think that the only one to develop intelligent life was a rocky ball a mere 8,000 miles wide on the edge of an obscure arm of the Milky Way?

But, who cares? I wasn't even curious. My interests were in inner space—spirituality, psychology, philosophy, ethics, and other abstractions of the mind. I loved science too, though my interest was less on mechanics like speed and trajectory than on things science rarely touches, such as theories of how the cosmos relates to consciousness and how it affects human thought and action. I loved the world of ideas. Outside of meditation, church, volunteer work, and spirituality-related activities, I had few interests. Whatever was in the illusory world of material existence, like Newtonian mechanics, business and commerce, world events, spectator sports, shopping, and such, was of no interest to me. I didn't even know who the current singers were and hadn't known the names of TV and movie stars since the days of Goldie Hawn and Robert Redford. So why should I care about something as frivolously unimportant as space aliens?

However, two percent of the population must know why for everything, and, Houston, I had a problem—I couldn't conquer the riddle of why Tom had told me this story. I didn't think it was real but it drove me crazy trying to figure it out.

"You haven't given me enough data to do any research, Tom—no facts, no key words, just this hare-brained story. Why should I spend hours researching something only to get it out of my head, when all it would take is for you to tell me the rest of this story?"

He didn't even address it. "Thanks for lunch, kid. See you at church."

As I often did when I was with him, I gritted my teeth. My lusting after answers and my ill temper painfully reminded me how far I had yet to go to reach my spiritual goals.

I finally had to admit that Tom wasn't going to give me any more answers and that I couldn't find a way to talk myself out of needing to know. I believed it had to be an illusion of some kind, some hidden form of romantic ideation that had gripped me. By romance, I mean more than sex and relationships. Romantic highs get triggered by things like movies and songs, art and fashions, fast cars, slick deals or delicious ideas—those feelings of excitement and mystery that make our hearts quicken. Sometimes such feelings are a clue to direction but I saw romance as based on illusion. Illusion has long been known to be the enemy of truth.

Illusions die in one of two ways. They either die slowly, such as when clues add up to a dawning realization that Santa Claus doesn't exist. Or, it happens suddenly, like when your older brother ridicules you for believing anything as childishly illogical as a fat man who climbs down four-inch-wide chimneys to leave free presents. But whether it happens slowly or all at once, it's the reality that kills them and, thus, kills the attachments. The quick deaths go poof! like a balloon poked with needles, and that was what I hoped to get from Tom, a quick poof! to make this whole issue go away.

Unfortunately, as in Gabriel Garcia Marquez's book, *100 Years of Solitude*, we usually must go all the way to the end before we escape. I protested. I didn't want to go all the way to the end. But, since Tom refused to provide explanations to kill the mystery, the fastest way to get to poof! was the hard way, to face this demon head-on—to give in and do the research. But research what? Use key phrases like, "Eloysia Deneb interplanetary war" or "Local woman saves galaxy"? Those were more likely to bring up comic books and space operas than it was to call up useful data.

But I had an idea. If I confirmed that everyone in the extraterrestrial/spaceship (UFO) field was loony and that there was no real merit to be found there, that might disconnect me. Indirect and laborious, yes, but it might help get it out of my system. It seemed to be my only choice.

Chapter

9

RESEARCH

Sitting in front of my Mac, I sighed and tapped the keyboard to wake it up. I quickly discovered was that Deneb was not a planet but a star. Nothing came up for Eloysia. As expected, the term *interplanetary war* produced a lot of links for fiction, nothing more. Not having any more keywords, I typed UFO in the search bar, then groaned. In .11 of a second, what flashed on the screen was even worse than I expected; over four million hits. (It would have horrified me to know that ten years later, that number would swell to ninety-four million, and ten years after that, another 100 million.) The next thing to catch my eye, the paid ad section, looked like instant proof of a mountain of data that was even nuttier than I'd expected.

Curious Crackhead: This free-baser craves knowledge! Especially about UFOs…

I sighed. Even in the mere act of seeking information, I had placed myself in a free-basing crackhead, loony-tunes class of inquirers.

The next paid hit had the tag line, *Area 51 UFO's Aliens Roswell...*

Roswell, Area 51, aliens... these terms seemed familiar but, like junk relegated to the attic, I'd lumped them contemptuously in the same mental bin with uneducated, superstitious people who couldn't distinguish fantasy from reality, and with conspiracy theorists—those irrational alarmists who find absurd plots even in ordinary circumstances.

The next hit went right for the bottom line:

Real UFOs: Your Favorite Brands. Low prices. Great Deals. Shopzilla. com.

I wish. It would save me a lot of time and trouble if I could just go to Shopzilla, type in UFO Truth, and get a list of where to find the best odds for real deals.

Down in the unpaid section, I skimmed through the links:

UFOs! UFO Folklore! UFO News! UFO Sightings! UFO Pictures! UFO Videos! UFO Reports of Flying Saucers! UFOs and aliens! Aliens and...!

As I scrolled through page after page of hits, the headlines blared out astonishing promises: *Secrets revealed! Learn the facts here! Get the truth about aliens and Area 51! Government cover-up! Captured spaceships! Are Aliens really Angels? Reptilians Discovered! Did Jesus visit other planets?! Discover the Supernatural for Yourself! Werewolves!*

Angels? Jesus? Werewolves? I'd had the computer on for less than five minutes and I already felt like I was in a den of emotional predators and economic weird-wolves sucking dollars from sensationalism. I could imagine lonely, uneducated people, the type who read *The Globe, The Star,* and *The Daily Mirror* to get their news the way others read *Newsweek* and *Forbes,* feasting on bleeding sensationalism with exclamation marks screaming like groupies at a rock concert.

Among things I don't trust, exclamation marks rank near the top. The exclamation mark kind of excitability would fall under Albert

Ellis' eleven signs of irrational thinking. I called it the used car sales approach to life, as if to say whatever is happening is, "A really big deal!" "Your one and only chance!" "The opportunity of a lifetime!" Then there are the awfulizing sensationalist descriptors like, "Horrible!" "Unforgivable!" and "Outrageous!" Spiritually mature people know that the less hyper the pace the more likely one can get into what athletes call the zone, or what TMers would call transcending to a more wholistic level— the calmer, clearer aspects where we can appreciate life in its fuller meanings, where interpretations of life are more likely to be true. Having experienced life from both sides of the exclamation mark, I'd much rather be older and wiser than young and excited, or worse yet, ignorant and stunned.

(Nothing hinted that times were coming that I'd have to eat those last words.)

"How's the research going?" Tom asked me the next day on the phone.

"Pure drivel," I said. "I was afraid to open any of the links."

"Why?"

"It all seemed so sleazy I was afraid my computer might get a virus."

He didn't appear to get it that I'd stooped to sarcasm.

"I think you'll be okay. Just don't click on any advertising links or send them your personal information."

I took a deep breath to hold back a retort. If I was stupid enough to be researching such a stupid topic, could I blame him if he thought I needed advice?

***

On the second day of Internet dumpster diving, I began by trying to ignore the exclamation marks, reading only in cautious bits and pieces, trying to stay on the surface. "Staying on the surface" is a practical, preliminary research technique. As taught in speed-reading classes, I scanned headlines, pictures, and graphs, skim-reading text to get the gist. This method would feed me names, places, dates, lingo, etc., thus creating a generalized mental map that would eventually provide directions for determining what to investigate in more depth. It would also keep me from getting sucked into any perspective or line of belief before I formed a big picture.

At MIU, I'd been accustomed to the world of rational, scientific, or at the very least, *considered* thinking. But I didn't know whether to laugh or pull aside my skirts as I waded through swamps and tides of gimmicky promotionalism and emotionally charged material. It made tabloids look respectable. Link after link promised the titillation of the unexplained, the sensational, the bizarre, everything from the garish to the ghoulish, and with things I would never have thought to associate with UFOs such as angels and demons. Next to headlines such as "UFO Sightings Verified" were links to "Vampires are Real!" and "Shop for Extraterrestrial Gifts Here!" Every site seemed to capitalize on a UFO craze I hadn't known existed, offering books claiming to be written from personal experiences, ET T-shirts, outer space jewelry, and UFO ringtones. But if headlines seemed as cacophonous as rumors of war, opening links put me on the front lines. The noise was bombarding— commercialism, preposterous claims, intense arguments, accusations and denials, mind-twisting ideas, hysteria. It was hard to bear over thirty minutes, or at most an hour, before my head was spinning.

"You still researching?" Tom asked again the following Sunday in church, smiling his inane smile. Was that grin a clue he was playing mind games? Acting out passive-aggressively? Trying to prove that my greater education was no match for his superior brain? If that was his game, he was winning, for I really was researching this wacky topic, wasn't I?

"Yes, thanks to you," I said. "It's wonderful to have a project to fill up the time when I have nothing else to do."

His expression didn't change. Both the irony and the sarcasm sailed right over his head.

I reminded myself that my attitude was unacceptable; mature people don't blame others for their choices, nor do they permit themselves to be rude. If others push our buttons it isn't their fault—it is we who own the buttons. Even if Tom was an idiot, I was the one with the button that couldn't stand a mystery, and I was the one who decided my only choice was to do research.

I sighed. It's one thing to have a philosophy; it's another to live by it.

***

The more I researched, the more questions multiplied so the more research I felt I needed to do.

"I did some research on Deneb," I told Tom the next time we met, "and on Eloysia, Lyra, Pleiades, Sirius, Procyon, Tau Ceti, Ummo, Andromeda, and Arcturus."

"Oh, yeah?" Tom said, cocking his head with surprised interest.

"Do you know what Deneb means?" I asked.

"No, tell me what Deneb means, Miss Smarts," he said, dipping his donut into his coffee.

"Deneb is an Arabic word meaning "tail" because it's in the tail of the Swan constellation. It's a white, class A supergiant with the luminosity of 54,000 suns, making our Sol look like a kerosine lamp in comparison. It's estimated to be at least 1,400 light-years from Earth."

Tom chuckled, "You really have been doing your homework."

"I also learned that it's highly unlikely any life forms can live in that system because it's so high in ultraviolent and gamma wavelengths. Any planets would be blasted away from it by solar winds, or what would more accurately be called a solar hurricane."

Tom shrugged. "It's too technical to explain but what we call Deneb is hidden in that system."

"But I bet you learned the names from watching *Star Trek*," I said, accusation oozing out around the edges like oil squeezing through a leaky gasket.

"*Star Trek?*" Tom asked, frowning. "What does *Star Trek* have to do with Deneb and Eloysia?"

"On "Where No Man has Gone Before," in 2378, Deneb IV and its population—the Bandi—signed a peace treaty which allowed the Federation of Planets to set up Star Base Farpoint Station. Then, Deneb was mentioned in the first episode of *Next Generation*, and there was an Earth colony on Deneb's Planet IV in Babylon 5. So," I ended smugly, "you've had lots of chances to hear the name."

Tom shrugged. "It would be hard to remember something like that from watching TV," he said. He might be right. I'd watched a lot of *Star Trek* in the early 70s but I had no memory of the name Deneb. But I bet a lot of Trekkies would know it.

"Are you a Trekkie?" I asked.

"What's a Trekkie?"

I guess that answered my question. "Never mind," I said, returning to my research findings. "I found no reference to Eloysia as a real planet but I did find a link to it in *Star Trek*."

"No kidding," Tom said. "That's amazing. What did it say about it?"

"Well, where you say the Eloysians are the good guys who are at the mercy of the Denebian bad guys, in *Star Trek*, the Deneb are Federation members and the Eloysians are Elasi pirates—the bad guys."

Tom huffed.

I grinned. "So, are you ready to confess that you got your information from TV, only you got the names backward?"

"Not at all," he said. "They're not storybook names."

"I didn't say they were storybook names. Real planet names have been used liberally in Sci-Fi. Besides the TV shows, Deneb was mentioned in not one but two of Isaac Asimov's stories," I said, shaking two fingers at him for emphasis, "and in the Marvel Comics Universe. Captain Future books claimed that Deneb was the source of the human race. So, you probably got the idea for the war between Deneb and Eloysia from one of those sources."

"You know I don't read," Tom said.

"Not even as a child?" I asked.

He shrugged.

"At least Deneb is a real star system. Eloysia is not."

"You better keep researching," Tom said, as dryly as before.

My purpose in challenging Tom with published uses of the names Deneb and Eloysia was to see if he reacted to it, offered some flicker of recognition or flash of guilt. But he neither flickered nor flashed. He just kept refusing to reveal the mystery.

Chapter

10

HISTORICAL OVERVIEW

I've learned that whatever one must do in life, however odious, the way to success is to be open-minded and just surrender to it. Positive things come out of such an attitude. But during the next weeks of on-off Internet dumpster diving, I found staying open-minded difficult. Wading through all the exclamation marks, wild stories, and multiple opinions felt like trying to uncover trade secrets from pimps and drug dealers, weirdos, and crackpots. Did I believe my findings? Of course not. But at least it gave me a place to start. Nothing I found referred to any successful human-alien DNA crosses, the existence of aliens on earth, or gave any clues why I might be needed to stop a war. But what began to emerge was a loose overview of the UFO scene— Roswell, the Kenneth Arnold story, Adamski, Kecksburg, and so on, all cold-case mysteries I had little interest in, all the way up to more recent incidents. Compared to the studied arguments in scientific disciplines, there was ferocity in ufology I found unsettling. It was less like proof and counter-proof than it was like the brawling of a dysfunctional family or conflicts in a soap opera. Without a menu, it was hard to tell who was who. Gradually, I began to sort out the major cast of players.

—UFO buffs, those who believed in UFOs, attended UFO conferences, had theories, claimed to know something everyone else didn't;

—Debunkers who scornfully claimed that anything UFO was a hoax or a misidentification of common, ordinary things such as clouds and birds, experimental planes and, of course, weather balloons;

—Conspiracy theorists who were up in arms saying that UFOs not only existed but the military/government was covering up what they knew for power, profit, manipulation of the masses, or other dishonest and immoral reasons;

— The military, who insisted that nothing was happening, that UFOs did not exist and they were not looking for them;

—The men-in-black who insisted that nothing was happening and if you talked about what wasn't happening something awful would happen to you;

—The media, who wrote tongue-in-cheek UFO reports in the weird news section side by side with Darwin Award stories;

—Mainstream science, spoke volumes by their silence, ignoring the whole thing or dismissing sightings as cloud inversions, satellites, or the planet Venus. And, lest we forget: weather balloons.

Like children arguing about who is right, instead of working together to solve the mystery, each faction not only argued its perspective but attacked the others with a fervor that went beyond my ken. No matter. I expected very soon that I'd gather enough evidence to fully confirm it was all irrational.

***

I asked Tom, "Have you ever seen a UFO?" I'd been in the church sanctuary that evening waiting to hear a guest speaker. Only minutes earlier, he'd had leaned over the chair next to me and said, "Mind if I sit here?" I'd been so proud when, years earlier, my therapist helped me overcome being deceptive, evasive, and posturing to learn how to become "authentic." But Tom triggered old behaviors. Trying to handle my animosity toward him with grace or honesty at church was the hardest—there was little privacy and rarely more than a few minutes between events. Instead, I embarrassed myself with hypocrisy. To his self-invitation, I replied, "Oh, no, I don't mind. Sit down." Moments before an event was hardly the time or place to be authentic and say, "No, you big fat slug, I don't even want to be seen on the same side of the church as you."

Almost before I could chastise myself for thinking such petty thoughts, I jumped from the moral frying pan into the fire—I saw a chance to exploit the situation. Manipulation is another deadly sin my therapist had helped me work through but Tom brought out the worst in me. I had the sudden thought that, if I let him sit down beside me, I might get some answers from him.

We spent a couple of minutes in polite chitchat about how his store was doing, then I asked about seeing UFOs He chuckled. "Many times."

There it was again, the unhelpful, unreadable answer in a tone that contained both a smokescreen of jocularity with vague hints he might be telling the truth.

"Have you been in one?" I pressed.

"Many times," he repeated, poker-faced, his eyes disclosing nothing.

As a writer, I know that details are needed to convey information but not everyone knows how to explain things well. Even when they think they are telling all, they don't realize they have said nothing. I couldn't tell if Tom's manner of speaking was because he was one of those, lacking communication skills, or if he was deliberately withholding. Whatever the cause, his answers on any topic were usually spoken in vague generalities. It made me impatient. "Come on, Tom, stop playing games."

"I'm not playing games," he said. "I told you I wasn't playing games."

"So, prove it. Why don't you show me one?"

"You can see them for yourself."

"How?"

"Just watch the skies; they're everywhere."

"If they're everywhere, then why isn't it public news?"

He chuckled. "Most people don't look. Even if they did, most people don't believe in them so they don't see them."

I scoffed. "You mean like the way we can't see fairies unless we believe in them?"

Tom shrugged. "Something like that."

"Your being so cryptic is frustrating. Instead of making me drag every bit of information out of you, why can't you just say things outright?"

He smiled, cocking his head with a look that could have either been the teasing look of a flirt or someone feeling mean-spirited satisfaction. "It wouldn't be any fun then, would it?"

That did it. I lost it. "I have no patience for this," I snapped, standing up to go hide in the classroom until I could work off my temper.

He laid his hand on my arm. "Come back," he said. "I'll stop teasing."

That wasn't exactly an apology, but I'd let it pass if it meant that he was going to tell me something useful. I frowned and sat back down, willing my spinning neurochemicals to settle down. It proved worth the effort.

"Many people see UFOs," he said. "You just don't hear about it much. Mostly they don't get reported because folks know that if they do, they're likely to be hushed up or ridiculed."

"But you said they didn't see them."

"What I meant was that most people don't see them because they don't understand what they're seeing, or they don't see them because they don't know where or how to look."

Excited to finally be getting some practical information, I said, "Tell me how to look."

"The best time to see UFOs is in the early morning or late evening—sunrise or sunset. That's when it's easiest to see them against the sky, toward the horizon…"

Just when I was getting some real information from Tom, a hand touched my shoulder. It was Sara, wanting to set up a phone appointment for discussing our fundraiser. I'd barely set a time when Joanne began introducing our guest speaker. I groaned. All hope of getting more out of Tom was lost.

***

With an 800-acre lake east of my cottage, I had a superb view of the sky. I began having tea on my screened-in veranda in the mornings and I shifted my meditation time a half hour early so I could scan the sky while having a sunset supper.

What I saw was: nothing.

Nothing.

Nothing.

Nothing.

Birds, planes, clouds, stars. A few will-o'-the-wisps, mosquito swarms, an occasional windborne Walmart bag, or an escaped party balloon. Down on the water, I saw fishermen in johnboats and teenagers on jet skis. Twice, I saw the evil eyes and snout of the alligator. I saw the magic of shifting light and shadow in sunrises and sunsets but nothing weird.

At least there was nothing weird until one morning when I found what appeared to be hundreds of sticks coming out of the lake. All those "sticks" rising out of the water were seriously weird. I stared at this surrealistic sight with waves of horror washing through me but my Rubik's Cube syndrome kicked in. I had to find out what they were. Trembling with fear of the unknown, I crept down to the beach until I was close enough to see that that they were turtles. Recognizing them as common creatures helped to lessen the fear but it didn't explain, *why*? In the silent dawn, with wisps of mist rising here and there, the sight reminded me of the angels on the beach in the movie, *City of Angels*, all facing the same direction. Only, instead of facing some mystical direction, like Mecca or the North Star, they were all facing southwest. The only thing in that direction was a power station. Even though I spent considerable time making inquiries of state, national, and other expert sources, no one could tell me why hundreds of turtles scattered around a lake would stick their heads out of the water, facing the same direction, at the same time. Strange, strange. But not the strange I was seeking.

"You're not looking right," Tom said in response to my grumbling.

"Then how am I supposed to look?"

"I can't tell you that," he said. "You have to figure it out for yourself."

He said that often, and I hated it when he did. He had given me the mystery but no clues, and now I had to figure it out for myself? This is a test, I'd tell myself. This is a spiritual test to see if I can overcome my negative feelings. But I was failing these spiritual tests all too often. Sometimes I'd get so frustrated with his enigmatic answers that I'd make up my mind to forget the whole thing. I'd tell myself that aliens didn't exist and for a few days, I managed to not think about UFOs or peoples of warring planets crying for my help.

But then I'd wake up in the middle of the night with *that* feeling again, that Rubik's Cube longing for answers. It was a *want* that reminded me of the scene from *Close Encounters* where Neary stares at a mound of mud similar to Devil's Mountain and murmurs, "This is important. This *means* something." That's how the want felt, like getting answers to this nebulous issue meant something. Then I'd stare at the skies again, searching for moving dots, or at the computer screen, searching through that sicko UFO trash. Or I'd be wondering—if Tom wanted me to know about space aliens, why wouldn't he be eager to tell me everything he knew? It made no sense. I wasn't getting anywhere, but neither could I let it go. It was driving me crazy.

It took maybe a week for me to quit looking. Rising from a chair on the veranda that last morning, I snorted in disgust. What would it prove if I saw a UFO? It would only prove that they existed but it wouldn't satisfy the crucial mystery of Tom's story. If aliens needed me, they'd just have to land on the beach and ring my doorbell. In the meantime, I'd keep researching, hoping that something would eventually make sense.

Chapter

11

THE GOV'MENT SEZ

Nothing provided clues regarding Tom's story that I was a half-breed alien who needed to stop a war, nor even to refute it. However, after months of investigation, the *in toto* evidence had begun to sway me toward a tenuous belief that UFOs were real and that aliens existed. At least it did until I read overviews of the *Condon Report*. The Condon Report was the study of the findings of Project Blue Book, the Air Force's 17-year investigation of 2,618 reports of UFOs. The report concluded that "Nothing has come from the study of UFOs in the past 21 years that has added to scientific knowledge… Further extensive study of UFOs probably cannot be justified in the expectation that science will be advanced thereby." Didn't this qualify as a final authority?

"The official government report says there's no such thing as UFOs," I said to Tom. I was picking crumbs of apple pie off my daisy-patterned sundress while people came and went at TGIF.

Tom, dressed in his usual Florida business casual, a tieless white shirt, rolled at the sleeves, with pressed slacks, was sipping his second cup of coffee.

"And you believed it?" he said, peering at me intently, his tone incredulous. "Did you actually read the report?"

I, the postgrad with research training and years of informal but dedicated research experience, felt irritated at being challenged by someone who didn't even read. What made his comment especially irksome was my instant recognition that he was right. Most of the time, I do thorough research and I don't accept authority just because it's authority. I admit that such skepticism made me unpopular with parents, teachers, and husbands, but it's a great attitude for someone who wants to know the truth. However, Tom's incredulity made me realize that in this case, I'd been all too happy to forget the growing evidence to the contrary, jump to the end of the story and buy the claims made by the *Condon Report*.

"Why shouldn't I believe it? The Air Force did two decades of investigation and Condon concluded that there was nothing of interest to require further investigation."

Tom made a wry face. "Oh, sure. Upwards of 3,000 cases of people who saw something so out of the ordinary that they took the time to report, but who are such fools that they can't recognize flocks of birds, odd clouds, and ordinary aircraft?"

His sarcasm was not lost on me. Like anyone with blinders, I'd ignored that same thought when I myself had it. I'd developed enough character that I could admit when I'd made an honest mistake, but it's hard to confess to making a stupid one, like being willing to jump to conclusions after reading only summaries. As people do when they're wrong, I argued. "Not just clouds and birds," I said. "Some were stars, satellites, reflections, and…" I finished lamely, "… weather balloons."

Tom snorted. "If all the unidentified objects that have been called weather balloons really existed, you'd think it was a hot air meeting. I can't believe you'd accept that. Have you ever seen a weather balloon?"

I nodded. It was a white sphere about four feet wide, released at a National Weather Service Demo Day. It darted upward then, caught by the wind, it rose in jerks until it was so high in the sky it looked like a dot. Twice a day, eight hundred weather stations around the world (including 90 in the US) release balloons at the same time. As they rise, they expand to as much as 40 feet across, rising as high as 17 miles before they burst, at which time a parachute carries the radio box back to earth. NASA and some universities also release weather balloons.

Still self-justifying, I said, "The meteorologist said that every time they release a weather balloon there's always a rash of UFO calls."

Tom just stared.

I ate crow—or to put it in vegetarian language—humble pie, and confessed. "All right, I didn't read the report in any depth. But, even if you're right, I have a hard time believing that a government board of inquiry could get everything wrong, or worse yet, that they would deliberately mislead the public. I find that simply unthinkable."

"Have you seen the data?"

This time, I didn't weasel out. Knowing I'd been doing just plain sloppy thinking, I growled in embarrassment. "I read a summary of it."

"Did you see the figures they gave, that 94 percent of the cases were 'solved'?"

"Yes, I read that."

"What about the other six percent? Did you ask about that?" Tom raised his eyebrow.

I opened my mouth to say something to justify myself, but nothing came out because I had no answer for why an official inquiry could not account for nearly a hundred cases while claiming they found nothing of interest. That's unscientific, like a doctor ignoring unexplained symptoms while saying you have nothing to worry about.

Tom continued. "And are you aware that one of the Blue Book researchers—an astronomer, I can't remember his name—said they had instructions to make up answers if they couldn't find one?"

My guess is he was referring to the astronomer and ufologist J. Allen Hynek, with the one giving instructions being the notoriously anti-UFO Major Hector Quintanilla, who considered it a punishment and demotion that he'd been assigned to head what he considered a silly project.

"Yes, but..."

"Did you see actual copies of the Blue Book reports when they released them to the public? Half the data was blacked out for 'security' reasons. If UFOs don't exist and if there isn't any threat to national security, then why would they need to classify any of it?"

The fact was, I hadn't wanted to see any copies. I'd jumped to conclusions to escape from this mystery, and I now presented my strongest argument for accepting the report. "After all those years of public investigation and months of inquiry by a scientific panel, it makes little sense to me how a government-funded report could have fooled everyone. Or why they would have wanted to fool anyone?"

"They didn't fool everyone," Tom snorted. "You can't fool the people who saw what they saw. What you can do is to make them look like fools in everyone else's eyes, or you can scare them with threats if they talk too much."

"Oh, come on, Tom," I said, sticking a napkin into my empty cup. "That death-threat stuff is so unrealistic that I can't buy it. Why should our own government threaten people who were talking about a new discovery?"

He sighed and rolled his eyes. "I thought you were more intelligent than this."

"More intelligent than what?"

"More intelligent than to buy one of the biggest frauds ever pulled over on the American public."

"Oh, I see. You're a conspiracy theorist!"

He sighed again. "No, I wouldn't call myself a conspiracy theorist—I'd just call myself too smart to buy what the government says about aliens and UFOs."

"That's a major contradiction, Tom. Weren't you recently arguing the government could do no wrong?" This harked back to an argument in last Sunday's class in which he had said that the US was superior to other nations and should be so respected.

"This is different," he said.

"How is it different?"

"It just is."

I groaned. "Come on, Tom, don't turn cryptic again."

"I'm not being cryptic."

"If you state an opinion as if you know something specific but provide no details to substantiate it, then what else would you call that except being cryptic?"

"I call it staying out of trouble."

What an irony that whatever drives us the craziest is what we're given to deal with. The marriage and relationship guru, Harville Hendricks, wouldn't have called it ironic; he would have said, "We marry our issues." Tom and I weren't married but we seemed to be trauma-bonded over disagreements. It reminded me of the saying, "when you're up to your ass in alligators it's hard to remember that you came to drain the swamp." I was so deep in annoyance that I had forgotten I was supposed to be looking for compassion, love, and forgiveness. "If you want to stay out of trouble, then why don't you explain all this to me so I don't have to struggle with this time-consuming research to understand why you told me I was a half-breed alien? Why is it you wouldn't trust the government on this issue?"

"Do you trust the government?" he asked.

"Who does? But science is rigorous, and it's hard to fake research," I said, entirely forgetting about frauds by tobacco and pharmaceutical companies.

He shrugged. "Well, why don't you just keep on investigating and see where it takes you."

"Tom," I groaned. "This is so aggravating. If you know something I don't know, then why don't you save me all this wasted time and just tell me?"

He leaned toward me. "You wouldn't believe me even if I did tell you."

Oh, dear.

Bingo.

He was right.

Speechless, I stared back at him across the table.

It was true. I didn't—couldn't, wouldn't—trust the judgments and opinions of a needy, uneducated, non-thinking, arch-conservative with a comb-over and a bankrupt store. But like a Sumo-sized martial arts expert, he had not only thrown me back on my own resources, he'd left me with a wave of uncertainty about my own underlying assumptions. If he could be this insightful, was it possible that I had misjudged him altogether?

Moments like this dangled the enigma in front of me in a fresh, red-hot mix of stinging distaste and a passionate want, a near-desperate need to know, a combination of stick and carrot that kept driving me forward. One moment I was convinced that, if only he would, he could clear up this alien business with a little explanation. Then, the next minute, with one little comment like, "you wouldn't believe me even if I did tell you," I found myself startled into a deeper perspective. The jaw-dropping truth was that he was right—I wouldn't believe anything he said. From the moment I met Tom, I'd mistrusted him as a person. Now I realized that, unless he introduced me directly to a band of aliens, nothing would make me believe his preposterous story. But now, even if he confessed that he'd been lying all along, I would suspect him of lying to get me to stop pestering him.

At the same moment, this insight clarified something else. Until now, I'd only half-hearted my "research." Trying to take the easy way out on the Condon report was a symptom of that. With Tom's last sentence, however, everything turned upside down—or right-side up. I realized that the UFO/alien question had quietly, insidiously, become not just an artificial mystery Tom had created, it had become *my* mystery. Somewhere I'd crossed the line from "What is the truth to Tom's story?" to "What *is* it that is happening in our skies?"

I stared at Tom, locked eye-to-eye in the semi-paralysis left by the wake of the revelation. Tom was right—the only answers I could count on were the ones I had yet to discover for myself.

***

When Tom dropped me off at home, I didn't head for the lake but to the computer. I typed *Condon Report* into the search bar and discovered how naïve I've been. Wiser minds than mine had not been willing to compromise their integrity. Peter Sturrock, a Stanford professor renowned for his work in astrophysics, had long ago questioned it. Reporting his findings in a book entitled *The UFO Enigma: A New Review of the Physical Evidence*, he wrote, "…[F]ar from supporting Condon's conclusions I thought the evidence presented in the report suggested that something was going on that needed study." Finding many discrepancies, he began a two-year research project. Also, the

American Institute of Aeronautics and Astronautics (AIAA) published a paper not only criticizing the Condon method of collecting evidence but noted that the conclusions often didn't match the cases. The AIAA claimed that (instead of a mere six percent) a whopping third were still unsolved. More than a serious scientific failure, *Blue Book* and the *Condon Report* appeared to be actual manipulation of facts.

After reading similar stories, I felt sick. How could scientific and governmental authorities be willing to be so unfaithful to their purposes? We want—need—to be able to trust authority, especially as it is a powerful and seductive persuader. A 1984 Harvard study demonstrated that if someone in charge told a research subject that it was okay to give another subject a lethal electrical shock, 37 out of 40 people did so, even when they could see the other person apparently screaming in pain. Some people read this research as a failure of individual character and that is true, but most people lack the time or ability to do real research for ourselves. We should be able to depend on authorities to provide opinions and directions to guide society.

I hadn't realized how deep my faith in science had been, especially government-funded science on issues important to the public. You will probably say I was naïve. But it wasn't the kind of naivete that left me surprised to learn that some politician had had his hand in the till or up his secretary's skirt. I was aware there were a lot of frauds, cover-ups, and every imaginable form of misconduct, from embezzlement by the county treasurer to Bush's weapons of mass destruction. I was also aware that science wasn't perfect, that it made mistakes, and that it needed to be examined carefully. Yet I'd assumed that impropriety was a deviation from the norm. I took it for granted that no matter how badly, slowly, stupidly, or corruptly the government behaved, the underlying principles were sound. I believed it was the matter of a few rotten apples in a fundamentally sound barrel.

But pieces of the puzzle were coalescing that I'd resisted seeing. Evidence was growing that something dark was happening. Stories had arisen time and again, across the decades, across the continent, how the government had not only refused to listen to witnesses about UFOs and abductions but had repeatedly ridiculed the people who made the claims, even threatened them with their lives, reputations, and careers if they talked about what they had seen. Regarding something as important scientifically, culturally, and even militarily as the existence of intelligent life from other worlds, this should be public news. But evidence indicated that our government had been lying to us. Scientists in positions of authority had been lying to us. The military had been lying to us. Why were our leaders not only keeping us in the dark but even skewing the results of scientific research? Why did they want to keep us ignorant? Wasn't ours the country of high ideals, pride, and honor? Didn't we stand for justice and human rights and protecting those weaker than ourselves? As scientists, wasn't our goal to find and protect the truth?

But, if so, then how can we account for the sloppy work done on *Project Blue Book* and the *Condon Report*? All along, I'd rejected stories of coverups as unlikely, especially when they portrayed the government in a sinister light. But the pattern had existed all the way back to Roswell, New Mexico, in 1947.

***

Roswell is a name both sacred and profane in ufology, the event that began an age on one hand and, on the other, became a battle cry for conspiracy theorists. The story goes that in early July 1947, one, two, or possibly even three UFOs crashed in a storm in the New Mexico desert north of Roswell. The most accepted storyline is that a spacecraft fell on the Brassel ranch, and another at a cliff some miles away. Roswell Army Air Field (RAAF) sent officers to investigate. In the next day's *Roswell Daily Record*, Army officials claimed to have recovered a crashed "flying disk." Rumors circulated about the discovery of amazing metal that recoiled to resume the original shape after being crushed, hieroglyphic-like writing on I-beams, and even four small humanoids. Supposedly, one or two survivors had been captured alive, one had been shot, and that bodies had been shipped to Wright Air Force base.

But the day after the news article, the RAAF suddenly changed its statement, claiming the object had been merely a crashed weather balloon. Almost as suddenly, a dead hush fell over the locals. The talk about whatever crashed would not be revived until 1980 when, after interviewing over 90 witnesses (many of whom claimed to have been threatened with their lives if they talked), Charles Berlitz and William L. Moore published the book, *The Roswell Incident*.

Even after all these years, the mystery of what happened there still burns. A 1997 CNN poll indicated that 80 percent of Americans believe it was a government cover-up about an extraterrestrial crash.

When I first read about Roswell, I was so naïve that I thought the idea of life threats from our government implausible. At the same time, I felt uneasy about the government's obvious resistance to disclosure. Even from my disinterested perspective, the "top-secret weather balloon" story was so patent it felt insulting.

I'd been in the military. I could easily imagine brass gathering behind closed doors with maybe a politician or two, having a solemn meeting at which it was decided that telling the truth might create a general panic, like what happened with Orson Welles' famous 1938 radio reading of *The War of the Worlds*. The public upheaval that happened then is still used today as a model for studying public reactions in a panic situation.

But the Roswell incident might also serve as a model of another kind, that of what happens when there's a cover-up. Nature doesn't like anything false. No matter who does it or what they hide, covering up the truth is like sticking a splinter under one's skin—even though it can't be seen, it festers, itches, and burns as the body tries to eject it. Likewise, a cover-up has a way of feeding the public's subconscious uneasiness, a feeling that just won't go away, often giving rise to theories that take on strange lives of their own. (It wouldn't surprise me to learn that today's intense disinformation-based mistrust of government might not be a long-term consequence of this.) We may not see the truth but, on some level, we intuitively know when something isn't right. Fads—swings of interest not grounded in practical facts—flame up and burn out. The reading of head bumps, swallowing goldfish, conical bras, and mortgaging one's home to buy tulip bulbs passed quickly out of public interest. But something with truth at its core tends to keep surfacing. The 75-year-old Roswell mystery has a definite flavor of a cover-up, something that burns and twitches too intensely in the public mind to be tossed off as nothing more than a tale told by a few crack-pot conspiracy theorists. The symptoms suggest that something of significance really did happen.

Even so, my initial impression was that the theorists were over the top when they claimed that individuals and families were told they might "just disappear into the desert" if they talked. I wasn't ready to believe, not then at least, that our government would threaten the civilians, even the children, it was their job to protect. That kind of talk cut the legs off any credibility witnesses otherwise might have had for me.

But isn't this exactly how beliefs begin to be changed, with evidence that at first seems unbelievable? Many things in our history were thought at first to be preposterous. If you read the history of Yellowstone, people fiercely disbelieved that such features were even possible. Likewise, as far back as Aristotle, people who believed that rocks could fall from the sky were ridiculed as crazies. It wasn't until 1804 that they were vindicated when such rocks were officially identified as meteorites. Giant pandas and giant squid were laughed off as mythical, and the first pelt of the duck-billed platypus sent back to England was cut up as scientists looked for proof of a hoax.

I still wasn't entirely convinced of the existence of beings from other planets, but one thing I was already convinced of, was that there were enough reports about them that the government should be addressing this issue publicly and science should be seriously investigating them rather than lying to the public.

*****

Another story that refused to die was about Area 51, home to a top-secret air base in Nevada. Even back in 2000, I found eleven million hits for it on the internet. (That was almost as many as the *Bible*, a number that would skyrocket to 46 million in less than five years, with another 400 million added five years after that.) As far as I could tell, all of those hits were headlined with double exclamation marks. Virtually every UFO/alien website I found promised the latest news about it.

At first, it went way over my head to understand what all the excitement was about. I know a bit about military secrets. When I was in the Navy, we made jokes about our job being so secret that even we didn't know what we were doing. With so much compartmentalization, there is more truth to that than humor. Area 51 is also like that, so secret that even though daily planes and busloads of employees come and go, acres of blazing lights at night, and nothing but satellite photos and average citizens with high-power binoculars who could see it, the government denied its existence until 2013 when employees brought a toxic waste lawsuit against it.

My initial reaction was, "So what's the big deal with there being a secret base? Isn't it logical that the military would have a secret base?" Yet countless UFO buffs and tourists make pilgrimages into the Nevada desert (where miles and miles consist of nothing but miles and miles) to try to see a base that officially doesn't exist. Admittedly, for a base that didn't exist, it makes you wonder why it is surrounded by thousands of motion detectors, armed patrols, and no-trespassing signs promising to kill you if you enter. But, for Pete's sake, why bother? The thought of driving through the desert hoping to catch a glimpse of something hidden reminds me of a childhood joke that says, "Why do they put fences around graveyards?" The answer is, "Because people are just dying to get in there." Does the fascination with Area 51 come because people can't bear to think someone is keeping secrets from them?

The more I dug, however, the more the mystery began to unfold, not into answers, but into more mystery, into a story so bizarre that it almost made sense. What launched Area 51 into public awareness was a man named Bob Lazar. On public television in 1989, Lazar claimed to be a Cal-Tech engineer who had worked not in Area 51 itself but at a site about 20 minutes south, an area designated Section Four (S4). S4, he said, was a hanger hidden inside a mountain, a site so secret it could only be reached by a bus with blacked-out windows. Lazar claimed his job in this hidden mountain hangar was to help reverse-engineer the nine captured alien spacecraft kept there. That got my attention. I half hoped such a cool story was true. I even got a little excited about it, a feeling I later understood to be a creepy sense of foreboding.

Lazar claimed that to qualify to be at S4, one practically had to have one's wazoo under a security clearance. To get clearance this high, he claimed to have signed an agreement to, among other things, have his phone tapped, his life watched, and his constitutional rights voided. Then, despite his special clearance, Lazar did the militarily unthinkable—he talked. He talked first to his friends, bragging no doubt, and took them to witness test flights of the human-made prototypes of the alien machines. As the story goes, the sightseers were discovered and Lazar was fired. A short time later, he went public, claiming he'd been threatened at gunpoint. The military denied even knowing the guy existed, and no one could find any proof—no records of degrees at Cal-Tech, no employee records of secret labs where he claimed to have worked prior to Area 51, nothing. Lazar claimed that the military or the FBI or CIA or the MIBs had apparently expunged the records.

Like the public, I was guilty of buying into an irrational argument about him, i.e., the ad hominin fallacy where a viewpoint is attacked not on its own merit but by blackening the character of the person who holds it. When I read that he had been arrested for pandering—in a state where prostitution is legal!—I had the thought, how can one have any confidence in a low-life like that? With the damning character faults and the lack of credibility regarding his credentials, I found Lazar's story deteriorating for me as well.

Even so, once again I wasn't without lingering concerns in the reverse direction. Knowing that clearances are both more and less than they are cracked up to be, I felt uneasy. In the Navy, I had a Secret security clearance. That's only a couple of steps higher than the average gossip saying, "Don't tell anyone but…" Even at the Secret level, far less than the clearance Lazar claimed to have, security is serious business. The Navfac (Naval Facility) building I worked in was fenced and guarded by armed Marines, hidden several miles away from the main base where I was stationed at Keflavik, Iceland. Like Lazar, we got there by bus with blackened windows, though ours hadn't been covered for security purposes but from sooty volcanic ash. Nobody cared. There was nothing to see anyway except dreary volcanic rocks.

As part of our responsibility to protect the secrecy, we had to learn firefighting skills because, in case of a blaze, non-classified fire personnel would not be allowed through our numeric-pad coded doors. Deeper into the bowels of the building, half-hidden behind our secret machines, were more coded doors. Only those with the next higher clearance, Top Secret, could go in there. They, of course, had to learn to do their own firefighting. If a fire broke out in their space, those of us without the higher security rating would be out in the cold watching with the regular firefighters.

In case of invasion or breach of security, we were also trained in various other measures, such as how and where to burn or otherwise destroy classified papers and equipment. There was a picture of an ax taped on certain machines in our workroom, identifying which needed to be destroyed in case, under pressure, we forgot what needed to be smashed. Disliking the military and my boring job, I remember more than once looking at those axes, half-wishing for an invasion so I could hack away at the damned things. But that's another story. What's important to pay attention to here is that even at low levels of security, the military takes itself very seriously. Classes solemnly emphasized the importance of keeping secret things secret. We were informed of stiff penalties for leaks such as a $10,000 fine, ten years in prison, court-martial up to and including being tried as a traitor, and/or dishonorable discharge. This included the pressing of criminal charges if, in case of invasion, we failed to shoot anyone who tried to enter the building.

As a Naval grunt shivering in Icelandic rain waiting for the bus to pick me up for work, I'd given the matter serious thought and decided that even though I felt responsible enough to not casually disclose classified information, I wasn't going to take a precious human life over a bunch of paper and machinery. But it appears others may not have that kind of conscience. Area 51 has posted signs that it will use deadly force if you cross the line, and Lazar claims that he was threatened at gunpoint. He certainly believed they were serious. "Coming forward to talk in public about my experiences at Area 51 is something I did to save my life," he told an interviewer. If no one knew what was happening, he might have ended up as a bunch of bones in the desert that could only be identified from dental records.

My experience with the military made me think Lazar's story might be plausible, though I wasn't ready to believe (at least not yet) that our government might have killed him without due process. Even after my own experiences in the military where I'd seen that if they didn't like you, they didn't play nice, I'd still clung to my belief that they played by the rule of law. However, as stories added up about Roswell and other places where people reported threats on their lives, I realized that as a dedicated spiritual seeker, my tendency to having idealistic expectations was probably naïve. Now the picture of reality was expanding to paint the government as being heavy-handed not just with those in the military but with civilians as well.

Feeling rattled, I closed the computer and walked to the veranda door, staring at the sunlight glittering on the lake, thinking, why? What was so important that the government would put out misleading reports? What was so important that it would threaten its own citizens in order to hide evidence? I put leashes on the dogs and walked to the lake. Sitting on the dock, watching the dogs chase frogs, I tried to sort out the conundrum. Again and again, the theme repeated itself— citizens sees an unidentified object. The military comes in then claims to find nothing but cleans the area with fine-tooth combs. Then stories leak out about witnesses claiming they were threatened if they talked about what they saw or experienced. That this had been reported all over the world was a valid phenomenological pattern—i.e., consistency in witness reports—that made it worthy of scientific notice. At the same time, in a milieu of ridicule that appeared to be coming from the government itself, almost no research was being done. The only news appeared dedicated to debunking the phenomenon, even if it had to use fraudulent methods.

I had to admit it—something was seriously wrong. This wasn't the outcome I'd expected when I'd begun investigating. I'd expected to quickly and easily prove that spaceships and aliens didn't exist and that both conspiracy theories and theorists were all nonsense. Like countless others who began their research expecting to be myth-busters, I'd started with the belief that those who claimed to have encounters with UFOs or other-worldly beings, were hoaxers, romantics, and fantasists, victims of exaggerated fears and hallucinations—all just nutcases. But, like other researchers, the more facts I learned, the more it appeared that I'd been seriously insulting to my fellow human beings. I'm sure there exist those who honestly can't tell the difference between a flying saucer and weather balloons, strange clouds, and flights of geese but it seemed unreasonable and illogical to suppose that *everyone* was a hoaxer, stupid, or crazy. Some people, as the saying goes, can't tell their hind end from a hole in the ground. But all the people all over the world who had reported sightings or experiences could not be madmen or fools. It was simply out of proportion with normal reality, to think that millions of UFO witnesses could be so ignorant, confused, mentally ill, or deliberately deceptive that they were *all* wrong.

What about alternative possibilities? Could UFO reports be caused by mass hypnosis? Delusion? Hysteria? LSD in the water? Epidemic brain farts? Public illusions had happened, including the deadly dancing plague of 1518, the "Great Fear" in France in 1789 (a panic based on fears of famine), the Salem Witch trials in the US, and Springheels Jack (a frightful character that haunted London for nearly a century). But such things were geographically isolated and short-lived while alien/ UFO reports spanned the entire globe, going as far back into pre-history as rock paintings. From the standpoint of phenomenological research methodology, it counts as validation that many of these witnesses were trained observers—pilots, military, police, and others with reputations at stake, including former President Jimmy Carter, Senator and Presidential Candidate Dennis Kucinich, U.S. Senator Richard Russell; American astronauts Buzz Aldren, James McDivitt, and Gordon Cooper; Russian Cosmonauts Major General Vladimir Kovalyonok and Victor Afanasyev; news anchor Walter Cronkite, and Clyde Tombaugh (the astronomer who discovered Pluto), as well as other respectable world citizens. Responsible people with responsible jobs in the public eye do not make claims that carry the potential to get themselves ridiculed.

The principles of the philosophy of science say that to be considered real a thing needs to be observable by multiple witnesses. Indeed, some sightings of unidentified flying objects include witnesses numbering in the hundreds, even hundreds of thousands, all the way up to millions. For instance, on nationwide TV, untold numbers witnessed four UFOs flying over Three Rivers Stadium at the nationally-televised Dallas Cowboys game in 1979. Hundreds observed an armada of ships over Farmington, New Mexico, in 1951. With the full cooperation and participation of their government, in 1989 and 1990, countless Belgium citizens reported multiple sightings. In 1997, thousands spotted a huge triangular craft over Phoenix, Arizona. And more. Lots more.

Another phenomenological consistency I found about UFO sightings was the intensity of emotional reactions. Observers saw something that was so startlingly different from known objects it upset or excited them, something so out of the ordinary they felt challenged to describe it. "I don't know what it was," they said. "It didn't look like anything I've ever known."

Exclamation marks are still red flags. But there's a difference between exclamation marks used by teenage girls or amateur writers and those applied to events that are outside our expectations of normal reality. Seeing the turtle fest in the lake was an event worthy of exclamation marks. Chills of horror had rattled me while my mind scrambled for some rational explanation for why hundreds of "sticks" rose out of the lake at the same time with their heads pointing in the same direction. The reality is, unexplainable phenomena are emotionally significant. If I got excited by turtles, I could only guess at how much more intense it would be to experience the high strangeness of non-human intelligent beings or constructed craft that didn't appear human-made. One of the first requirements of true science is witnesses, and in such cases, the exclamation mark reaction becomes legitimate phenomenological evidence that something exists that needs to be accounted for. Where there are so many witnesses, it is not in proportion with normal reality to dismiss them as no more than irrational people who panic over weather balloons. When so much evidence emerges, there needs to be an inquiry. Yet, what explanation did we have for why science, the media, and the general population castigated observers instead of finding answers to these disturbing questions?

My early assumption was that when I'd done enough research it would exonerate the government and military, exonerate science and scientists, and demonstrate that citizens making these claims were merely crazies. But, like Neo taking the pill that lets him see reality, once we break out of the box of our rigidified expectations, there's no way to get back in. The evidence had been falling more on the side that UFOs and aliens existed, and that science and the government were doing things to cover it up. Clearly, something was happening and I had to ask, why? How do we account for this?

Watching the gentle waves break on the sand, I realized again that what I'd viewed as Tom's mystery had become my mystery. I needed to know what was happening in the world that was terrifying people, and what it was the government was hiding. As much as I'd wished for the *Condon Report* to be the last word, I had no choice but to continue researching, this time with a new commitment to finding the truth … for myself.

Chapter

12

WHY DOES IT HAVE
TO BE SNAKES?

O ther than the disdain I began with, and the grief I felt losing my faith in science and the government, two other things triggered strong emotional reactions. One was crop circles.

The fervor about crop circles began in the 1970s and 1980s, mostly around Wiltshire County, England, in the Stonehenge area. Beginning with simple circles, over time they became elaborate geometrical shapes, some hundreds of feet across. Occurring overnight, they appeared in cereal crops like wheat and canola, to a lesser extent in corn, ice, and snow. Eventually, over sixty countries reported them. On examination, it was found that, without damaging the plant, the grains are forced down and the nodes on lower portions of the plants "blown" as if by a microwave. Magnetic anomalies cause compasses to spin, gyro problems in airplanes flying overhead, and malfunctions of electronic equipment on the ground. Mathematicians discovered fractal geometry in the designs. Visitors claim to experience disorientation or spiritual euphoria inside them. Farmers complain but crop yields increase by as much as 400 percent.

Debunkers claimed the designs are frauds, anomalies of Earth energies, accidents created by downwash from helicopters, and from such things as the ravages of mating hedgehogs. I had to laugh at such explanations. When have you ever seen helicopters create anything except clouds of dust and debris? As for animals, I'd watched a documentary showing an elephant painting a sketch of another elephant, and I'd read a book called *Why Cats Paint*, showing art supposedly painted by cats. Skeptics claimed those were only random marking behavior but the work appeared to have an intelligent, intentional design. But hedgehogs creating fractals a hundred feet wide? Deer stomping out precise representations of Pi to the 10th number? It was like claiming the Mona Lisa was created by an outbreak of mold or a lizard dragging its tail through paint.

Still, I'd be guilty of limited thinking to say that extraordinary designs could only be made by conscious intent. Fractals—exquisite repeating patterns—are found in broccoli, cauliflower, ferns and other leaves, in mountain ranges, rivers, and fiords, even in lightening. However, the flawless intricacy, the apparent intentionality, and the precise outlines in crop circles make it unlikely they are accidents of nature. Calling them such would be like otherworldly beings claiming that the etched metal messages we sent out in the Arecibo and Voyager satellites were only distortions caused by small-body space rocks.

Like many others, I found crop circles enchanting. If beings from another world had made these breath-taking, intricate designs, then it showed not only technical advancement but aesthetic greatness. The beauty filled me with love and a desire to meet with beings who had such imagination and artistic ability.

But if aliens created them, then why? In the "musical tones" scene in *Close Encounters,* the scientists and the mothership conduct a symphonic interchange. With lights and tones flashing between ship and backboard, an amazed technician asks, "What are we saying to each other?"

"Seems they're trying to teach us a basic tonal vocabulary," someone answers. With a grin, he adds, "it's the first day of school, fellas." Could it be that crop circles are how aliens attempt to open dialogue?

Then I read that a couple of Brits named Bob and Dave claimed to have been creating the circles in the dark of night using a board with an attached hand-held rope, stepping on it to mash the grain down. I was as shocked and saddened by that as I had been by the dishonesty of the *Condon Report.* When very few can draw a perfect circle, I can't imagine anyone creating huge works of perfect geometry night after night without ever making mistakes, art worthy of great masters, while their wives claimed to be unaware they were even gone. But, hey, what did I know? With so much point-counterpoint one found in ufology, it's hard to distinguish truth from non-truth.

***

Then there were abductions. Where I found crop circles enchanting and uplifting, a mere glance at the word *abductions* riveted me with cold chills. That was the other source of intense emotionality. In *Raiders of the Lost Ark,* Indiana Jones peers into the depths of the Well of Souls and then rolls away. With understated horror, he looks up to the Heavens and says, "Snakes! Why does it always have to be snakes?" Every time I encountered the word abduction, it was like that. Instantaneous and intense, a ripple of horror would shoot up my spine and I'd think, *No, not that, please, anything but that.* Mental doors slammed shut and I wrapped denial around me like a security blanket.

Denial is an interesting thing. Alcoholics Anonymous explains it well, pointing out that in families where alcoholism is present, it is like having an elephant or a dead body in the room. Everyone just pretends it isn't there. That's how I dealt with abductions—I was so terrified of it that I just blanked out and pretended it didn't exist. In therapy, I'd developed good skills in handling fear so it was puzzling how anything could make me this frightened. Yet, every time I did research, that word reached out to me like a gnarled hand from the grave, filling me with primordial terror. To deal with it, I either read it as a buzzword or, if there was too much detail, I moved on to a new site while pretending abductions were something made up by the crazies or the sci-fi writers, telling myself I'd deal with it later.

But now that the UFO mystery had become my mystery, didn't I have to open the door to that dismaying question, Were aliens evil beings who were snatching us?

Until now, I felt insulated by the assumption that if beings from other planets existed, the "Powers That Be" (i.e. the "deciders," people smarter, more powerful, more educated than me) would all get together and figure out the best way to handle it. Unless I had a major part to play in negotiating peace between planets (highly unlikely) I assumed that my place in the scheme of things would be so far in the background that it made me invisible, just as I was now invisible in Earth politics and Earth wars. It was always someone else on the floor of the Senate or on the front lines, not me. While soldiers were facing legitimate fears slogging through the swamps in Vietnam, facing sniper fire, foot rot, and live snakes, the worst things I'd had to battle was a dysfunctional Command and an abusive time schedule.

Like that, I assumed that if aliens landed, I'd be watching it on television news or reading about it in a three-month-old magazine in a doctor's waiting room. I assumed the atmosphere would be positive, like on *Star Trek* where Captain Kirk proclaims to newly-encountered beings, "We come in peace!" Or, as it had happened in *Close Encounters of the Third Kind,* everyone would stare at the mothership in respectful awe and happy excitement. I assumed that our government, the scientific community, and important citizens from our universities and professional organizations would welcome them with fanfare and handshaking, curious and eager to meet our neighbors from space, who had also come in peace. I assumed it would be a case of noble Earthlings meeting noble beings from space. Right?

But the word abduction shifted all my assumptions from welcoming galas and happy-ending *Close Encounters* scripts into monster movies. Even fleetingly opening the cover to peer into my own Well of Souls, all possibilities of monsters flooded into my imagination—slobbering, slimy insects who prey on humans, sucking their blood until nothing but a husk remained, or snarling reptilians who drag living, gasping humans into caves to eat them, limb by limb, perhaps even while the victims scream and writhe. Might they be sadists who played mind games with their horrified captives, laughing at our terror? And what possibilities existed I hadn't even thought of?

Despite my care to avoid any mention of abductions, sometimes I got caught off guard and stepped into the thick of it before I realized it. In reading Glen Campbell, the king of Area 51 researchers, I stumbled onto a paragraph that gave me nightmares. Following a prolonged hiatus, he wrote, "They [the aliens] were now mutilating cattle, making crop circles, abducting large numbers of humans (mostly female) and doing lecherous things to them, inserting implants into people's bodies, intruding psychically into their minds, harassing motorists, causing power blackouts, sending out agents in human form to intimidate witnesses, and colluding with the government at the highest levels."

His words were even more chilling because, even though Campbell was informal and tongue-in-cheek, his was one of the first voices I heard in the UFO field that had inspired a fledgling trust. If this man thought abductions were happening, then might they really be true? In the same world in which I'd had my *Maha* experience, with its bliss, wonder, beauty, and truth, how could something exist as monstrous as abductions by aliens? And where the artistic and mathematical beauty of crop circles suggested interplanetary visitors were advanced, intelligent, cultured, and ready to interact peacefully with humans, the idea of abductions, implants, and surgeries without anesthesia suggested animalistic horrors. I kept telling myself that Campbell had made those ideas up to be dramatic or was secretly an alarmist fear monger or else he was repeating the stories he'd heard from the crazies.

I didn't dare ask Tom about it. He'd either say that, yes, obviously abductions were happening, or he'd say yes, I was being silly. But whatever he said, I wouldn't believe him, so why bother asking? The real reason I didn't ask was fear—what if he told me things I didn't want to know?

But I also knew that a fear held at bay eventually buries itself in the unconscious where it splinters to become the source of other fears— the invisible monster that creates unidentified anxieties, phobias, compulsions, depressions, obsessions, rages, imaginary demons in the dark, ghouls lurking in shadows, and who knows what mental and emotional torques. People who fail to face their inner demons sometimes become the brutes guilty of chronic domestic torment, even the Hitlers and Pol Pots who project their fears onto the faces of others and then try to eliminate them in the belief they were doing it only to defend themselves. All of us have primordial dreads, our terrors of unknowns filled with the worst things we can imagine. These are often archetypal, inbred in both the collective unconscious and individual psyche. It is this that chills us when we see Degas' painting of *Saturn Devouring his Son*, his face smeared with the blood from the headless body, or *Hell* by Hans Memling. Shadows in alleys and stairwells make promises to come alive with rape, torture, and murder. Deep in our unconscious, we have nightmares of elevators in free fall, airplanes crashing, death by fire or water, and for me (punch-my-buttons-why-don't-you) the most chilling thought I'd ever had: abduction by aliens.

The idea was so terrifying I felt light-headed just thinking about it.

Among the Internet's facts and fiction, I had no trustworthy source to consult for guidance. Tom was the only person I knew who had ever even talked about aliens and his descriptions of the "bad guys" were that they were very bad indeed—war-mongers, pillagers, cold-blooded murderers of harmless, peace-loving peoples. Now the fire in my belly to know had brought me face to face with what we fear above all—the unknown. For me, the unknown had a name: *alien abduction*. But, the Hound of Heaven follows the scent of fear and I knew I could run to the ends of the Earth and never escape it. That's why psychologists say the way out is through. Once I admitted that this was my mystery, one I must figure out for myself, I realized I had no choice but to face this terror head-on. Sitting in front of the computer, staring at the cursor blinking in the address bar, my fingers clammy on the keys, I wondered, did I dare?

The standard instruction when one is in a high place is, "Don't look down." Emotionally, I distanced myself as much as possible, compartmentalized the fears and, taking a deep breath, and typed *alien abduction* in the search bar.

Let the games begin.

***

The abduction theme began in 1961 with what is often called the Zeta Reticuli Incident—the abduction of Barney and Betty Hill. According to their story, the Hills, a middle-aged couple, were traveling in New Hampshire one night, when, suddenly it was two hours later and they were 35 miles further down the road with no recall of how they got there. Afterward, both began having snatches of strange memories and haunting nightmares about strange beings performing painful medical experiments. Hoping to make sense of the craziness, the Hills met with Benjamin Simon, a Boston psychiatrist, who spent several sessions hypnotizing them. Simon concluded that the Hill's belief that they had been abducted was sincere, but that they had created a mutual delusion stemming from Betty's sexual fantasies.

On the surface, it seemed like a reasonable theory. Still, I had to wonder if Simon himself was in denial. Psychiatrists are only human and, in the early 60s when no published information existed about aliens, what responsible professional would suppose such a wild story even *could* be true? Even now, decades later, it seemed far-fetched to me. If aliens captured humans, wouldn't it make more sense to eat them right on the spot, zoom off with them to a BYO café or a zoo or science lab, on another planet? Or hold them as hostages to negotiate Earth's surrender? Or leave their mutilated bodies strewn around as carelessly as abandoned tires? But, according to the story, the aliens did none of these things. They only set the Hills back on the road. More like a mystery tour than a bloodbath.

My mind balked against the storyline of being experimented on and having one's memory erased. It seemed too much like sci-fi in which the writers try to think of every weird, breath-sucking, terrifying scenario they can, like eating brains out of a monkey's skull or the Ray Bradbury story about a psychic boy making a rat eat itself, or weird stuff that happens in the da te da [spooky sound effects] *Twilight Zone*. Didn't *Playboy* or some BDSM magazine have short stories somewhere about someone being forced to have sex in a spaceship? "Oh! They were beastly! They swept me up like an iron filing before a magnet! Then they strapped me onto a cold, hard table and poked strange things into my paralyzed body!" The kicker was that most abductees claimed they had no memories of these until they were retrieved through hypnosis. Could the whole thing be a Freudian delusion created by people in deep denial of their sexuality? Or were the victims publicity seekers? Hill's tale opened the doors for many similar reports. Was the "alien abduction on a dark, lonely road" a path to public recognition? Without witnesses, one can claim anything, right?

But some cases had witnesses. For instance, two years after the Hills claimed to have had their experience, the lights in the Andreasson house in Massachusetts flickered and went out. Betty, her seven children, and both her parents watched as five small humanoid beings bounced into the house. Then, poof! No memories of what happened next. A decade later, Betty answered an ad from a UFO researcher. Allowing herself to be hypnotized, an astounding saga unfolded. According to her narrative from fourteen hours of regressive hypnosis, she spent four hours in a spacecraft where small beings gave her a physical examination and subjected her to numerous tests. The human probing of her testimony amounted to over 500 pages of reports, intense scrutiny from two lie detector tests, and several scientists from different disciplines, including a UFO investigator, an M.D., and a psychiatrist.

Respectable people such as Professor Emeritus of the University of Wyoming, Dr. Leo Sprinkle, had explored and documented similar events, such as from police officer Harold Schrimer. Schrimer claimed to have been given a tour of a spacccraft he'd found sucking electricity from a transformer. After tests and hypnosis, Sprinkle wrote that Schrimer "believed in the reality of the events he described."

That phrase, "believed in the reality of the events," lingered uneasily. Those or similar words were used to describe the Andreasson story, in Dr. Simon's analysis about the Hills, and by others who examined abductees' stories. Patterns are what researchers look for, and this was one of the first logical patterns I found in ufology, that even responsible people sincerely believed their stories of abduction.

Another pattern was the tone. The tone of reports said something intense had happened to the victims, something strange and confusing, unlike anything they'd ever experienced before. It's well-known that witnesses don't always report the same story. One says the light turned red before the car moved into the intersection. One says the car ran the light as it turned red. Another says he didn't notice the light. But if a child was mangled at that intersection, witnesses don't tell the story deadpan. Their faces wrinkle with distress. They may tense, and their eyes may narrow or well up with tears. Their voices become strained, angry, or sad. Even when details don't match, these telltale emotional cues are signs that something meaningful happened. The tone in abduction stories is like that. It conveys that something impacted these victims, something of such intensity that it left them traumatized. Something was happening that was out of the ordinary.

***

Movies almost always tell distorted stories but they can provide clues to new questions. Wanting a break from so much expository reading, I checked out a library copy of the 1993 movie *Fire in the Sky*. Just as witnesses described, it showed Arizona logger Travis Walton being sucked up into a spaceship in an Arizona forest. Then it showed him waking up encased in a slimy cocoon among stacks of thousands of cocoons filled with dead or dying humans, on which the evil aliens feed or breed. It left me as terrified as a child. Desperate to know the truth, I spent precious bucks from my limited income to buy Walton's memoir by the same name, where I learned that those horrible scenes weren't true. Walton wrote that he allowed it because it reflected the degree of his actual terror. The reality was that, even though Walton's was the most documented abduction on record, he didn't remember a lot of details.

First, I was relieved, then angry. This is one of the problems in ufology—there is so much distortion for sensationalism, profit, or fiddling with people's minds. It makes it hard to stay grounded and impossible to test each piece of data.

One argument against abduction was that it simply didn't fit into the picture I'd gotten about life when I'd had my *Maha* experience, where I'd seen that the universe was essentially good, loving, and intelligent. Yet, the more I researched, the more primordial fear I felt. It's a good thing I didn't know then that I was just a memory away from finding out just how much more I had to be afraid of.

Chapter

13

ICELANDIC CHILLS

―――――――――

"You want to hear a funny story?" I asked Tom.

Instantly I regretted asking. I'd opened my mouth to tell him what, until that moment, I'd always thought of as a joke. I'd not recalled it in years but instantly I'd realized it might have a different meaning than the way I'd remembered.

Tom and I had volunteered to stuff envelopes for the church, a mindless, repetitious thing that allowed us to do mindless chit-chat. We were at his tenth-floor condo sitting in the glassed-in balcony overlooking Lake Jackson, sharing the fresh lemonade he'd made. Below us, the lake was framed in lush greenery dotted with red, yellow, and pink flowers. The sun glittered merrily on the water, sending reflected light through elephant ear leaves and wicker deck chairs to create pretty patterns across the walls and my cream-colored slacks. The feeling that day was how I imagine a good marriage to be: the companionable comfort that comes from friendship and shared memories. Our good memories weren't about each other but of happy times at Unity with beloved friends. For some miraculous reason, we had not argued once. He was not trying to discredit TM as cult nonsense, and I hadn't been pestering him for answers to space questions. Had the relaxed atmosphere permitted some inner guard to fail at his duties, allowing the old memory to arise?

"A funny story?" Tom asked.

"By funny, I mean odd."

A chill of apprehension made me aware that I should think this through in private before speaking further. "On second thought, I think I shouldn't talk about it."

"Why not?"

"Because I spoke before thinking. Let's rewind and go on to something else."

"You can't do that. Once you start something, it's not fair to withhold it."

I frowned. Hadn't he done that to me with this story that I was an alien who needed to help ancestral planets end a war, then refused to tell me the rest of the story? But it would do no good to say that. He wouldn't get the connection.

"If I said it was wise to ignore it, you couldn't just let it pass?"

"No way," he said, reaching for his lemonade while grinning with that smug look he'd get whenever he'd caught me at something blamable. Had I not felt unnerved, that look was so familiar it might have made me feel almost affectionate.

"Okay, okay," I sighed, thinking I'd just downplay it. "It's just that you aren't the first person who has told me an alien story."

"Oh, yeah?" he said, halting his glass in mid-air, giving me his full attention.

"Yeah. When I was in the Navy, there was a guy that…"

***

I was stationed at the Icelandic NATO base, mid-1970s. There was little to differentiate one day from another, same boring duties, dull meals, and daily bus ride across miles of gray rocks to work in a square, windowless building. I remembered Luke because his calm, unaffected presence was in sharp contrast to the edgy excitement of the party-hardy younger swabs experiencing their first freedoms as adults, the groggy hypomania (craziness caused by lack of sleep and/or lack of darkness) that most of us experienced, and the general dysfunctionality at the command. In my memory snapshot, he stood just inside the door, peering across the room with its banks of humming, clicking machines. He looked close to my age, around 30, and appeared fully present. Brown hair, chiseled features. He stood erect, his stance like a cat's—easy in his skin, owning himself and the surrounding space, almost noble. I don't recall feeling any of the awkwardness, dislike, or one-up/one-down anxiety I felt around officers but he showed more confidence than a common sailor. Morale was too low for anyone to report that the door could be forced, but even if he'd come in without authorization, it didn't explain why he was there. I suspect now it was to find me.

The next time I looked, he was gone.

A day or two later, he reappeared and asked me to have dinner with him at the base restaurant. I recognized that he was not the type to be interested in a ditzy hippie. I said yes in part because I was curious, and in part, because I wanted to eat at that restaurant. I'd been a vegetarian for two years and, on military chow, I was often hungry. The recruiter who advised me that I'd do okay as a vegetarian apparently wasn't aware that the navy puts meat into most everything. Something made me so dislike the idea of eating meat from crotch-scratching Navy cooks that I've half-seriously wondered if it was like the warning to Demeter's daughter, Persephone, to eat nothing while she was in Hades. When her will power flagged and she ate six pomegranate seeds, it created the immutable sentence of living six months each year in Hades. Had I eaten meat in Iceland, might I never have escaped from that hell? But the base restaurant Luke named was not military—it was Icelandic, with the food cooked and served by natives. When the pale-skinned, blue-eyed server asked for our order, Luke suggested that I shouldn't leave Iceland without tasting its fresh fish. Since it wasn't military, I was willing.

Surrounded by the guttural lilt and growl of English spoken with Old Norse accents, there are two things I recall about the hour or so I spent with him. One was how wonderful fresh fish was, and the other was Luke's extraordinary story, the one I was about to tell Tom.

***

"When I was in the Navy, I met a guy named Luke. He told me…" I hesitated. The more I remembered, the more disquieted I felt.

"Come on, out with it," Tom said, leaning closer to nudge me with his elbow. "You can trust me with your secrets."

He fancied himself to be a counselor of sorts. Most likely his callers were needy ladies thinking a retailer would be a catch, but Tom took himself seriously. But I had no secret. My hesitation was because, the more I remembered, the more uneasy I felt. Still, not knowing how to stop without being rude, I caved under the pressure.

"Luke said that spaceships were flying over the base with beings who were trying to bring world peace."

Tom's usual happy-dumb-dog expression now had a hint of focus-frown.

"He said that he'd been helping them, sharing his mind with them. He said it was 'important work,' and that in sharing his mind, he experienced 'all kinds of insights and understandings about life.'"

My people-watching skills were less developed then, but as Luke had talked, I watched his face for flickers of tension, shifts in his eyes, and the telling movements of the hands and torso. In Tom's case truth seemed to be short threads woven through—and mostly hidden by—multiple fogs and uncertainties. But Luke's signal-to-noise ratio had been true, a perfectly clean line. While we waited for our fish, he sat easily in his chair, his hands folded on the table in front of him, no signs of being ill at ease, no nervousness. His gaze was steady; his voice was clear, unwavering, not a red flag anywhere. His demeanor was serious, almost solemn; I don't recall him smiling except when he reported the bit about having "all kinds of insights and understandings about life." He told his story without inserting hesitancy fillers like "… uh…" or "…well…" Nothing gave reason to doubt his authenticity.

All ears now, Tom asked, "What more did he say?"

"He said, 'My time is almost up.' He said someone was needed to take his place."

"What did that mean?"

"He probably meant his tour of duty was almost over and that he was shopping for a replacement."

"What did you think of that?" Tom chuckled.

"I thought he was confused. I thought he was having a spiritual experience like the one I'd had and the only way he could explain it to himself was to think that someone was sharing his mind."

Tom looked pained. "How can anyone confuse extraterrestrials with spiritual experiences?"

"He said they gave him knowledge and insights about life. I assumed that he was referring to omniscience, like what in Sanskrit is called *Ritam Bhara Pragya*. It means that level that only knows the truth. I'd had a direct experience of that, where I'd seen and comprehended huge amounts of knowledge in seconds so I knew it was a natural phenomenon. And when he talked about mind-sharing, I assumed he was talking about witnessing."

"Witnessing? You mean like what Christians call 'witnessing for Christ'?"

"No. That is only a figure of speech for proselytizing. Witnessing the way I'm using it is a neuro-physiological phenomenon that happens in higher states of consciousness." I explained that witnessing is a condition in which one experiences both local and non-local consciousness at the same time. Local consciousness means ordinary cognition through the senses, intellect, and so on, the same as everyone experiences. Non-local consciousness refers to the universal, non-egoic consciousness. "The result is like Divinity watching the small-self act in the world as if in a drama, hence the descriptor, witnessing."

"That makes no sense. Why would anyone want to do that?"

"Wanting isn't the right word," I said. "It's something that happens naturally when the conditions are right for it. Witnessing is a by-product of a perfectly functioning nervous system." I tried to explain that, instead of being ego-centered, where we think the world is happening to us, in witnessing it seems like God or our larger Self is watching the mind-body act spontaneously. It's usually associated with blissful feelings. "I didn't believe in aliens so enlightenment was the only context I had for understanding Luke's claim that someone was 'sharing his head.'"

Tom harrumphed. "I thought that was mental illness."

I was patient. I understood that to someone who's never had the experience, the concept is incomprehensible. "No, that disassociation." Disassociation is a break between body and consciousness, like when a child is being molested. The mind has difficulty handling that reality, so consciousness splits off. In contrast, witnessing is what happens when consciousness and body are fully integrated. "Witnessing isn't a symptom of mental illness but of higher stages of human development."

"Like having cameras in your head?" Tom chuckled, referring to the story I'd told him about the drunk on the bus.

"No, that's schizophrenia. In that state, consciousness is distorted. Witnessing happens when the mind-body is pure and coordinated and developed enough that it can see reality from the point of view of the complete universe."

Tom only looked cynical.

"Okay," I said, finally impatient, "even if I can't explain it, can you understand that it's something I understand? I didn't believe in aliens. I thought they were a joke so I assumed that Luke was confused. The only experience that I could relate his description to was enlightenment. If I hadn't interpreted it like that, most likely I would have thought he was mentally imbalanced because I certainly didn't believe in aliens."

This is a good example of how we often force-fit new information into existing paradigms. Since I hadn't accepted the key concept then that aliens existed, I could only understand Luke's story as if it were a premature breakthrough into enlightenment, one less complete, less explanatory to him than mine had been to me. I assumed that the idea of someone sharing his mind was his rationalization to explain his unusual experiences.

"So, what did you do?"

"I tried to tell him about TM."

Tom leaned back in his chair and looked at me like I was an idiot. "If someone was telling me there was an extraterrestrial sharing his head, it would never occur to me to give him a TM lecture."

I sighed. Now that I had some background knowledge for understanding that aliens really do exist, I understood why he would think I was an idiot. "When you believe someone has had a spiritual experience, isn't that the time to share practical information about how they can get more of it? I was excited for Luke. I assumed when he had the full experience, he would realize that what he'd interpreted as an alien sharing his mind had been cosmic witnessing."

"Did you argue with him as you argue with me?"

"No, I didn't argue. If I'd believed his story was about aliens, I would most likely have freaked out." I looked out over the lake, suddenly swept with a painful sense of lost opportunity. "Considering what I'd learned, I have to wonder," I said.

"You think it might be true?"

"I never once thought about it in any serious way," I said. But now that I'd learned so much about ufology, I realized it might be true. Aliens were reported to be telepathic and UFOs were known to hang around military bases.

"Did he say outright that he wanted you to take over his job, sharing his mind with aliens?"

"He made it clear he was looking for a replacement but, apparently, I blew the interview. I'd done most of the talking, trying to explain that his experiences were fragments of higher consciousness and that he needed to learn TM in order to expand on it. When I finally run out of steam…"

I was taken aback by the pieces that were falling together, remembering Luke's air of self-possessed authenticity. He'd dropped his eyes as if he had gone inward. Had he been consulting his alien? When he opened his eyes back to me, he was still calm, still self-possessed. There had been no tone of frustration or argument. To Tom, I said, "He did this pregnant pause and said, 'You're too involved in TM to help us.'"

Tom chuckled derisively. "I couldn't have said it better myself."

I frowned. Tom just didn't get it about TM. He didn't know how difficult it had been to make sense of life after having experienced multiple dimensions of reality with no help to sort it out. Also, this event had happened before therapy and I was still seriously dysfunctional. The stabilization and growth TM had brought me was priceless. I wouldn't have traded that for anything. But it was hopeless to explain this to Tom. I just finished with, "That's all there was to it. He didn't argue, didn't try to persuade, didn't offer any rewards. He just folded his napkin and paid the check. We left the restaurant, and I never saw him again."

Tom snorted. "I bet you're sorry now that you were so 'caught up in TM.'"

I leaned back in my chair. "Tom, I've never regretted my involvement with TM. I keep trying to tell you, it saved my life. What I do regret is not asking more questions."

"Why didn't you?" Tom asked. "I'd have kept him there until midnight asking questions"

"I didn't ask because I didn't believe him. Even if I had believed him, I was too socially backward to even know I could ask." A wave of almost painful regret hit me. Now that I had some knowledge and understanding about ufology, I'd give a lot to be able to ask Luke questions.

"So, that makes twice that beings from other planets have asked for your help," Tom said. "What do you think of that?"

Anxiety ran its fingernails down my spine. "I don't want to think about it," I said. I glanced at my watch. "I think what I better think about is going home. It's getting late."

Tom sighed. "I don't see how you can keep running away."

I didn't know what he meant by "running away" but I grinned. "I do it like this." I stood up, picked my purse up off the floor, and said,

"Do you want to carry these church things to my car or do you want to bring them later?"

"I'll bring them later," he said, waving me away with what looked like a frustrated grimace.

Chapter

14

WHY ME?

D riving home, I marveled at how I hadn't made the connection sooner between Luke's story and Tom's. It made me wonder, had I forgotten or misunderstood other life events? Searching though childhood memories, I recalled Mom asking me as an adult if I remembered who "Totchur" was. She said that as a three-year-old, I talked constantly about my friend by that name. Indeed, some people report meeting ETs as small children.

But where that story was too vague to be meaningful, something weird did happen when I was ten or eleven, and my brothers, Steve and John, were nine and five. Dad had carved wooden airplanes for us. It was night but, as rural kids, we were not afraid of the dark. We knew every inch of our small town, population 200, by heart. About fifty feet west of our house, a gravel road branched off and ran a block north before it made an S curve toward the one-room country school we attended—probably one of the last schools in Missouri where all eight grades were in the same room. The only house on that gravel road, sitting at the first curve, was Nadine's. As our telephone service provider, she had a one-person panel in her house for pushing and pulling wires into, saying, "Number, please," and "One moment, please." Again, probably one of the last in Missouri. Our plan was to run up the gravel road to Nadine's and then turn around to run home, letting the south breeze turn the propellers.

When we reached Nadine's, I noticed what appeared to be a red smokey ball sitting on her chimney. But it was the wrong time of year for a fire. With the summer weather, Nadine's door was open and I could see through the screen door into her home. Almost as if the ball had lost interest in peering down the chimney in favor of more animated game, the ball moved toward us, growing larger as it came. By the time it reached the road it had grown to perhaps eight or ten feet high and six or eight feet wide, and had become opaque, solid-looking. Glossy white "poles" began blipping down the middle of it. Blip, blip, blip.

In a tone like "Let's pretend," Stevie said, "Run! It's a ghost!" Maybe we were just country dumb but he didn't sound afraid, nor was I. I turned and started running toward home, holding my airplane up to see the propeller turn in the light reflected off the white gravel.

Suddenly Johnny shrieked. I turned to find the red light hard on our heels. I grabbed his hand and, with all three of us now screaming at the top of our lungs, we sprinted for home. The light, nebulous and smokey again, moved to our left and raced along the fence beside us. Would it cut us off at the turn?

Having heard our screeches, both parents were waiting on the porch. The light turned the corner with us and strung itself along about thirty feet of the fence opposite the house. Mom and Dad saw it, too. After a few minutes of just watching, our ever-cheeky mother put it to the test. With Steve and me clinging to her, she walked down the highway toward the gravel road. The light moved with us. When we moved back toward home, so did the light. Then we watched it from the relative safety inside the house. After a while it disappeared, leaving nothing behind but the old sagging fence and a mystery. The next day, Mom checked the newspapers but found nothing. She called the weather station but they reported no anomalies. None of the neighbors had seen it. Some months later, there was a news article about children in a trailer court being burned by a mysterious red light. We never learned anything more.

UFO-related lights are usually described as fast-moving balls that zip around swiftly and erratically, then disappear. I'd never read of shape-shifting lights with glassy poles. But what else could it have been? No one even had theories.

Other than vaguely recalled, slim possibilities, I couldn't recall any other weird thing that might relate to aliens or provide explanations for what happened with Luke. It did raise the question again, if Tom's story was true, then why would aliens be interested in me?

***

"Why me?" I asked Tom. It was a couple of days after our meeting at his condo and he was driving me home from the theater where we had watched *Star Wars: Attack of the Clones*.

"What did you think of the movie?" Tom responded.

His sidestep miffed me. It's insulting to distract a child that way, more so for a middle-aged woman. But maybe if I played his game, I might have a better chance of coming back around to the question a second time.

"Great graphics but lots of cheese. What did you think about it?"

"I liked it."

"Why did you like it?"

"Humm, I don't know. I just liked it."

How typical that he wouldn't—or couldn't—express himself in more detail.

He dimmed the car lights for an oncoming car. Then, as if he'd read my thoughts, he added, "I thought Padme was gorgeous. The Genosian arena fight scene was good, too."

The Genosian fight had turned my stomach—chaining humans to be shredded by monsters five times their size? That's even less sport than watching Christians run from lions. Somewhere I'd read that most movies are made for adolescent males, but it would have been rude to say that. I just said, "Padme really was beautiful, wasn't she?"

With the other car now behind us, Tom flicked the high beams back on. Even though the row after row of orange trees offered few landmarks, I knew from the time passed that the drive was almost over. If I was going to get any information out of him, I had to try now. "Why me, Tom?"

"Can't we just enjoy the ride home without getting into that stuff?" he said.

"I need to know," I said.

"I thought you decided you couldn't trust anyone's opinion but your own. Why ask me?"

"The internet doesn't explain anything personal. Only you know the answer to that."

"You already know why," he said.

"If I know why, then why is it I don't know what you say I know?"

"Because you're apparently not thinking about the obvious."

"Okay, I admit sometimes I can't see the forest for the trees. Give me a clue."

He said nothing for a few tenths of a mile.

When he finally spoke, I wasn't prepared for his answer. "I hate to make it so easy, but what if I said 'black and white'?"

Black and white?

Black and white?

How was this possible? Tom—Tom the argumentative nobody had shocked me again with an insight that went straight to the heart of the question.

From the beginning, he'd told me why—because I was half-and-half of warring interplanetary races. I'd dismissed that explanation but now the meaning popped into vivid relief. The hair stood up on the back of my neck. I turned my head away from Tom to stare unseeing into the darkness, into the quantum mystery his words had thrown me into. The Eloysians were the good guys and the Deneb were bad guys—the extremes of good and bad. And then there was me; beyond the ordinary capabilities of the average person, didn't I understand the extremes of black and white, of positive and negative?

***

"Let's see if I can figure out a way to explain this to you," Jim, my therapist, had said a decade earlier. Where Tom's short body was off-putting, I found Jim's appealing, broad-shouldered and muscular. His dark eyes looked like they could see into your soul, not piercing the way mine did, probing for truth, but patient and understanding, inviting. After thinking a few seconds, he stretched his arms outward on each side of himself, his hands just behind the line of his peripheral vision. "It's like this," he said. "It's like you see things as either one side or the other, but not both at the same time." He waggled the fingers of one hand and then the other, demonstrating that to see either, he'd have to turn his head. He couldn't see both at the same time. "In psychological jargon, it's called splitting."

"Splitting," I said, more rote-reciting than understanding

He nodded.

"Splitting means, you're almost like two people. It's like sometimes you see yourself as being all good, but then suddenly you make a mistake and you see yourself as being a total failure. When you are on one side, you forget the other exists. Does this make sense?"

I nodded. I recognized the experience.

"That's what splitting means, that the world seems to be all-good or all-bad, all-white or all-black, with no grays in between."

Few things are more difficult than accepting that one's understanding is distorted—unless it might be admitting it. "Have the courage to be imperfect," Jim had said early on. Indeed, it took courage to admit to having faults, even to oneself. But if being wrong is one of the worst feelings in the world, one of the best is experiencing the aha! that makes the world happier and more understandable, more doable, to hear the "click" of "aha!" as the pieces fall into place. To find ways to sort confusions into orderly paths of meanings, to have conflicts reduced to healthy simplicities, to find a world that made increasing sense, for that I'd become willing to suffer the humiliations of admitting that I needed to change.

Good and bad, Jim had said. Black and white. That had a ring of truth. Almost like being two people. That's how it had been. Passionate romances fried into ashes by sudden rages, the rages fired by a sudden, bitter disillusionment. Great hopes one day to be followed by abject despair the next. How did he know me so well? Was he psychic?

I felt my face flush. Looking down at the carpet, I said, "I've tried hard to overcome the bad side."

"Overcoming it isn't the goal. This isn't about getting rid of any part of yourself."

I looked back up, astonished. "Why wouldn't we want to be rid of what is so destructive?"

"It's not that we condone the destructiveness. It's that we own it. The operative word here is not 'elimination,' but 'integration'. If you can accept that what you call badness exists at the same time as your more positive attributes, then something interesting happens—usually the badness becomes less extreme."

"But why wouldn't we want to be all-good?"

"That's not the way life works. Everyone is part good, part not-so-good. If we try to believe we're all good, then it's like we're pretending; we're in denial about the reality of who we are. If those negative parts that we are trying to deny can't come out through normal channels, then pressure builds until it squeezes out in abnormal ways."

"How do I deal with it?"

"Integrate. It's about letting each side, the good and the bad, the black and the white, see each other. Like making friends with yourself."

"That sounds good, but how does that happen?"

"When you find yourself thinking that things are either all good or all bad, then see it as a symptom, a signal, that you aren't in a rational state. Then start looking around to see the other side, too." Jim spread his arms and moved them a little more forward so now he could see both at the same time. He waggled his fingers again, smiling at me encouragingly. "Just be patient—it will take time."

***

It did take time. Years. During that experience of development, I'd seen that, given time (and awakenings from TM), anyone can change and grow. Tom said that being half good-half bad meant that I could "talk to them, get them to stop the war." In learning to see degrees of gray in myself, I had also learned to see it in others. Was that why aliens thought I could help, because I knew that Divinity lay at the heart of everyone?

But why wouldn't they prefer professional peacemakers like, say, Marshall Rosenberg, the internationally famous mediator who founded Nonviolent Communication? Could it be that even though Rosenberg was more skilled, my enlightenment experience had left me less enmeshed in the limitations of the material world, more open to possibilities, deeper in faith that even bad people could change? Been there, done that, came back with the map. The enlightenment experience had left me grounded in the sacred underpinnings of reality. I felt my eyebrows raise as I realized that intelligent beings anywhere in the universe would necessarily share the same underlying natural laws that govern humans. Was this the real reason Tom pursued me, because, deeper than my dislike for him, he felt my respect for the sacredness of his inner being? If I could overcome my fear of them, might extraterrestrials also respond to such total respect?

Also, having endured layers of shocks regarding the existence of beings outside our culture of knowledge gave me an advantage. Without that understanding and experience, experts who lacked such preparation would be distracted by high strangeness, disgust, fear, and other potentially disabling emotions. Under such circumstances, could it be that, being steps ahead, I could work more efficiently to bring peace? Where *they* just waiting for me to overcome my fears so that I could do the work?

For the first time, I considered the possibility that I'd underestimated what I might have to offer. A lot of movies and novels portray an ordinary person thrust into extraordinary situations, where someone called Stupid, Asleep, or Nobody is picked out of the muck to be transformed into Hero. As reported by Joseph Campbell, author of *Hero of a Thousand Faces*, it's the classic hero tale, told the world over in countless languages and cultures. Campbell wrote, "the hero ventures forth from the world of common day into a region of supernatural wonder, fabulous forces are there encountered and a decisive victory is won: the hero comes back from his mysterious adventure with the power to bestow boons on his fellow man." George Lucas used this theme as background to create *Star Wars*.

One theme is that, if the hero doesn't go voluntarily, then he or she is forced by circumstances. After his initial refusal to join the rebellion, destruction of his home and the death of his aunt and uncle forced Luke Skywalker into his journey. As an ordinary naïve nobody, was I being forced (or, as Tom said, "brought along") to venture into the world of the hero?

At least in the movies, Stupid becomes Hero because he or she has at least a smattering of skills uniquely suited to the situation. In *The Last Starfighter*, for instance, Alex Rogan, a college-age kid who helps his mom in her trailer park, is tapped to fight the vicious Xur of the Ko-Dan Armada. Alex's qualifying skill is that for years he's been blasting away at an arcade game that turns out to be a simulation for actual weaponry needed to fight the Ko-Dan.

In real life, George Takei, who played Sulu in *Star Trek*, had so internalized his control panel that, like the Galaxy Quest crew, he automatically knew which buttons to push in any given situation. Likewise, in *Galaxy Quest*, the dysfunctional cast of a *Star Trek*-type TV series gets tagged by aliens to help in their war with the villainous warlord, Sarris. When the actors realize they are not there as paid actors for an amateur video but to fight actual battles with an actual villain, fear at first freezes them into paralysis. However, given that the tangible ship the aliens provide is an exact copy of their production mock-up, they found themselves adapting quickly. For battle strategies, they use tricks they'd learned from past scripts. "Remember how we handled the bad guy in Episode 41?"

Practice, practice, practice, that is what gives us skills portable to other situations, because knowledge *evolves*. If Tom, the guns-and-ammo jingoist, had asked me to fight the Deneb, to "blow them out of the water" as he recommended for Earth terrorists, I would have failed. Developing the skills to kill had never been on my bucket list.

But he hadn't asked me to fight a war; he'd asked me to stop one. He'd asked me to be a peacemaker, to protect peaceful victims from angry aggressors, to bring balance and integration to black and white extremes. In that scenario, I had the compassion, years of amateur experience, a lot of practice in communication skills, and the right educational background to build on. Hadn't I even saved my own life using such tools? When an enraged addict had tried to kill me, it took four hours for me to talk him down using reflective listening, a technique of repeating back what others are saying to let them know they are heard. If one is sincerely caring, then even in dangerous or tense situations, such techniques are powerful. Proof of that was that, even as a beginning non-professional, it had worked. Even wild animals respond positively to that kind of attention. So, what if I had more value than I knew? Maryanne Williamson wrote, "Our deepest fear is that we are powerful beyond measure. It is our light, not our darkness, that most frightens us. We ask ourselves, Who am I to be brilliant, gorgeous, talented, fabulous?" If others thought that I was the right person to do the job, then wouldn't it be logical to suppose I might reach inside myself to do it?

Thinking about mediating in an interplanetary war, I felt longing awaken in me, the longing for meaning, the longing to contribute in some great way. I'd always discounted that longing as if it was nothing more than the romance one feels watching a movie, wanting to be a hero even when you're not. Movies momentarily inspire us to seek the Holy Grail of greatness so we can somehow make life better for everyone. Isn't that desire built-in? Don't we all want the courage and nobility to do heroic things? If, on a small scale, I could take the hatred and turn it into love, use skills of communication and caring to turn violence into peace, why couldn't I attempt to heal entire planets if the work was given to me to do?

I had not one shred of evidence for believing a war was happening except Tom's story... well, now I had to add Luke's, too... and I certainly had no reason to believe that I was the "one" needed to stop it. Pretty stupid to even think about it, I thought. Even so, I felt goosebumps.

The crunch of the tires as Tom turned into my driveway brought me out of my thoughts.

"Nice movie," Tom said.

I'd forgotten all about the movie. "Yes, it was. Thanks for taking me." My voice sounded a little hoarse.

"Sure thing, kid. I'll walk you to the door." I must have wobbled a little as we walked up the path. "Are you okay? Not too much of a shock?"

"No… no, I'm okay," I protested, wondering for the millionth time if I was out of my mind.

Chapter

15

THROUGH THE TELESCOPE: ASTRONOMERS AND UFOS

A fter seeing an endorphin-inspiring movie, I usually slept well. But this night I tossed and turned. So many unanswered questions, with wondering if I was a fool still topping the list. You probably think I'm foolish, too, don't you? Most people would have dismissed this whole story as nonsense from the very beginning.

But most people still evaluate reality in terms of classical Newtonian mechanics. That's the billiard ball kind of physics that restricts us to concrete facts and figures rather than waves of probability found in quantum mechanics. Newtonian physics is the bread and butter of daily life. It's how we navigate the mechanical plane of existence, what we use to judge what is real and what isn't. By Newton's standards, we can agree that Tom's tale was absurd.

In quantum physics and higher dimensions of consciousness, however, the picture is far more fluid while still being fully real.

There, we see the interplay between gravity, electromagnetism, and the strong and weak atomic forces. We see how, rising out of the "nothingness" of the unified field, these four forces work together to structure all of creation. This happens in layers. Electrons add up to molecules, molecules add up to cells, cells add up to such things as organs, then these add up to become humans (or plants or rocks or birds or whatever) on the surface. On that level, following the laws of Newtonian mechanics, all things appear separate.

This is a casual way of explaining deep physics and I'm not expecting you to understand based on no more than that, but that's how it works. Humans walk around in the Newton level but the finished products are only on the surface of life. If you follow the trail backwards, you go back to the field of pure possibilities. From there, everything and anything becomes possible, including such seemingly bizarre phenomena such as the simultaneous existence of all time, infinite dimensions, multiple layers of truth, and the absolute fact of omniscience. Newton would say a brick is a brick and is therefore "real," but reality is not only the brick that you can hold in your hand but the electrons that compose it, the fire in the kiln, the mood of the brickmakers, and the pure concept that began it all. From that level, those elements could just as easily become a ceramic bowl or a fine art statue or the left arm of an alligator. From the linear Newton world, quantum physics (and developed consciousness) looks like magic.

But, it isn't magic. It's only a more abstract order of natural law. It's just a larger understanding of how the universe works. Having seen it directly during the *Maha* experience, I knew that anything—literally anything—is possible. Having seen it even once had left me more porous, more open to the unusual, and more willing to consider alternatives. I wasn't tied to linear Newtonian thinking, because I knew that reality exists *beyond* that level. That was why I couldn't automatically shut the door to these far-out possibilities.

That was also why I was so attentive to rings of truth. If one were to measure the sound vibrations on a junky car and compare it to those on a Tesla, the first would be full of muddy, blurred lines and the second would show clear, distinct lines. Like that, if we are pure enough to know how to listen, when something is false, it sounds muddy. When it is true, it rings as clearly as a bell.

In Tom's case, that ring my intuition heard had been neither clear nor consistent. To shift the comparison from hearing to vision in order to make it understandable, I would describe what I heard as resembling what happens when the wind flicks back the leaves of a tree but, out of the corner of your eye, you *think* you saw a light. It was just enough to tickle my interest. It left me feeling alert, wishing it would happen again so I could be sure. Even when Newtonian logic said to quit, that ring kept me moving forward, leaving me sensing that, if only I could pinpoint it, something of value existed that I needed to discover.

***

In contrast, one very solid Newtonian bit of logic consistently brought Tom's story and questions about vague rings to a dead halt. That thought was that no entities were going to bank on an unknown. If I was truly needed to help aliens, then wouldn't this require them to have met me face to face? I had no memories of anything like that, of course, but in that weird world of ufology, having no memory is not proof. The argument repeated ad infinitum states that "absence of evidence is not evidence of absence." Less than ten percent of abductees/contactees have memories accessible to them outside of hypnosis. Was it possible I'd met with aliens and had no memory of it?

When I imagined being face to face with bug-eyed humanoids, I couldn't have felt more primordial alarm than if I'd found a snake in my bed. Merely imagining a spaceship over the lake had left me unsettled for hours. The more I'd learned since, the more frightened I became. But I wasn't the type to be afraid of imaginary things and, unless it had to do with potential husbands, I also wasn't the type to get caught up in flights of fancy. So why was I so scared?

Bud Hopkins, who's been called the father of abduction research, had created a list of 52 symptoms of Post Abduction Syndrome (PAS). I checked off half the boxes. Had another person scored that high, they might have been convinced they'd been abducted but I saw that most of the items were no different than symptoms of ordinary PTSD. Only two things on that list related exclusively to alien abduction: implants and missing time. (Implants are rice-sized foreign objects found in the body.) If I had implants I didn't know it, and I felt certain I had no missing time. Most abductions happen at night but wouldn't I have noticed something intuitively? Or something out of the ordinary— clothes on wrong, sleeping in a different place, or blood on the sheets? A shiver ran through me. I did recall, twice, finding odd spots of blood on a sheet or pillowcase. I told myself there was a rational explanation, like a scab breaking off or a fingernail cut, and dismissed it. I waved all that away as inconsequential. Because of all this ruminating, I was missing time right now: sleep time.

***

I came awake to a gray pre-dawn, aching and irritable from not getting enough sleep. After meditating, I was fixing a fruit bowl for breakfast when it hit me—if any trustworthy scientists had seen UFOs, wouldn't they be astronomers? Why hadn't I thought of this when I read about Peter Sturrock, the astronomer who'd argued with the *Condon Report?* I abandoned the fruit, turned on the computer, and typed "astronomers and UFOs" into Google. In .46 seconds, what flashed onto the screen were respectable names with respectable letters behind them, connected to respectable universities.

It didn't take long to see that even scientists were quarreling about ufology. But scientists have always argued. It was how they exchanged ideas to get the truth. What made their quarreling different from UFO armchair theorists was that they did it with educated facts rather than exclamation marks. The major point of contention regarding UFOs was that, because of the limitations imposed by the speed of light, space flight over long distances was out of the question. This argument claimed visitors couldn't come to earth because it would require upwards of centuries to traverse distances between planets. To understand this, let's start small. We live in what astronomers call the Local Bubble, which consists of all the stars and planets within five parsecs (16 light years) from Earth. At the speed of light, the minimum time it would take to reach the star closest to Earth, the red dwarf star Proxima Centaur would be four years. Everything else is much, much further.

Our best distance accomplishment so far is Voyager II, launched in 1977. Despite the existence of hyper-drives in movies, Voyager II's speed is the equivalent of a covered-wagon crossing the prairies. If we could go at the speed of light, we could get to Pluto from Earth in twelve minutes. But using our primitive Newtonian technology, after twelve *years* Voyager II had barely reached Neptune. It's expected that to even reach Mars at clunky non-light speeds, it will take around nine months.

On a bigger scale, the issue becomes almost too large to grasp. A light year is ten trillion kilometers (about six trillion miles). The Andromeda Galaxy—the nearest big galaxy to us—is (brace yourself) over two and a half million light years away. But there's more. A German supercomputer estimated at least another 500 billion galaxies exist beyond those that are visible to us, adding at least another dozen billion light years further out.

So, there you have it. Distances like these are what makes many scientists believe that space travel is impossible. But how can our thinking be so limited? Do we think progress stops at our present level of knowledge? That kind of thinking would have prevented us from creating heavier-than-air flying machines, breaking the sound barrier, or sending men to the moon. But here's the secret key to understand— science advances. Each step builds on all that has gone before. A man using a horse and buggy would laugh to think of anyone reaching the moon. But where it truly was impossible to reach the moon in 1900, countless layers of research and development took us from the automobile to airplanes to jets to rockets to the moon 69 years later. So, why should we think science will stop where it is now? The speed of light is fixed, yes, but SOL only limits things that are limited by light or limited by Newtonian thinking. A thought, for instance, is far faster than the speed of light. Likewise, gravity is only barely understood. And dimensionality is a whole new ball game, barely touched even by the most advanced physicists. Rapid travel through space isn't impossible, it's only that humans haven't discovered or developed it yet…or gotten that knowledge from the aliens. In 2022, it is estimated that human knowledge is doubling every 12 hours, so why doubt that "instant" space travel is possible, especially as alien spaceships are apparently doing it.

Of course, naysayers will continue to make supercilious challenges, including reminding us yet again that Alan Hale, the co-discoverer of the Hale-Bopp comet, said that three principles must be met to evaluate the existence of spaceships and aliens.

1. Extraordinary claims require extraordinary evidence.

2. The burden of proof is on the positive, meaning that he who makes the claim must provide the proof.

3. Occam's Razor, i.e., the simplest explanation, which fits all the observed facts, is probably the correct answer.

As a lover of the philosophy of science, I certainly agree with those points. But I would counter with, how much proof is enough? We need to consider what Philip Coppens (*The Ancient Alien Question*) said about how different people have different requirements for belief. Just look at how, despite irrefutable evidence to the contrary, some people insist the Earth is flat or that it has only existed for 6,000 years. Even with the presentation of a pelt, the extraordinary claim about the duck-billed platypus was unresolved because the pelt was believed to be a hoax. Despite reports from sailors and suction cup marks on sperm whales that argued that giant squid exist, scoffers claimed them to be mythological until 2004. If people are not ready to believe, they will find reasons to disbelieve even when proof argues otherwise.

It is like that in ufology. Whether it is videos, eyewitness reports, multiple witnesses, burn marks, radiation effects, implants, and even medical and scientific endorsements, the proofs provided by ufology are more often refuted than accepted. One of the best cases that demonstrates this resistance in the face of evidence is the Rendlesham Forest Incident. Known as the British Roswell, the case met every criterion as evidence. The first requirement for proof is witnesses. On the Rendlesham US Air Base, several military personnel, including the base commander, Deputy Lieutenant Colonel Charles I. Halt, and others collectively saw a glowing craft on the ground. Another requirement is physical proof. After the craft left, they found burn marks and broken branches on the trees, indentions on the ground where the craft had been sitting (for which plaster casts still exist), and a higher radiation count. At the same time, local animals were spooked. Less evidence has been used to send people to death row. Yet, for years, this has been considered insufficient as proof that an alien ship landed there.

When I began researching, I fully expected to discover that aliens *didn't* exist. Now I find less intelligence in the denial than in the positive. Naysayers often use Occam's Razor to argue that there always exists "simpler," more prosaic explanation for UFO evidence. But where Occam's Razor is a valuable scientific perspective, many "simple" explanations don't fit the evidence. For instance, I was taken aback that the "prosaic" answer to the Rendlesham evidence was the accusation that what witnesses claimed were glowing lights on a craft were actually the light from a lighthouse some miles distance. If you were familiar with a lighthouse, as the airbase crew were, do you think you couldn't tell the difference between it and lights on a spaceship? Occam's razor can only be applied if it is adequate to address all the data, which the lighthouse theory failed to do.

Another "prosaic" response was from the notorious UFO debunker, Philip Klass. He dismissed the indentions found at Rendlesham as "fairy rings." But which is the simpler explanation, that the evenly spaced, precisely-sized indentions were due to the random peccadillos of nature or that they were marks left behind by a mechanical craft's stabilizing legs? In cases like this, it takes more elaborate imagination to think of alternatives than it does to have one simple explanation— that a spaceship, as directly witnessed by several responsible humans, had landed there.

Astronomer J. Allen Hynek famously said, "Ridicule has no place in science." Yet, naysayers can be identified by their common feature: ridicule. They scoff, scorn, and mock on a surface level while lacking the depth of knowledge known to long-time researchers. The fact remains that, unless you're enlightened or dealing in pure numbers, absolute truth rarely exists. Like the doubts about the platypus pelt, if one refuses to believe, then one can't see the truth even when it is in one's face.

Astronomers, on the other hand, are experts in what goes on in our skies. Unlike the general public, they would not be confused by odd clouds or the planet Venus. In 1952, Hynek, an astronomer and one of the founding fathers of ufology, did an informal poll among 44 fellow scientists. Of those, 25 percent claimed to have seen lights moving across the sky "much faster than a plane and much slower than a meteor." One claimed to have seen "a cluster of five ball-bearing-like objects" moving rapidly across the sky and disappearing but, like most scientists, didn't want his name released. Hynek wrote, "This is a characteristic of scientists in general when speaking about subjects which are not in their own immediate field of concern." This would explain why many scientists don't speak out more about UFOs.

Peter Sturrock also did a poll, finding sixty-two astronomers who admitted observing something relevant to the UFO phenomenon while lacking prosaic explanations.

Astronomer Clyde Tombaugh, the discoverer of Pluto, not only reported UFO sightings but called for scientific research regarding them. But in an atmosphere of ridicule, who would fund such research?

Because ufology at first appeared to be such a sleazy business, I'd assumed no respectable scientist would be interested. But how many times do we make assumptions simply because we failed to inquire? Now that I had finally inquired, I was excited to read rational and objective discussions about unidentified objects in our skies. I was further astounded to find that formal scientific interest went back much further in time. In April 1910, a British paper reported that a two-day conference was held at the Royal Society of London, titled, "The Detection of Extraterrestrial Life and the Consequences for Science and Society." This paper also reported an astrobiology conference in Texas at which they would discuss new methods of detecting aliens. Science has observed more than the public is aware.

By the time I put the computer to sleep, it was nearly 2:00 in the afternoon. Excitement and fascination had kept me working. But, with a poor night's sleep and no breakfast, my eyes were bleary with fatigue and I was light-headed with hunger. I made a sandwich with a freshly picked avocado and headed for the Florida sunshine on the veranda.

I loved my screened veranda and the comfort of its yellow and white rattan furniture. With a happy tummy, I lay down on its sofa, stuffing a bolster under my head. The birds warbled background songs and the sun was twinkling on the lake while I closed my eyes.

Until now, I'd held Tom's tale at arm's length the way one would hold a muddy dog, not wanting to get splattered. But having trustworthy scientists (rather than only internet theorists) say they too had seen UFOs, I was ready to go to the next level, to ask myself emotionally, what if it is true that I am being groomed for a galaxy-class mission? I had no way to find out directly but what would I learn if I tested myself with a gedankenexperiment?

A *gedankenexperiment*, German for thought experiment, is an investigation in one's head. Einstein made this form of research famous. He examined how gravity works by imagining an elevator in space and studying the insights he gained from it to come up with the world-changing relativity theory. Other famous thought experiments that solved theoretical problems included Maxwell's demon and Schrödinger's cat. We lesser mortals often use similar imagination techniques to think, "If I say this, then how would they respond?" Or, we ask ourselves, "What is the worst thing that can happen?" Then, with as much realism as possible, we visualize it. Psychologists use this approach to help desensitize people with phobias, having them imagine themselves in situations that frighten them, such as facing dogs or airplanes or their mother-in-law. Research has shown that for athletes, picturing themselves performing in detail is almost as effective as actual practice. If intelligent, mature people used imagination so successfully, why couldn't I? A thought experiment isn't daydreaming per se, not a wishful-thinking fantasy, but a careful test of "if this happened, then what's the logical step?"

In the pleasant drift of a near doze, I opened my mind to the question, how would I react if I was called on to mediate between intergalactic cultures?

Chapter

16

GEDANKENEXPERIMENT: IMAGINATION IN SEARCH OF REALITY

Where to begin? To do diplomacy with aliens meant I'd have to imagine meeting them in person. The thought made me shudder. How could I possibly mediate with creatures who terrified me? Rick Archer told me that Maharishi, in his few comments about beings from other worlds, had laughingly said that the gathering at the Mos Eisley cantina in *Star Wars* was nothing compared to the reality of the numbers of beings who actually existed. It was too fearful to imagine. I decided that, instead of envisioning scary, foreign-looking creatures, I'd imagine myself meeting with the tall, blond-haired, blue-eyed, human-appearing aliens—the "Nordics." Instantly, I saw them staring back with eyes that were intelligent, knowing, and highly developed. Clearly, this was already out of my league. The idea they needed a human to mediate for them was laughable.

But what if the problem race was one more primitive? As a writer, I often thought of myself as a step-down transformer, someone who could translate big, abstract ideas into simpler language. If the more advanced beings needed a translator between them and the less evolved, I might be useful in that situation. For that role, I'm sorry to say what came to mind was humans. Humans—the creatures who had such a history of raping and pillaging and who were so stupid that they were trashing and sickening their own planet certainly didn't seem very evolved, did they?

I imagined three Nordic types sitting on one side of a large oval table standing in as the Eloysians: Ett, Boef, and Kam. On the other side, I imagined three humans: Bob, Sally, and George standing in as the Deneb, lusting for the gold on Eloysia likw US corporations raid and pillage the Amazon and other places around the world. Like Amazon tribes, the Eloysians had no standing army, no slick lawyers, no powerful politicians. They're defenseless. Wasn't this exactly the situation Tom had painted about the Eloysians and Deneb? If so, then this was another game-over scenario—game-over because power-hungry, profit-lusting humans can't be reasoned with. They can only be out-maneuvered and I had no skills at that sort of thing.

But Tom had said the reason that I was needed was because my DNA was half of both sides, half good, half bad. Didn't I have the power to understand because I also had been like that at one time—greedy, violent, disrespecting of others? And wasn't I proof that we have the power to change, grow, and develop in character and consciousness? Bob, Sally, and George might appear to be evil on the surface but deep inside them, they too are Divinity incarnate, disconnected by layers of error, ignorance, and lack of character development. What if, instead of focusing on their greed, I would focus on the inner truth of who they were at their most sacred level?

This had worked not only in sweet little church groups but in deadly situations as well. Joe, the guy who tried to kill me years earlier, had been a big man, six-foot tall and at least 180 pounds. He'd trapped me against a wall and started choking me. Somehow, I had the presence of mind to know that if I struggled, tomorrow's news would report him as my killer. Even if I'd had a gun or known martial arts, it was highly unlikely that I could have bested him. I did the only thing I could do—I looked into his soul. Whether that woke up some sense in him or if he found some on his own, he stopped choking me and began hitting and cursing me instead. The latter was better than being dead. I stayed calm, at least outwardly. I didn't fight back. Even when said things that were untrue, I didn't argue. Knowing he must be in a lot of pain to be so irrationally enraged, I felt genuine compassion for him. Fortunately, my ex-husband had taught me a technique called "reflective listening." It's very simple but very powerful—you repeat back whatever the other person is saying. Typically, when someone disagrees with us, we respond by insisting that they are wrong and we are right. In turn, they argue that it is we who are wrong. As humorously expressed by author Robert McCloskey, it's a situation of "I know that you believe you understand what you think I said, but I'm not sure you realize that what you heard is not what I meant." In this technique, however, instead of being defensive and insisting on getting our own points across, we only repeat back whatever they have said, as word for word as possible. That reduces misunderstandings, increases clarity, and promotes a sense of connection. We say, "What I heard you say is…" and then end with, "Did I understand you correctly?" This doesn't mean we have to agree with them, it only confirms to them that we listened, and to ourselves, that we heard. When people feel heard, the fight tends to go out of them and they become more receptive, more willing to cooperate. Anger de-escalates so that rational discussion then becomes possible. Even though Joe's outward behavior was despicable, I didn't focus on condemning him. Who changes just become someone criticizes? Instead, I respected the core, that precious "I" at the heart of everyone, and he felt it. In psychology, this attitude is called non-judgmental acceptance or unconditional positive regard. It's powerful in promoting spontaneous change. In Joe's case, it took maybe twenty minutes before he gradually stopped being violent, then maybe another three hours of me repeating his words back to him before he finally nodded off and I was able to escape.

Unless you experience how deep, how intimate, we can get using these non-violent techniques, you won't be able to understand why, rather than traumatic, the incident registered in memory as priceless. It was a very one-sided conversation but it allowed me see deep inside him, to understand why he was like he was. His development had been arrested at the age of nine when he'd discovered drugs. Now 40 or so, having the maturity of a nine-year-old meant he couldn't hold down a job or have normal relationships. It was a miserable life. A serious part of his tragedy was that, years earlier, he'd watched his wife blow her brains out in front of him and he still struggled with the horror of it. I am not a therapist so I can't be sure, but I truly believe some healing happened for him that night. You can't see that precious inner core without being moved, yet we rarely listen long enough to see it until, as happened in this case, we are forced to do so. We'd rather be "right" than to be loving.

Marshall Rosenberg, the famous mediator who founded Non-violent Communication, said that, even when mediating between murderous African tribes, if he could get both sides to understand the needs of the other, then he could get a resolution in twenty minutes. Likewise, the famous moral psychologist Jonathan Haidt, author of *The Righteous Mind: Why Good People are Divided over Politics and Religion*, argued that both political sides have *legitimate* needs. Battles ensue because we usually fail to inquire about—much less care about—those legitimate needs. If we could take the time to respect each other sufficiently to listen, our political wars would end.

Could I use understandings like this to get a resolution in this case? I didn't see how raping someone else's planet could be considered legitimate but if I let Bob, Sally, and George tell their story while I listened from the heart, might a way emerge to reduce the conflict? I wanted to dislike them for their crudity the same way I disliked Tom, but would respectful listening soften them enough that they could then respect others? I didn't know if it was possible but, sitting there in imagination between the two opposing sides, considering all this, I felt my heart quicken with interest. I was practical enough to know that it wouldn't be smart to apply but if the Eloysians rang my doorbell to offer me the job, I'd be willing to give it my best shot.

And, wouldn't it be fun to try?

Chapter

17

WISHING IT WAS TRUE

"I don't care if your story is true, or not," I chuckled to Tom. "I just wish it was." We'd been on a late afternoon walk and had sat down at the city park lake to watch kids play at the water's edge. I don't know when it happened but I'd stopped feeling embarrassed to be seen with him in public. At least that showed some progress in my character development.

The thought experiment hadn't removed my real-life terror of aliens but it had left me with a romantic high. By romance, I don't mean sensuous fascination for another person but the kind of high that one feels for slick cars, cool clothes, and hot business deals. Fans feel it for stars and college students feel it when they sign astronomical loans dreaming of their future. Such highs are what drive us to buy products associated with movies and to spend small fortunes inside video games for items that don't even exist. I was having it from fantasizing about doing diplomacy with warring planets.

The kicker was that I was almost as scared of romance as I was of aliens. I knew it for what it is, an illusion. Whether it is the lover-sex thing, the glorious spirit of adventure one feels thinking about things like the barnstormers in the early days of airplanes, the romance of swash-buckling musketeers, or inspirations from movies such as *Star Wars, The Last Starfighter,* and *The Matrix,* where one identifies with greatness and heroism.

But it's all temporary insanity. During a romantic high, one's biochemistry produces the most delicious of its neurochemicals—increased testosterone (sex drive), dopamine (reward-seeking), and oxytocin (the cuddle chemical), all fueled by norepinephrine (an adrenalin-like substance that fires a larger-than-life feeling). These cause us to see the world through rapture-colored glasses. They're what makes your lover's shambolic bachelor pad look quaintly charming.

And, if it's high, then isn't it logical that what goes up must come down? Until we're enlightened, no bliss is permanent. On average, romantic relationships crash about a year after one believes one has married the dream. That's when the body normalizes, bringing the mind down with it. For some, the glow fades gradually; for others, there's a sudden crash that corresponds in intensity to the height of the high—the pure misery of disillusionment that leaves you feeling betrayed not by your own silly dreams but by the lover or the con-artist or the illusory hopes.

I thought I was too smart to get caught up in romance, especially as I knew the secret weapon against it—feed it reality. I had fully expected research in ufology to *poof!* all that nonsense about UFOs and Tom's tale. But what had gotten poofed was entirely unexpected: my faith in things I thought were inviolable. I'd learned that scientists could be warped for profit and that my government was darker than I'd ever imagined. All the King's horses and all the King's men couldn't have put my innocence back together again. Then, when I'd imagined a test for myself, expecting I would fail, it had instead snagged my heart with wishful thinking. No, I absolutely didn't believe a bit of it; I just wanted to.

Tom spread his arms across the back of the wooden bench. "So, you want to believe now, do you?"

"I only said I *wished* it was true."

"And why do you want to believe."

I hadn't told him about the gedankenexperiment because I didn't think he would understand. I figured he'd just tease. "It just feels like something I've wanted my whole life. Deep down, I've always felt I had some mission to do. Maybe it's to bring peace to the world."

"Bet you didn't think it would be 'worlds,'" he chuckled again.

"I certainly didn't."

"Humm," was all he said.

I turned my head to look at him, to see if his face explained what he meant by *humm*. He was smiling that enigmatic half-smile of his, the one that might be a "gotcha" or a master's satisfaction at seeing his pupil finally seeing the light. Or maybe he was just enjoying watching toddlers immersed in the importance of patting wet sand.

Not looking at me, he asked, "Did you ever wonder where you got that drive?"

"To do something important? Doesn't everyone feel that way?"

"No. Some people just want to watch TV or go to baseball games."

I knew that one of the symptoms on the abduction list was feeling you had something important to do but I shrugged. I was too suspicious of my illusory high to take anything too seriously. Just for fun, I asked, "So when do they come to get me?"

Tom chuckled again and looked at me with those vague, watery eyes. "It may not be long now. I have a meeting with them soon."

"Soon?"

He nodded. "In Georgia. Next week. I'll tell you more after that."

I was surprised that he was so forthcoming. "What happens in Georgia?"

"Oh, we'll just have to wait and see," he said, his voice singsong with a coy tease.

Even buoyed by dazzle chemicals, I felt a wave of irritation. I didn't inquire further. I knew that if I grilled him, he would only clam up and I'd end up frustrated. I still didn't believe him. I just wanted to. "I need to get home," I sighed.

Chapter

18

RICK'S REPORT

I love philosophical arguments. By this, I don't mean heated battles but arguments in the name of truth, the way a dog argues with a bone, trying it from this angle then that, to get to the marrow. In ufology, however, the arguments were more like a pack of dogs wanting to own the bone or the quarreling in family disputes that requires police intervention. As one wit said, next to breathing, sex, and beer, the need to be right is the single most important aspect of life. That appeared to be the case in ufology. With only the heated point and counterpoints to go on, all I had after a year of exploration was what's called a stage one conclusion—a generalized overview leaning toward the belief that, most likely, UFOs *did* exist. Conventional or "prosaic" explanations did little to convince me they didn't. Most often, those were shallow at best, irrational at worst. Regardless who made the claim, a fireball that makes two ninety-degree turns is not a meteor or a weather balloon. Governmental denial, making it a joke, or downplaying reports from responsible people was patently insufficient.

Likewise, there were too many redacted lines on formerly classified documents, too many instances of multiple witnesses, too much trace evidence, supportive details, and unexplained loose ends for me to believe that nothing was happening. But neither was anything so rock-solid that it was beyond being attacked by virulent naysayers and my own chronic doubts. I was sick of all those conflicting opinions. I liked to do my own investigations but by now I recognized that scrabbling around in the murk on the Internet wasn't going to deliver anything deeper than what I'd already learned. I was ready for the next level—to consult people whose opinions I respected—my friends in the TM movement. As a member of a chat group that didn't fear tackling hard questions such as "Is the Unified Field Absolute?" and "How does one identify different states of consciousness in practical application?" I asked, "Have any of you heard any Holy people speaking about extraterrestrials, space ships, etc.?" By "Holy people" I knew they'd understand I meant people enlightened enough to experience *Ritam Bhara Pragya* (omniscience).

Other than a couple of sarcastic quips, no one responded except Rick Archer, a former classmate at Maharishi University. One goldmine answer was all I needed, and he gave me that. I had confidence in Rick. He had a reputation for being knowledgeable and, having known him for over 30 years, I'd come to trust his judgment. Like most responsible TM teachers, he was careful to say only what he had either seen himself or knew from trustworthy sources. He posted that Maharishi referred to extraterrestrials as "the truck drivers of the universe."

I was astonished. Did Maharishi really say that?

I immediately sent Rick a personal message asking where he got that information. He responded that he'd heard it himself, directly from Maharishi. He volunteered more. "A friend of mine was on a meditation course when he and other participants saw a UFO flying outside their dorm rooms. In the lecture hall, Maharishi asked, 'How many got up early this morning?' Most raised their hands. 'And how many looked out the window?' Maharishi asked. Fewer hands raised, but still some. Then Maharishi chuckled and started the meeting with no further explanation."

If Maharishi said it, this was gold to me. The reason I held him in such high regard as a source of information was that his descriptions of enlightenment matched perfectly with my own experiences during omniscience. Also, he'd proved himself in the big picture. Every time I followed his teachings, it brought remarkable benefits. If such a man had treated the concept of extraterrestrials with his signature sense of humor while appearing to accept them as "normal," didn't that indicate that ETs weren't monsters?

When I asked Rick for more information, he wrote, "I'd recommend a book by Joy Gilbert entitled *It's Time to Remember*. I think she might be a former TM teacher."

Bingo! If it was true that she was a former teacher, then she probably shared the same values as Rick and me—having a deep concern for truth in the context of universal reality. I immediately ordered her book from Amazon.

Within days, two things happened that not only brought my research to a dead halt, it made me pack up and flee Florida.

Chapter

19

A TIME TO REMEMBER—THE JOY GILBERT STORY

T he same day Tom left for Georgia to supposedly meet with extraterrestrials (haha), the UPS truck drove up with my book. Abandoning the dishes, I dried my hands and had it torn out of the package almost before he'd gotten out of the drive. I sat sideways on my sunny yellow couch, back against the overstuffed arm, knees drawn up, to read. I was not disappointed. By the time I went to bed, the book had answered my most important questions about aliens.

Gilbert wrote with artless simplicity. Beginning with her shock and disbelief when she was "taken" in Oregon in 1993, her experiences left her feeling she was "immersed in some absurd science fiction film."

"After going to bed at night, I'd lie motionless in the dark, my body rigid with fear… I'd feel them in the shadows, waiting for me to drift off into sleep."

As so many do (and as I had done in the beginning), Gilbert believed those involved in UFO phenomena were probably mentally deficient and that alien experiences reported from hypnosis were fabrications. But in checking out books and documents from university and public libraries, rather than discover they were silly riffraff, she found representatives of the full range of society, "doctors, scientists, psychologists, psychiatrists, police officers, pilots, homemakers, celebrities, utility workers, and even high-ranking government officials." The patterns they reported were consistent with her own experience—"seeing a ray or beam of light; an examining table; being physically probed, ova harvesting in females and sperm collecting in males; missing time; recalling being taken beginning in early childhood; psychic phenomena; scars from unknown origins; memories or evidence of superior surgical techniques and procedures, implants, and unique dreams, the content of which seemed to be purposeful communicating."

Most of what I'd read portrayed aliens as dangerous and abusive but Gilbert claimed that when she stopped panicking, she discovered she was safe in their hands. She realized they were her *friends* (italics hers) and that the picture of reality they espoused was quite positive. She saw that they were doing "necessary, even healing work" that aided her spiritual development. Think of how wild birds and animals panic while humans try to help them. Like that, Gilbert wrote that the way humans interpret such experiences depends more on attitude and state of consciousness than on actual events. According to her, the calmer and more present we are, the more likely we are to understand that extraterrestrials aren't bad guys but benign helpers.

She realized her friends were interdimensional. "I sensed their presence with me at all times… Imparting knowledge to me, they were always kind and loving…Their playful humor and infinite love flowed into me, soothing my anxiety [and] giving me feelings of absolute acceptance and unconditional love." She realized the universe was even more vast than she'd believed. "[Ours] was not the only dimension. These [human bodies] were not the only forms."

Where unbelieving therapists have sometimes labeled experiencers as schizophrenic, bipolar, or delusional, Gilbert's therapist verified she was mentally healthy. He pointed out that respectable researchers, such as Harvard's Dr. John Mack, recognized that so-called abduction experiences weren't delusions. Under hypnosis, Gilbert recalled many "abductions" in which ETs checked her body for disease. She even received medical interventions.

She described how mind and body work together to create our perception of reality, and how fear creates a contraction of consciousness. Contraction is the source of unhappiness. In contrast, expansion produces bliss and happiness. Spiritual development, she found, was a matter of *remembering* deeper levels of who we are. The expansion she acquired from her friends helped her to remember more. These positive cycles awakened her to larger dimensions, larger realities. She wrote, "If our beliefs are limited, we see the world as being full of separate individual things but when beliefs are not limited, then we see that there is no separation between us. It isn't that there is [me] and you, but that we all belong to the same creation. We swim in a sea of ever-present Love, not as thought but as a living reality."

What Gilbert described was very much like what I'd experienced during higher consciousness. Enlightenment isn't some exotic place, not something one merely believes in, but the next stage of human evolution, a very desirable state that gets nurtured and developed with meditation, good health, attention and intention. And, in Gilbert's case at least, enlightenment got developed with a little help from her *friends*. Could it be that, instead of being monsters, aliens were already enlightened and were actually helpers in our human journey towards awakening? Gilbert claimed that being taken and surgically altered had benefited her, given her new abilities, improved her health, and brought new ability to enjoy life. They "allowed me to see the truth.

My awareness moved from one level of consciousness into new realms, new frontiers of understanding. As my fear gave way... I now see the pure flow of creation through everything."

A Time To Remember would not have satisfied those looking for hardcore "proof," nor would it satisfy those who believed they had been forcibly abducted by monsters. But it fit with what I knew about reality. Her words matched with my own direct cosmic experience. Her book had been exactly what I needed. Gilbert's wrote, "Peace will be the main process of development among the people who will inhabit the Earth in the New Age. Many who have been called to serve during this transition will feel the joy in being with the *friends* who are now making themselves known, to share knowledge with us at this time."

By the time I closed the book, the mystery about aliens and UFOs felt solved. "Playful humor and infinite love," Gilbert had written. How different that sounded from the sensationalism and fear-mongering I'd found on the Internet. It appeared that abductions were not for cruel or self-serving experimentation but were a gift to experiencers.

I'd read somewhere that, "Reason is a whore; it will lie with anything." Any statement of belief can be argued from either side. In contrast, expanded consciousness sees the truth, the whole truth, like an *aha!* According to Gilbert, beings from other dimensions belong to that larger, more fundamentally real state of consciousness where truth is not clouded by impurities and the limitations of reason. I trusted that Gilbert was telling the truth.

But, to my profound consternation, it didn't erase the fear. The thought of being taken still left me feeling like jiggling Jell-O. I'd often said I'd do anything to expand consciousness but I'm embarrassed to confess that I felt glad that abductions happened to other people, not to me.

Still, I was satisfied to accept that ETs were not monsters. Closing the book, it felt like my feet were solidly back on the ground. I felt like

I now had a realistic map, one too grounded for such silly imaginary responsibilities as thinking I might be needed to end intragalactic wars. It put me back on the sidelines, an unimportant nobody, safe in a world in which aliens weren't evil. I slept soundly that night.

I suppose I needed the rest before tackling what was to come.

Chapter

20

THUNK

I've said that the best weapon against romance (or fear, or any other misconception) is to feed it reality. After reading Gilbert's book, I felt a click of acceptance as many pieces of the puzzle fell together. All my gedankenexperiment-inspired fantasies collapsed and the world once again felt like it was playing by rules I understood. Gilbert's perspectives were at least similar to other UFO researchers who also believed that ETs were a "multidimensional paraphysical phenomenon." I dismissed lingering doubts in order to go with that analysis, especially since it assured me that I was no longer in danger of being abducted. I found it strange that the fear hadn't gone away but I shrugged that off as a personal quirk. There were other questions I couldn't answer either, such as why was the government so secretive about UFOs? But what could I do about it? The smart thing was to simply stop asking the question. Just let it go. That left only one burning question—Why had Tom told me this wild story that I was a half-and-half alien who needed to end an interplanetary war? I told myself I was ready to let that go, too. Maybe that story was just *his* personal quirk.

What I didn't know was that admitting that I wished his story was true would prove to be the catalyst to bring the whole house of cards to a crashing collapse. Apparently, Tom took it as an encouragement to feed me BS. Before he left for Georgia, he'd started telling me more about his "mission." I listened, not believing anything but no longer arguing, just seeing what he would say.

"You'll be amazed at the people you'll meet," he said.

"People? Do they call themselves 'people'?" I asked.

Tom corrected himself. "Oh, right, that's what I meant—beings. Some of them are people — from Earth, you know. A lot of people are in on these things, but you're right, some beings aren't human."

I held my breath hoping he'd disclose something useful. He didn't, so I asked, "So, whereabouts in Georgia is this meeting?"

"Upstate. Hidden in the woods. We have a secret place there."

"We?" I asked. "Who is this 'we'"?

"That's for me to know and you to find out soon enough."

I tried to ignore the wave of irritation at the tease.

"We'll meet inside a ship," he said.

"What's it like on a ship?"

"They're much bigger than they look. There's plenty of room inside."

That might be true. I'd read a theory that spaceships were dimensional and were larger inside than they looked outside. Bob Lazar described the "sport model" spaceship he worked on as bare bones, no sleeping places, not even bathrooms. The way he described it sounded like the interior had been melted into place. Was that a set-up for dimensionality?

"What's inside them?"

"Nothing. It's all done with mind control." I'd read that as well, that inside crashed/recovered ships they'd found headbands believed to be used for mind-controlling the crafts.

"How does one pack for a trip with them?"

"Oh, don't worry about packing. They provide everything."

I smiled. My mood was such that I was ready to leave for the base on the dark side of the moon…but not planning on it.

***

The same day Tom left for Georgia, Gilbert's book arrived and, within hours, reality popped my fantasy bubble. I didn't mind. I'm essentially a realist. I let it all go the same way one lets go of a visit to a theme park—you have fun while you're there but when vacation is over, you come back to practical life.

When he called me a couple of days later, Tom didn't know about the thought experiment or Gilbert's book. "What's happening at the meetings?" I said, knowing there was no meeting but curious about what he would say.

"Oh, lots and lots," he said in his usual vague terms. "It was a great meeting."

"Why wasn't I invited?"

"Because you aren't ready yet."

I hated it when he said things like that. "You can't tell me at least a little?"

"I'll tell you later," he insisted, his pseudo-cheery tone conveying that he was enjoying his little game.

His openness finally gave me one thing I'd hoped for all along. Before, his story had always been too vague to get an accurate read.

Now, it was no longer vague. He'd dropped his disguises and the cosmic wave function collapsed, leaving him visible for what he was. Truth reverberates like crystal while falsehood sounds like Walmart glass hit with a fingernail, *thunk*. It was such a rock-solid *thunk* that I felt embarrassed for him—a grown man lying like a child, thinking no one else could see it.

Worse—oh, much worse—the mysteries shrunk into a puddle of silliness and I could see *myself* for what *I* was—a gullible idiot. For whatever reason—most likely for making a fool of "Ms. Smarts," to prove that she was not as smart as he was—Tom had played with my gullibility and I had gotten caught up in his little con game. It takes two to work a con, one to offer it, and one to buy it. But even understanding my part in it, I nearly hated him for his. Deeper than just being conned, the feeling was that I'd lost the moon.

I believe in karma. It is irrational to blame others when they are messengers for returning what we have called back to ourselves. Knowing this, my reaction surprised me—I found myself filled with loathing and black rage. I felt betrayed. I was far from perfect but my intentions had been honest while he'd been manipulating just enough that I could never be sure.

After I got the rage under control, I felt numb. I stared at the lake, took the dogs on walks, dangled my feet in the cool water, pondered. It had taken nearly two years to get to the bottom of it, all wasted life, all because Tom was a liar and I was a fool.

When Tom called again, in his pseudo-cheerful voice he said, "I'll be back tomorrow. I'm coming in on a starship."

"Coming in on a starship," I repeated flatly.

"Yep. Right to the door," he said. *Thunk.*

"But what about your van?" I asked, pointing out the obvious. "You drove there, didn't you?"

Small pause.

Then, "Oh, that will get delivered later," he said. *Thunk.*

I've known people a lot meaner than Tom but he had played me for a fool worse than anyone ever had. You'll say you knew it all along. You might agree that I got what I deserved. But with the mystery now bleeding out its life's blood, it felt as tragic as if I'd been betrayed by a lover.

I didn't throw a fit. I didn't castigate or lecture. I didn't tell him the con was over. I didn't even know how to address the issue. I just said, "Okay, Tom. I'll see you when you get back."

Too late, I saw the wrongness of maintaining secrecy about our "relationship." A favorite Maharishi quote has always been, "Do what you know to be right, don't do anything you know to be wrong." Anything that leaves us without a clear conscience is a moral mistake and a call for bad karma. It was right that I wanted to overcome my dislike of Tom but wrong to let embarrassment stop me from freely admitting to my Unity friends that I was seeing him outside of the church. Likewise, I should have been more open about researching ufology. Some reticence to tell others had come from Tom's claim that talking might endanger him or to possibly make a fool of him by disclosing his beliefs about aliens. But I had to admit it—the biggest reason I kept the secret was that I hadn't wanted my beloved friends to think I was a dingbat.

Well, obviously, I was a dingbat. Not only was I a dingbat, it had left me with no one to talk to about it. At this late date, if I told anyone what a fool I'd been, they wouldn't comfort me by saying, "Oh you poor dear. What a cad that man has been to you." No; they'd look askance and say, "And you fell for that?"

The truth is, some people will believe anything. In 1976, it was announced on BBC radio by British astronomer Patrick Moore that, for anyone who wanted to participate, a once-in-a-lifetime experience would happen. At 9:47 on that morning, the planet Pluto would pass behind Jupiter, temporarily causing a gravitational effect from the alignment that would lessen the Earth's gravity. If listeners jumped into the air at the exact moment, they would experience an odd floating sensation. Even though it was an April Fool's joke, immediately after 9:47, the radio station began to receive *hundreds* of phone calls from listeners claiming to have felt it. One caller reported that she and eleven friends had floated around the room.

Hadn't I been exactly that kind of gullible? How could anyone fall for a story that they were needed to stop a war between planets?

Absurd.

Absurd.

Absurd.

There is a Chinese saying, that the more arrogant the person, the easier they can be made into a mark.

Apparently, I was very, very arrogant.

I didn't leave the house for a week. I didn't answer my phone. I meditated extra to find comfort and healing in the silence. I walked the dogs. I took long paddle boat rides on the soothing waters of the lake. I sat on the porch, staring at the sky or the trees or the sandy beach. Finally, watching the ospreys fly over the lake I loved so much, the pair that I'd seen make love in the air then nest and raise their young in a tree just yards from my cottage, I understood what I had to do. Perhaps another person would have shrugged it off as a lesson learned. But I doubted I had learned enough that I wouldn't be equally gullible in the future. Before I could ever trust myself again, I needed to work on developing greater wisdom and character. I knew where I needed to go to get that.

I rose from the couch on the veranda and went through the French doors with their lovely view of the lake, wiped the sand off my feet, then picked up the phone and called a realtor. "I want to sell my cottage on Lake Lotela," I said.

***

"You're what?" Joanne said, a pained expression on her face.

"I've decided to move back to Fairfield," I repeated. Afraid I might see hurt in her eyes, afraid I might cry, I kept my eyes focused downward. Across from me, I could see Tom's belly plopped over the table but I didn't want to see his facial expression either. I hadn't been answering my phone so this was the first he'd learned of my plans. Typically, I would have been courteous enough to give warning but I felt too fragile to even talk to him.

"Where's Fairfield," Mr. Butler asked.

"Fairfield, Iowa," I said, "Thousands of TMers live there around the University that Maharishi founded, my alma mater. I lived there on and off since the '70s."

"Woman, with so many people up north dying to come down here," Jim said, "don't you think you're out of your mind?"

I nodded. I knew I was out of my mind, but not for the reason he was saying. "I know, it sounds crazy," I said. "You're the dearest people in the world, and I don't know how I'll live without you. But I've realized that's where I need to be." If my dearly beloved friends knew what a dupe I'd been, they too might have agreed that I needed more of TM's intelligence-producing meditation programs. Aren't you also shaking your head, saying you knew all along that Tom was a fraud? Or maybe you're even saying something like what Tom would say, something scornful like, see, meditation didn't make you as smart as you thought it did. But at least I'm not wrong about that. Meditating doesn't make you fail-proof, it just makes you smarter than you were yesterday. I needed to get smarter yet.

I tried to comfort myself that I hadn't been entirely a fool. I had heard something so thin and fine that, like the distant whispers of angels, it had been hard to know for sure that I'd heard it. It suggested I might be of real service. All of us have the potential to achieve greatness; that part wasn't fantasy. It speaks to us on a deep level and it sounds like the priceless thing it is, a spark of truth. If we follow it, it leads to significance. Unfortunately, many—like me—fall victim to believing, too soon, that we have found it.

***

In January 2003, my U-Haul truck sat in the driveway, my car on a dolly behind it. Dawn had just begun to spread across the lake, throwing light through tall, curtainless windows to find only emptiness in what was now someone else's cottage. How dearly I would miss this place. How dearly I would miss the lake. How dearly I would miss my Unity friends. A few blocks away on Highway 27, traffic was light; only a few snowbird stragglers arrived in Florida this late in the season. I would take 27 to go in what many said was the wrong direction— north, back to the snow and ice of long, cold winters. But it was also the direction of sanity, just the next logical step toward awakening consciousness sufficiently that I'd never make the same mistake again.

"You shouldn't do this," Tom said, his tone somber. He'd volunteered to pick up boxes of donations for the church rummage sale and to secure the straps on the car dolly. The timber in his voice was no different from the times he'd talked about flying saucers and wars between planets—sincerity glinting like silver through the density of the base metal. But I'd seen enough of the base that I now ignored the silver.

"Shouldn't do what?" I asked. I knew very well what he meant. Not only had I failed to overcome my dislike, I was failing now even to be polite.

"You shouldn't leave," he said. "If you go back, you'll just fade into the background."

I didn't answer. I tried to ignore the cold chills his words brought. I didn't want to hear any more vague rings.

"We need you," he said.

"You lied to me, Tom," I said, throwing some last odds and ends into the donations box. In Iowa, I wouldn't need a bamboo towel holder or a reef-and-fishes statuette.

"I was trying to protect you," he said.

"Lying isn't protecting."

"But you said you wanted to believe."

I ceased sealing the box to stand up and stare at him with my hands on my hips, feeling the anger in my gut explode fire out through my eyes. "Yes, I said that. But that was a wish, Tom, not an appeal. How many times did I say that the most important thing is truth? Honesty is the basis for relationships."

"People can't always be honest," he said limply.

I glared at him. "Honesty is the first law of maturity, but I think you can't even be honest with yourself, much less with someone else." I wasn't thinking of how dishonest I'd been with my Unity friends by not telling them about seeing Tom, nor how, by not being straightforward about my dislike for him, I'd been dishonest with him. Or even how dishonest I'd been with myself, thinking that I might overcome my negative feelings.

He looked away from me, toward the lake. "Maybe there are things you don't understand," he said.

"What I do understand is that people of character don't lie. I also understand that if I've been fool enough to believe such lies, then 1300 miles north is probably just enough distance to protect myself from believing them again."

Tom looked like a sad dog. He turned to pick up the box and my overnight bag. "You're needed here," he said as we walked toward the U-Haul.

Another ripple of anxiety fluttered through me, as it did every time he said stuff like that. But I was done. I took my bag from him and tossed it, along with one last bag of fresh oranges, into the truck cab and pulled myself up into it.

Cold as a north wind, I said, "Bye, Tom. Send me a postcard from Eloysia."

Pulling out of the driveway, I could see him in the truck's mirror, an overinflated Michelin Tire Man standing forlornly against the magenta dawn. He'd never said so, but I suspected he was in love with me. If his heart was breaking, then isn't that what he deserved? But smugness is a form of arrogance and arrogance is a sign that you're headed for a fall.

I should have known that.

Part

II

Chapter

21

HELLO ITS TOM AGAIN

Since TM develops intellect and awakens creativity, TMers flourished and Fairfield flowered into a cutting-edge mecca for the arts, education, business, and scientific research with multi-million-dollar grants, more restaurants per capita than San Francisco, sustainable eco everything. As I walked around after my arrival, slipping on snow and shivering in a too-thin coat, I marveled at seeing so much light in the faces of enlightened denizens getting tea at Cafe Paradiso, attending book signings at Revelations, or shopping for organic food at Everybody's grocery.

I'd looked forward to renewing old acquaintances but besides being a fool for believing Tom's story, I also seemed to be one for seeing the potential in run-down houses. This time, instead of a cute Florida cracker cottage with promise, I'd bought an architectural catastrophe full of oddly shaped rooms and weird construction. It would have been smarter to have torn it down and bought a yurt. Five miles north of Maharishi International University and Fairfield proper, my new house sat across the county highway from Maharishi Vedic City where hundreds of upscale citizens lived in lovely Vastu homes, leaving me isolated in "no man's land." The questions that had driven me out of Flori-duh went away, not because the alien issue had been resolved but because I'd closed my mind to it. I was too busy to think about anything except the next emergency. I spent more time yelling at lower-skilled workers (all I could afford) than I did about compassion and non-violent communication, extraterrestrials, or Jabba the Hutt. Instead of a lake and luscious greenery, I was surrounded by two acres of abandoned construction trash, old vehicles, and the you-name-it the previous owner had left behind, and miles of flat, featureless farmland. Also, there was snow. And dust. And wind. With no trees or buildings to stop it, the northwest wind ate at my property and my bones with near-gale force. My body protested the chill and my heart ached for trees. But who moves to Iowa for the weather? Or the scenery? I considered it penance for having been such a silly twit.

At least now I was part of a community I could trust, people who talked inner peace, not outer space. I missed my Unity friends but I was back in the Domes, the football-field-sized housing for life-transforming TM programs where I hoped to gain a little more wisdom. I expected Tom and his story to slide into a mere anecdote to be told at parties for their oddity value, the way I used to tell the tale about Luke in Iceland. "Speaking of strange stories, did I tell you about the time a guy in Florida told me that I was an alien who was needed to stop a galactic war? Crazy. No, no, don't be silly. Of course, I didn't believe him."

***

A year after I left Florida, work on the old house was slowly progressing into mid-spring or early summer when the phone rang inside the clothes dryer. The roof had been torn off for replacing at the same time the water lines were also being replaced so the washer and dryer had been moved to the patio. That meant, in case of rain, the safest place to keep the landline telephone was inside the clothes dryer. I expected the call to be from the electrician, or the box store telling me to expect delivery of my shingles. But, as disorienting as a call from Mars, it was Tom.

"Sorry you left Florida yet?" he asked, his tone just like the Tom I remembered—half overly friendly, half mocking. How did he get my phone number?

"We were talking about you in church, so I thought I'd call you."

Swept with a wave of love for my friends back in Florida, I was too off-guard to say, "Tom, didn't I make it clear I wanted nothing more to do with you, you lying conman?" Instead, I heard myself enthuse, "Oh! How is everyone doing?!"

At the end of our conversation, I managed to politely say "Thanks for calling but considering our differences, wouldn't you agree that we shouldn't communicate again?" His response was that he began calling every few days. It was a mystery why he persisted, although not the kind that took up mental room; I needed that space for more important things like calculating square footage for insulation or screwing up the courage to fire another ne'r-do-well worker. Had I known what was coming, I would have started simply hanging up.

Chapter

22

AND TOM YET AGAIN

A couple of times, in a manner more like sparring than courting, Tom shuffled obliquely around the subject of marriage. Even if I'd been interested, I told him more than once that I'd never marry anyone who didn't practice TM. Unless a mate experienced the same rapid growth, he would be at odds with my lifestyle and its goals. I'd have had better luck talking to my pet chickens. When I told him that meditating raised IQ, he said he didn't want more intelligence. "I might have to think too much," he said. I was too astounded to know how to respond. I asked him why he was interested in me. His answer was even more astonishing "You're nearly perfect." This from the man who criticized me mercilessly in Florida?

My response was to tell him if I was "nearly perfect," it was because I'd spent all those years practicing TM until I got that way. He responded that I was throwing my life away in a cult. I tried explaining how his concept of a cult was flawed. The popular connotation of the word cult is full of expectations about strange people in strange clothes who have strange beliefs fostered on them by some mind-control sicko with packages of Flavor-aid, even while the critic fails to realize that they themselves follow scamming stock market gurus, Armageddon preachers, or crazy people who believe in UFOs.

The fact is, by definition, anyone who holds passionate beliefs is a member of a cult. You're a cult member if you're a straight-ticket voter, passionately pro-abortion, pro-gun, or pro-organic foods; if you never miss a baseball game, or if you faithfully buy every book ever written by Stephen King. You belong to a cult if you believe your dogma is superior to others, if you turn up your nose at all but name-brand clothing, or if you refuse to buy anything except American-made. Advertising cults use every manipulative technique known to science and psychology to make us hunger for their products. Got indigestion? Just take this pricey pill instead of eating right. Don't feel happy enough? Then opt for product ownership instead of a satisfying inner life. Feeling frustrated by civil problems? Then blame the other party rather than cooperate to find solutions. Approximately a hundred thousand ads a day cross our sensory field—even written on the clothes we wear!—day after endless day, molding opinions, desires, and values. But even in such a hyped-up environment, research says that TMers are above average as independent thinkers. Tom dismissed the stats to argue that doing TM meant I was giving up my American freedoms.

I bet you're saying, if meditation makes you so smart, then why are you still talking to this guy? At least I'd gotten smart enough to not buy any more of Tom's alien story. If Tom brought it up, I'd drop all pretext of politeness and snap, "If you say one more word about that I'm going to hang up." Maybe I was going to learn boundaries after all.

Likely he persisted in calling because he was lonely. He reminded me of a dog I had who'd been so severely abused that she couldn't trust humans. Her only friend was a bitchy cat. Whenever I'd let the dog outside, she would race eagerly to find her, wagging her tail and bouncing around with joy the way a normal dog does. But the cat didn't want any part of it. She hissed and clawed like a diva abusing the paparazzi. I finally found the dog a home with multiple animals for her to be friends with instead of a single human and her sassy feline. For the same compassionate reasons, I told Tom more than once that he should get a girlfriend and stop calling me. But the phone would ring and I'd be startled to hear his pseudo-cheerful voice yet again. "How you doing, kid!" he'd say as if we were long-lost best friends.

Our chats were tedious. TMers traded insights, anecdotes about healings, personal awakenings, and progress towards world peace. Some had become best-selling authors. Several became millionaires. Some went on educational junkets, outings to exotic places like Manchu Pichu, or Ayurveda clinics in India. Some had success stories about helping end poverty or war.

In contrast, conversations with Tom were achingly mundane. He described Florida weather in a tone tinged with "see what you're missing" and I responded with gruff comments about weather that was tolerable. He'd talk about his failing store. I'd mention burning a head-high pile of construction debris. He'd tell me he filed bankruptcy and had retired to south Texas where an Army buddy lived, and I'd report that I'd given a poetry reading. This ho-hum rarely extended beyond two or three consecutive volleys on any one topic.

One night, however, something came out of our conversation that was of cosmic proportions.

Chapter

23

OBSESSED

It was June of '04, at night. I'd been searching for instructions on how to get floor tiles to lay straight between off-center walls, when the phone rang. It was Tom. Not wanting to waste time with chitchat, I tucked the phone between my ear and shoulder and started tidying up the patio by the light of the open door, sliding a metal chair under the picnic table.

What's that noise?" Tom asked.

"I'm straightening up the patio," I said.

"You're outside?"

I quipped, "Yep, 'no rest for the wicked,' as my grandmother used to say."

He ignored both my martyrdom and Grandma's quote. "Seen any starships lately?"

Common among those who can't solve their communication

problems, both of us had become guilty of making half-hidden accusatory stabs. I couldn't tell if his question about starships was intended as humor or was a stickpin of veiled sarcasm. I grunted with disgust, grabbed a carboard box for picking up loose screws, and returned the stickpin. "No, of course not, I'm much too busy to pay any attention to such silly ideas."

"You want to see one?"

Involuntarily, I looked up. It was a gorgeous night with a clover-smelling wind. The Milky Way twinkled in majestic silence. On my grandparents' farm in my early childhood, one could drown in the sea of stars. Now stars are drowned in the glare of streetlights, halogen security bulbs, and countless other forms of synthetic light. "The theft of darkness," National Geographic called it, noting that it has made it increasingly difficult for astronomers to view the stars. My concerns were less for astronomers than for my loss of one of life's greatest wonders: the night sky. This far from town, at least, it was dark enough to see some of the glitter of our spiral galaxy. My awe did little to soften my sarcasm. "Oh sure; I'm dying to see one."

Tom chuckled. "Are you looking up?"

"Yes," I said. "It's beautiful,"

"There are spaceships up there," he said.

"I don't want to hear this, Tom." I dropped my eyes to the patio to resume picking up screws.

"You still don't believe me, do you?" he asked.

I sighed. "Until they land in front of me, I'm not interested, Tom."

"You better be careful what you say. That could happen, you know."

I don't know why such things still had the power to make my neck hairs stand up. I ignored it. "Don't bore me with this," I said.

"How can UFOs be boring?" he asked, his voice lilting with tease.

"UFOs wouldn't be boring if I had honest information about them. It's only boring when it's riddles and lies."

"Humm. Would you be more interested if you could see one for yourself?"

"What do you mean?"

"Just what I said. You want to see a flying saucer?"

I should end this before I got overly irritated, I thought. But demon curiosity tugged. "Sure," I drawled, not believing. "Can you produce one?"

"What direction are you facing now?"

"East."

"Stay standing east but look up to the south."

I looked up south.

"Now watch carefully because it's easy to miss small lights among all those stars."

I saw it. A moving light about three o'clock high, big enough there was no trouble distinguishing it from a star, speeding north.

"You see that light? The one that's headed north? It's not blinking the way an airplane does—it's just a steady, even light, moving fast. You see it?"

Indeed, the light was steady, not blinking, faster than a jet.

"Now watch because…" In the middle of his sentence, the light made an abrupt right-angle turn, upward and eastward while Tom continued talking, "it's going to make a right turn and…"

There were 1,193 miles between Tom's trailer and me. Yet he'd predicted it as surely as if he was standing next to me. Like an overloaded computer, my mind crashed. I dropped the box, took a step backward, and fell into a deck chair, blinking at the spot where the light had just blinked out. What *was* that light? How could he have known it was there? He hadn't even known that I was outdoors until I told him. I was dumbfounded.

"Are you still there?" Tom asked.

"Yes…I'm here," I said.

"Did you see it turn to the East?"

"How did you know it would do that?"

"I just know these things."

"Tom!" I snapped, exploding out of the chair. "You know I hate your riddles and half-answers. Why don't you just give me a straightforward explanation and stop playing mind games?"

"That would take the fun out of it," he chuckled. "Don't you enjoy a good mystery?"

"No! Your kind of mystery is never fun, only frustrating and irrational."

"What's more rational than seeing what you just saw with your own eyes?"

"I saw a light make an impossible turn. That doesn't tell me what it was or how you knew it was going to happen."

In mock disbelief, he said, "You saw it do just what I said it would do. I can't get much more straightforward than that."

"Tom!"

He must have realized from the way I spit out his name that I couldn't be pushed much further. He switched to a more serious tone. "Okay, it was a spaceship. Believe me now?"

"No," I snapped. "Seeing a light was strange but it's just data—it doesn't explain what it was or how you knew it was there." Where I had been trained to see and describe things in minute details, he seemed to not understand why anyone needed more than face value.

His tone was incredulous. "You saw it yourself and you still don't believe it?"

For someone with Rubik's Cube syndrome, a mystery of this caliber was enough to cause PTSD. Nearly whining, I prayed he wouldn't abandon me with it. "Tom, don't tease. Explain this. How did you know there was a light? What was it and how did you know what it would do?"

He chuckled. "I told you, I'm in on these things."

"If you don't tell me more than this, I'm going to hang up."

There was a small silence, as if he realized that I was serious. Then he said, "They're Eloysian patrols. They pass over your place at ten, then again at four in the morning to make sure you are all right."

"Patrols," I parroted. Like clothes tumbling in a dryer, questions rolled around in my mind. Protected from what and by whom? If I needed protection, how could a twice-nightly patrol lasting less than a few seconds serve the purpose? How could my well-being be determined from so high up? On the other hand, if "they" were telepathic, telepathy works from anywhere. Why waste fuel flying over my house?

A wave of black frustration rocked me. I saw the silliness of his "explanation." Obviously, it was another lie. Simultaneously, I realized that, all lies aside, I'd been jerked into yet another unresolvable mystery. Either Tom was deliberately withholding information or he was incapable of explaining. It didn't matter which, the anguish of having this new conundrum fostered on me was beyond tolerance. I snapped, "That does it, Tom. Since you can't explain this, I'm hanging up."

I heard him say, "But..." before I jammed my thumb into the off button and banged the phone against my head several times in Rubik's Cube angst. I turned in a circle, looking at the sky in a torment of longing, knowing perfectly well there would be nothing there except shimmering light from million-year-old stars, the mechanical blinks of passing planes, and the barely visible stream of jet trails. In wordless supplications, I begged the universe for a replay, begged to see it again in slow-mo so I could figure out was it was. But, like that cruel Christian admonishment that says "Jesus passeth but once, not to come again," there was no replay. Nothing in the sky appeared out of the ordinary.

With a half-howl, half-whine of protest, I stalked into the house and slammed the phone into its cradle. If Tom wanted me to believe alien stories, he had proved his point with this perfectly timed event. But, why? –why! why! why! —did he have to make it such a maddening puzzle? To someone like me, there was nothing crueler than a mystery that can't be solved.

While I groaned with defeat, the need for answers burned hot and visceral. This new mystery didn't have a fragile dependence on a vaguely heard ring of truth. This time, it was in my face. From over a thousand miles away, someone had predicted what I was going to see with my own two eyes while leaving me with no way to understand it.

I knew what was going to happen next—the wheel of questions would spin around and around at a maddening pace and, finding no answers, it was going to make me obsess until it drove me crazy. The kindest thing I could do would be to postpone it for as long as possible. I brushed my teeth so hard it hurt, took a sleeping pill, and told my mind—in the same tone a drill sergeant shouts at a bumbling recruit (with exclamation marks)—absolutely, DO NOT THINK ABOUT LIGHTS IN THE SKY! To literally blanket the ache, I turned the AC down to 65 degrees so I could sleep with a cover over my head. I stuck ear plugs into my ears, covered my eyes with a light shield, and crawled into bed chanting the Lord's prayer over and over to keep myself from thinking until the pills slid me into blessed unconsciousness.

***

The burning need to solve mysteries does not necessarily yield to reason. Despite yelling at myself to not think about it, and despite the semi-paralysis caused by the pills, at exactly 4:00 A.M.—the time Tom said the second patrol would pass—Rubik's Cube *want* pressured me awake and dragged me out to the patio like someone possessed. I knew I would not find any patrols yet there I was, blinking hard to keep my dry eyes open, shifting from one foot to another on the chilled concrete patio, staring at the sky.

Nothing.

Nothing.

Nothing.

Only stars, stars, and more stars. No moving lights, not even airplanes at this time of the morning. The moon had risen, a lovely quarter moon but, in the stillness, nothing else moved. My neck aching from the strain, I finally gave up and went back to bed. At least there were enough of the sleeping pills left in my system that, after a half-hour of tossing, I fell back into sleep.

By morning, awakening to stare at the ceiling, I knew that Rubik's Cube syndrome had trapped me again. This time it was more than a tale told by an idiot signifying nothing. This time, it was a tale told by an idiot that signified *something.* I'd seen that something with my own eyes and I couldn't stop the gut-deep craving to see it again, or see one like it, and to find out, *what was it?* I wasn't ready to accept that it was a spaceship and I certainly didn't believe it was a patrol but that wasn't even the biggest mystery. The biggest mystery was, how did Tom know it was there?

***

The carpenter came at ten to install trim around doorways—work above my skill level. Instead of protecting his focus so I could get as much efficiency as possible out of his pricey fees, I was still obsessing about the light. I distracted him with my story so much that he had to measure the doorframe a second time. "Was it a satellite?" he asked?

"It couldn't have been a satellite," I said. "It made a 90-degree turn without even slowing down, then disappeared."

"Ninety degrees," he whistled. "That's steep." He reached down and picked up his carpenter's square from the tarp laid under his ladder. "Like this?" he asked, drawing his finger around the sharp corner of the square.

"Yes, exactly like that," I said. "No arc at all."

He whistled. "I've never heard of anything that could turn like that." He paused, stared at the square, and then he said, "Did it explode? Anything that turned that sharp would explode."

Indeed, ordinary machinery couldn't have survived it. Referring to the chevron shaped flying machines he'd seen making abrupt turns around the mountains, Kenneth Arnold, the man who gave us the name "flying saucer" back in 1947, said, "If that… was a manned vehicle, it would have been impossible for humans to survive the gravitational pressure."

I shook my head again. "No. It didn't explode. It just blinked out."

We locked eyes, both of us slowly shaking our heads, marveling at the mystery.

***

The philosophy of science says that to be valid an experiment or occurrence must be repeatable. This creates a problem for ufology because sightings are like lightning—they rarely strike twice at the same place or time. The light Tom predicted had the appearance of being under intelligent control. To verify that I really did see what I thought I saw, I needed to see at least one more. I dismissed the part about it being a patrol. That was nuts. Yet, night after night, it was as if I had obsessive-compulsive disorder. At ten PM and then again at four in the morning, I'd run outside to stare at the sky, shifting uncomfortably on the chilly cement, staring hard at the sky, afraid if I'd come seconds too late or leave seconds too soon. I also started watching for them at dawn and sunset, the times Tom said UFOs were easiest to spot. No one needed to tell me this was senseless. Yet, like someone with a spit brain where the logical left doesn't know what the non-verbal right is doing, the mystery burned out of control. I used to like that part of me that is driven to solve puzzles, what I call the Rubik's Cube syndrome. But it had stopped being fun. On a ten-point scale, the need-to-know had ratcheted up to eleven-point-seven and I was sick of it. More than once, I resorted to drastic measures such as sticking my head in the sink and turning on cold water until I could think about something besides lights in the sky. Then, against all reason, at 10:00 PM and 4:00 AM, there'd I be once again, straining my eyes and my neck looking for lights. It was surreal. I saw the sky glowing over Fairfield. A field away from my property, I saw the searchlight at our local airport sweeping around and around. An occasional startled bird would cry out while, overhead, the Milky Way glittered softly. Cave men had watched the sky turn at the same pace. There was nothing new for me to see. Airplanes, jets, stars, moon, insects, nothing more.

Well, there actually was something more: satellites and space junk. From the day the USSR started the space age in 1957 with Sputnik, we started trashing the sky. In only six decades we put upwards of a half-million objects in orbit around the Earth, including 6,542 satellites (half of which don't work), an astronaut's tool kit worth $100,000, severed bolts, paint chips, and fragments of satellites that crashed into each other, broke up, exploded, or were deliberately shot down. The list of dead satellites includes at least three that were collateral damage from a 1962 Soviet nuclear test explosion. (That event created an artificial radiation belt around the Earth and killed a third of extant low-altitude satellites.) In 2008, the U.S. did a "full death-star treatment" for a failed reconnaissance satellite, spending several million dollars to shoot it down because (should it fail to burn up after it hit Earth's atmosphere) it contained enough deadly hydrazine fuel to create a gas cloud two football fields in size. The Russians and the Chinese thought the fuel was less likely a legitimate threat than an excuse to play war games, to test ASAT (Anti-Satellite) weapons. I suspect it was true. Looking at the photo of the Joint Chiefs watching the shoot-down, one can see the glee on their faces. Clearly, it is true—the difference between men and boys is the price of their toys.

Satellites are big business. Seventy-three countries or independent groups own satellites. The U.S. is the giant with over 2,800, but the list also includes satellites from Iraq, Kazakhstan, Azerbaijan, and other countries where you thought they derived the GNP from goat cheese. Even North Korea. Only 800 of the working satellites can step aside if necessary to avoid a collision.

The US Department of Defense uses the Space Surveillance Network (SSN) to track not just working satellites but 27,000 other objects in orbit around the Earth the size of a baseball or larger, including one carrying the ashes of Gene Roddenberry, creator of *Star Trek*. SSN also tracks a priceless antique—a satellite launched in 1958. Most space junk is invisible to the naked eye, but the International Space Station has nearly an acre of solar panels, making it the brightest light in the night sky.

But not one of those things could make 90-degree turns, nor could they explain how Tom could have predicted it as I watched.

Chapter

CULTURE SHOCK

The 90-degree turn and Tom's prediction didn't prove it was a spaceship but it was strong evidence that re-awoke my fears about alien abduction, worse than before. In her book, *Feel the Fear and Do It Anyway*, Susan Jeffers wrote that we are almost always afraid of anything new. Her advice was to have faith that one could handle whatever it was. I'd used that advice so often in various aspects of life that it reminded me of the Ray Montaigne song, Empty, "I've looked my demons in the eyes so many times, I must admit, you kinda' bore me." I was good at handling fear.

But this was more like a phobia, and it had resurfaced with a vengeance. Intellectually, I'd accepted Joy Gilbert's explanations that her *friends* were benign and beneficial. Until I saw Tom's light, however, my perspective had been that of a theorist, a researcher trying to stay detached and objective, someone who merely *thought* about aliens. But seeing a light that appeared to be under intelligent control shifted it from thought to immediate reality. *They* became viscerally real.

Shifts from intellectual understanding to cognitive immediacy can happen to us at any time, on any subject. It's like when I realized that money isn't everything. I'd heard that saying all my life, of course, as have you. One day, it shifted from being something I understood in my head to something I understood in my heart. Like sliding from one dimension into another, I suddenly realized that the value of a thing was not financial worth but beauty, usefulness, and desirability. The cost was just the price, not the value.

Like that, seeing that light with my own eyes, the reality shifted from concept to something that penetrated my gut.

They're here.

They exist.

They're landing wherever they want.

They're abducting people.

They might even abduct me.

Joy Gilbert called them *friends*. I only knew them as aliens, strangers, outsiders—a terrifying, unpredictable otherness. Incongruously, I was also passionately driven to confirm the light, to understand it, so I kept peering at the skies to try to find more.

One night, staring upward, I recalled the children's chant: I see the moon, and the moon sees me. Despite the fear, I'd been operating under the assumption, "they're out there and I'm down here. I'm safe." But awareness struck me like a physical force—if I saw them, would they, being telepathic, also see me? Would they know I was looking for them and...oh, my God... see it as a summons or invitation to... come get me? Adrenalin reflex sprung me out of the lounger and into the house. I flipped the deadbolt and shut off the lights so no one knew I was home. As I had a month earlier, I took a sleeping pill, turned the AC down, put plugs in my ears, and went to bed, trying to make myself forget about a universe that was suddenly too big for me to comprehend, one that included beings from other worlds who had abruptly become as real in awareness as the people next door.

***

The next morning, I blinked through sleep-dry eyes to scan the room. Nothing seemed out of place and I was pretty sure I hadn't been abducted. Experiencers have reported waking up to find themselves in nightclothes belonging to someone else, or even outside on the lawn. Nothing seemed amiss now, except that I was sick with fear. After leaving Florida, I'd closed my mind as tightly as the spaces between the stones at Manchu Pichu against thoughts of beings from other planets, other dimensions. Now strangeness was multiplying like rabbits, bringing it all back to the forefront of consciousness, with spurs on. How does a rational mind deal with being told twice in one life by two different men a continent apart that I was wanted by space aliens? What did it mean that I was told that I *was* an alien? How was I supposed to deal with having seen a light make an impossible high-speed turn while someone in Texas predicted it? Forcing its way past defenses, denials, and rationalizations, that 90-degree light had been the doorbell announcing *they are here*. I sat up in bed and meditated, hoping that would make it all go away. Had it been a mood, meditation would likely have transformed it. But, it didn't.

Plan B, I decided, was to follow the rule that says, "In times of stress, do normal things." I decided to paint the lattice that hung at the corners of the house. I planned to grow morning glories or roses there, something to give the boxy little cottage some color and character. I grabbed the old T-shirt I used for painting and put on jean shorts. In mid-zip, the thought that had bolted me out of the deck chair the night before resurfaced—the thought that telepathy might inform aliens I'd been looking for them. I, a survivor of significant abuse, I who had hitch-hiked and camped alone back in the hippie days, I who had joined the Navy and dared to break through the mold to put myself through college, I who had not feared tackling impossible old houses, now found myself agoraphobic at the idea of going outside.

Being "psychic" is not strange or oddball. Anyone can do it. I couldn't predict anything as complicated as lottery numbers but I'd had so many experiences of intuition in daily life that I took it for granted. Decades ago, when I was first trying to understand such things, I'd hold a stranger's keys and see what could be learned about their owner. Upwards of 80 percent of the time I could sense everything from their marital status to their psychological quirks. Then, in the Maha experience, the omniscience experience demonstrated that it's possible to know the truth of anything from inside oneself. The only reason that most people aren't psychic is that, not believing in it, they ignore it. Learning telepathy is like learning belly dancing—it requires locating muscles you didn't know you had, then developing them enough to be useful. Thought is faster than light and more penetrating. To those who can use intuition, the entire universe becomes accessible, fluid, and connected. Physics calls this quantum entanglement, describing it as, "you tickle it here, it laughs over there." Thousands of reports say that ETs use telepathy to communicate. So why wasn't it reasonable to think that, by thinking about them, I might make a connection? And, we all know what happens if you're told, "Don't think about pink elephants"—you can't think anything else. I couldn't stop thinking that if I thought about them, it might bring their attention, so I couldn't stop thinking about them when I desperately didn't want to think about them.

I didn't feel well at all.

***

Instead of potentially exposing myself to them by going outdoors, I began one of the unfinished indoor projects—fitting the metal edging onto the arc I'd cut in the carpet to give the entry/living room a finished look. But I couldn't stay focused enough to do the job right. I gave that up to make a list of the work that still needed to be done, but I kept drifting off. I thought about calling my mother. But what would I say, "Hey, Mom, did you know there are flying saucers that…"? I tried a video but was so distracted I didn't even understand the words. I tried working the edging again only to find myself just staring.

Suddenly, I understood. The restlessness, disorientation, anxiety, vague nausea and sense of disconnect were all symptoms of *culture shock*—the feeling of disorientation when one meets an unfamiliar culture, way of life, or set of attitudes. All of us have experienced shocks and tremors that rattle the dishes and windows of what we believe to be reality. Some shocks, like unexpected deaths, losing a job, or the realization that one's husband is philandering, are so intense one's internal world collapses. My shock was bigger than any of those. My entire Earth-centered worldview had been shot down.

If you don't know what culture shock is, try living with a different ethnic group for a while. You drink coffee; they drink tea. You expect Wi-Fi; they have toilets in the floor. You are aghast to see cooks squatting over food with unwashed hands, appalled to be fed grasshoppers or snakes, and white-knuckled to experienced drivers in countries where traffic control happens only through vehicular accidents. Craving the ease of familiarity, travelers get irritable, depressed, anxious, and homesick. Like them, I craved the comfort of the familiar, of my old worldview in which only humans existed, in which only what happened on Earth mattered, where I understood the parameters of reality. But those were gone.

My awakening to the existence of aliens had happened in layers, each layer bringing some new shock that left me having to rearrange my mind and my worldview. But these rearrangements had all been perceived through an Earth-centered lens so they were built on a familiar foundation. The last step—the one that connected me viscerally to the existence of beings from other worlds, had been such a violent upheaval that it had flung me into outer space without a map. My Earth, that solid ball of support under my feet, had shrunk from being the center of existence into a tiny, tiny dot on the edge of an unimportant arm of the Milky Way. The galaxy itself had shrunk into near-invisibility among billions of others. On Earth, we still use the human body for measurements, using words and concepts like arms-length, and thumb-sized. How then, can we relate to the conceptual models needed to understand a universe that is 28 billion light-years wide, so huge that it contains a sun that five billion times larger than Sol. As an intellectual explorer, I'd felt at home with multiple world views and countless strange things—duck-billed platypuses, 40-foot-long squid, disquieting things like worms found frozen in glaciers from thousands of years ago that come alive when thawed, blood rains, rainbow-colored mountains, the discovery that Viagra reduces jet lag in hamsters, even the existence of humans who can fly. These are ultimately acceptable because we recognize them as aspects of Mother Earth.

But how does one expand enough to grasp the meaning of life in the vastness of space? Where would I begin to understand non-Earth cultures, non-Earth values, non-Earthly perceptions, a universe teeming with lifeforms I'd never seen?

Only a few centuries ago, one lived in small villages where the name for anyone you had not known your entire life was *stranger*, an alien, someone to be feared. They built walled cities to protect themselves from *aliens*. Then we became state-centered, then country-centered, and now world-centered. What once seemed weird becomes familiar, ordinary, natural, interesting, valuable. But those shocks existed on planet Earth. What shocks must we endure to accept the culture of other planets? Other dimensions? Can we adjust our understanding to accept that non-human beings exist who are much more advanced than we are? How do we handle knowing they are here, now, on Earth?

This new weltanschauung—this worldview, this universe-view—in which beings from other planets and/or from other dimensions lived and moved around on Earth was almost beyond my ability to grasp. No respectable person I knew even talked about stuff like this. This unknown country was not on any maps; not even in *Wikipedia* except as something to ridicule. I had to deal with it alone, a stranger in a strange land. Was this what people felt when they first heard Copernicus' theory that Earth wasn't the center of the universe? Is this what sailors felt on the Nina, the Pinta, and the Santa Maria, believing in sea monsters, months away from their known universe with no land in sight? Some people reported feeling this kind of shock when their belief in the sanctity of American soil had been blown off their maps following 9/11. Some experienced the vertigo of shifting into a larger reality when they saw the IBM Powers of Ten video, the Mandelbrot Set, or other infinite fractal videos. Some reported it when seeing the Hubble Deep Field photo, the one that showed thousands of galaxies in a small section of space previously assumed to be entirely dark. The enlightenment experience—when I'd seen that multiple dimensions of human development existed—had been a major shock when I had to come to terms afterwards but even that had had historical precedence and Earth perspectives. Now, I felt I was floating without a tether in outer space. Instead of a place of refuge as it was before, Mother Earth had shrunk into a pale blue dot hanging in infinite parsecs of space that might be teeming with lifeforms I couldn't even conceive.

Like Cypher in *The Matrix*, I wanted the security of my old, Earth-centered universe back, the one behind the insulating fat-layers of intellectualization, emotional distance, and disbelief. As if for the first time, I had to ask:

Who are these beings?

Where did they come from?

What did they want?

And, having twice in my life been asked to help them, I also had to ask, what did they want with me?

***

I jumped up out of these thoughts to do something, anything, to relieve the anxiety. I grabbed the broom and swept at the sheetrock dust covering the floor. Too tense to be gentle, I only raised a fine white cloud while thinking, *they* must be an advanced culture, much more advanced than ours to fly here, to levitate themselves and their abductees, to go in and out of dimensions, to do precise surgical procedures. And what more did I yet not know? The unknown loomed vast—orders of magnitude of vast. Like the swarms of brooms carrying buckets of water in Disney's *Sorcerer's Apprentice*, visions of potentially dangerous possibilities swarmed into my mind. What was their agenda? For the first time, not from my head but from my guts, I thought, was their goal to conquer and enslave us? As often as I had trouble dealing with authority on Earth, how could I deal with authorities from another world? Might they have ray guns to melt me down to elemental components or mental powers to zap me into the next dimension?

I tried to make myself sweep the floor more gently. After all, what better time to sweep, do laundry, and water houseplants than during an alien invasion? No, I realized, they weren't lined up on the horizon ready to do armed battle. We had been "invaded" long, long ago, long before I was aware they even existed, all the way back to the indigenous tribes who drew pictures of them on boulders. Maybe they were even here first. But, like becoming aware that money wasn't everything, for the first time I comprehended how little I knew about them. Such enormous unknowns!

Do normal things. Stay on a routine. Get some exercise. Talk to others. These were tools I'd learned for handling anxiety. Oh, how dearly I wanted to talk to others, to hear someone I could trust to say, "Don't be silly—you're letting your imagination get the best of you." But in 2004, ordinary people didn't talk about such things. In Florida, church events had allowed friendships to flourish. Here I'd neglected to renew friendships or make new ones. I'd told myself I'd wait until the house looked good enough for guests, until I wasn't so exhausted, until I had more time, then I'd be more social. But, even if I had made friends, who could be so trusted that I could confess to having terrors about space aliens? Most people thought UFOs were jokes, only for the dingbats.

Maybe, if cover-ups by the government were true, was this why they'd been afraid to let the public know? Wasn't my personal reaction proof that disclosure might cause panic?

No, not so. If a trustworthy authority could explain what was happening, then I wouldn't be so distressed. Real authorities would have normalized the information, helped us to understand it, and not left it up to common citizens to have to figure it out for themselves. But the authorities—those who knew the real truths—were beyond reach under the deepest of black covers, with many of those who had tried to reach them having been found dead under suspicious circumstances.

I felt so ill I gave up and went to bed. I shuttered the blinds and pulled the blankets and comforter up to my chin. To distract myself, I tried to read *How to Handle a Problem Horse.* My half-Arab mare was a problem horse, bolting at the least shaking of the wind. Like attracts like, I thought bitterly. I read the same paragraph a half dozen times and still didn't know what it said. I gave up, covered my head, assumed the prenatal position, wrapping my arms around my knees. When all else fails, hug yourself.

In the comforting quiet of the darkened room, a rational thought finally came. What was happening was a form of transcendence, a matter of *going beyond.* In the largest sense, transcendence means to go beyond thinking into silence. That's what happens in TM. Regular transcendence expands the mind so that, in activity, we experience transcendence in action. As the blockages disappear and the mind expands, we awaken from smaller modes of understanding into larger ones. When enough smaller changes add up, it leads to what Thomas Kuhn, author of *The Structure of Scientific Revolutions*, would have called a *paradigm shift*. A paradigm shift happens when the preponderance of evidence is so great that the larger picture becomes the new normal. The new viewpoint is so obviously correct that there is no going back to the old view. But because it is still new, we may be uncertain how it all fits together. New visions often begin with confusion and arguments about what it means and how it works. This happened at the turn of the 20th century when science transcended the limitations of Newtonian Mechanics to the larger but still unmapped world of relativity and quantum physics. It is called growth, progress, evolution of knowledge, expansion of experience.

But, when reality has cracked open and one is flying into the unknown, most of us don't calmly think, yes, this is a significant change and I'm transcending into a larger reality. It doesn't feel like progress. It feels more like being lost.

Chapter

25

LANDING IN MY BACKYARD

I bet you think I am a silly old woman. I wouldn't deny it. But those who have seen me accomplish things in life despite handicaps often call me courageous. They've seen me be unrelenting in working through fears. Until now, the only thing I'd been phobic about was tornados. Having been through two of them, that fear was reasonable, wouldn't you agree?

The first one caught me and my kids, ages eight and five, from behind. We were in a Volkswagen bug and I'd just turned into a service station when suddenly the car started rocking wildly. Coming from the direction of the wind like thousands of murderous birds from Hitchcock's movie, gravel and debris pecked furiously at the rear and passenger-side windows. The safety glass crazed, held together only by the inner plastic, blinding us to whatever might come next. While the kids screamed, the wind was so intense that it drove straw between the rim and the rubber, driving air out of the tires. Metal roofing from across the street screeched across the top of the car and crashed into the station wall. A couple of feet lower and it would have cut off our heads. The station disintegrated in front of us, the windows blew out, the roof ripped off, the sides splintered from projectiles. An attendant tried to reach us, bracing himself with a hand on each side of the door casing, his hair and shirt whipping furiously until the wind blew him backward and a tree crashed into the door. The whirling violence then passed on to take at least one life and do millions of dollars' worth of damage. Had it set down even six feet sooner, we most likely wouldn't have survived.

The next big scare happened soon afterward. Weathermen called it a "tornadic cyclone," where multiple tornadoes spawn inside a larger churning wind. After warning sirens woke me, I raced to get the kids out of bed and into the bathtub, covering them with sofa cushions. With no room for me, I listened to the old house creak and groan in the roaring wind while glass smashed and the floors trembled. Six inches of hail hammered down in a roaring glissando. A tree crashed in through the back door and I swear I felt the old house shift on its rock foundation. Three people died that day.

Afterward, I'd panic over little more than darkening skies. Franklin Roosevelt said, "[T]he only thing we have to fear is fear itself." A boxer told me that the only thing that scared him was seeing fear in the eyes of his opponents because, he said, fear made them unpredictable. Fear of fear made me unpredictable. I did crazy things trying to overcome it such as riding my bicycle through thunder and lightning storms. I jumped off a 30-foot building into the Gulf (it felt more like it was 250 feet) because I was sick with fear of it. If the guys dared to do it, then wasn't I a coward if I didn't? When the first jump didn't cure me, I jumped off a second time. Whatever I was afraid of, I would force myself to do. It wasn't smart and I had broken bones to prove it.

Finally, I comprehended that fear is not necessarily a sign of cowardice and that force was not the answer. Sometimes fear is life's warning that "It's not time to do that yet." Rather than force it, the best way to overcome fear is to use step-by-step growth of familiarity where we gradually develop skill and strength to do things intelligently and appropriately.

Sometimes, of course, we find ourselves in situations where there isn't time for further development. Sometimes, win or lose, we must face something terrifying because it is necessary. In World War II a woman had to close a steel door to protect her children from gunfire. To close the door meant she had to reach outside to grab the handle, thus exposing herself to a hail of bullets. That was where I found myself now, knowing I must have the courage to face this head-on. The morning after the big, unnerving culture shock, I awoke with one clear thought: I must not run.

As a teenager, I liked Shell Scott detective books. One incident left a lasting impression. Shell found himself flattened against the wall on an upper-story building ledge, dazed from some earlier crises while being shot at from below. It looked like certain death, if not from the bullets, then from a fall. Momentarily frozen in panic, he had the clarity of mind to determine that if he was going to die, it would not be because he had given up. Grit ended his paralysis and he begin inching his way forward on the ledge toward safety.

The memory of that incident often motivated me to keep moving even when I was afraid, and I used it now. Even if taking action meant that I would attract aliens, I would go down fighting rather than endure being so afraid that I wouldn't even go outside. I would do another gedankenexperiment. I would set up a situation in imagination to face fear the way soldiers drill to face war—to familiarize myself with the sights, sounds, thoughts, and feelings that one would have if the real thing happened. Better to sort it out in practice than under the pressure of actual events.

The last time I'd looked for lights in the sky, I'd brought a pillow, a pashmina shawl, and herbal tea to get comfortable in a lounge chair.

But this experiment wasn't the kind that called for tea and pillows. I was going to use imagination in a way that might open my psyche to real aliens. Honoring the *Art of War's* first rule, I studied the landscape to pick the best place to stand and I plotted escape routes. Even knowing that locks didn't stop them, I flipped the deadbolt on the door several times until I got it—for speed, the motion was all in the wrist. Grasping for anything to give me courage, I wore no-nonsense jeans, my sturdiest track shoes, and my favorite T-shirt—the one that read, *Damn the torpedoes.* Despite the August heat, I protected my defenseless skin with a light jacket. To cover my head and neck while leaving vision unimpeded, I wore a ball cap with the brim towards the back. I drank plenty of water so I'd be well-hydrated. To avoid being light-blinded or leave myself outlined in glare, I turned off all the lights.

When it was fully dark, I took my stance just beyond the fence, leaving the gate open. If the experiment got too tense or if it attracted *them*, I had a clear path back to the house. The sky was clear, with just enough breeze to keep the mosquitoes away. I spread my feet to give myself solid balance then faced the graveled parking lot where there was enough room to land a 30-foot spacecraft. Taking a deep breath, I began trying to picture a round, silver craft setting down between me and the cornfield.

To overcome fear, the gedankenexperiment had to feel real. But to feel real meant I had to allow the terror to surface. I was scared that thinking about them might bring them. But I had to take that chance. In real life, others had seen spacecraft drop in front of them and had lived to tell about it. If they'd faced such an alien situation with no warning, I could do this when the challenge was mental…at least at first. Should there be any truth to Tom's tale, then someday a spaceship might really come for me. If it happened, if panic didn't cost me life or limb, it would at least cost me rationality, dignity, and the pricelessness of conscious awareness. I remembered a friend in childbirth. Lips white, sweat beaded on her forehead. But she remained silent and

210 Diplomat to the Galaxy

unbowed. When I praised her for bravery, she said, "My only choice is to break down or have dignity. I will at least have dignity." Even if I died in the teeth of an eight-foot praying mantis-type alien, I was resolute; I would do this, and I would at least have the dignity of not panicking.

The searchlight from the airport swept through the air, proving it was all pretense. It took a dozen more sweeps before imagination held and, instead of seeing the big metal shed or the deep shadow of the cornfield, I "saw" light glint off the metallic surface of a ship. Now I was getting what I'd worked for—a sense of reality so intense that in my mind's eye I saw the ship lower itself less than twenty feet from me, authentic enough to trigger an adrenaline rush, ragged breath, and a pounding heart. In a blue glow, a tripod of legs slithered down from its underbelly. Just like the description of UFOs around the world, it was silent; I heard nothing except the crunch of gravel as the feet settled.

It's one thing to have an intellectual belief, a theory, an idea that intelligent life exists somewhere in the vast reaches of space, *out there* somewhere. But it's another to meet it face to face. Tricked into believing, my brain released biochemical and emotional effects as if it was an actual event. All sense of safety and security blew away. My first impulse was to run, to escape. But I found myself rooted to the spot, too scared to run. I felt overwhelmed with the deepest sense of aloneness I'd ever experienced

"We are ultimately alone," Rev. Andy said in one of his lessons. "Even surrounded by others, we still must face our fears by ourselves. No one can do it but us."

I was not only alone, I was isolated. On the west, my house blocked any view from the highway. Cedar trees blocked visibility on the south. Acres of tall corn hid me on the other two sides. Against the backdrop of airport lights, even a craft with lights blazing could land and no one would notice.

My first impulse was to call someone, anyone, for help. But who? The county sheriff? My neighbors? My mother? Even if rescuers arrived this instant, even if they didn't also panic, how could they protect me against beings with abilities to paralyze onlookers and to transport people through walls and windows? There would be no help.

In mind's eye, the craft was a stereotypical UFO, about 30 feet in diameter, oval, seamless, metallic, with a domed top. A hatch slithered open and a ramp slid toward the gravel. I held my breath. My heart thundered. Hair prickled. Shivers raced down my spine. Sweat made my hands clammy. What was going to come down that ramp?

Webster defines terror as "fear that agitates body and mind; violent dread, fright." Primal terror arises from the deepest, scariest things our imagination can conjure, with the greatest dread being the fear of death, when we must cross into the great unknown. If we tend toward fear rather than courage, there are no ceilings in the unknown, no boundaries sufficient to contain imaginary possibilities. This is the same mortal dread we feel in our knee-jerk reactions to snakes, spiders, rats, heights, dark water, or deep holes. Children feel it when they imagine things in the dark. People in the middle-ages had it about cats and witches. Earlier centuries had it about falling off the edge of the flat world. It would be unkind to laugh but what triggered one woman's primal terror was her belief that landing a man on the moon would bring the world to an end. For me, the unknown was whatever was going to come out of that spaceship. Would it be slobbering insectoid monsters like in the movie, *Aliens*? Soulless little gray beings armed with medical probes? Galactic hunters looking for something to butcher and eat or to make into slaves or zoo specimens? What if they wanted bodies for laboratory experiments, maybe to dissect while still alive? (Weren't these the same things that humans do to animals used for research?)

"That's ridiculous. Animals don't have feelings," a horse trainer told me days earlier, responding to my comment that my Arab mare was unhappy. I'd even read about zoo managers and lab scientists who claimed that those who thought animals had feelings were only anthropomorphizing them—giving them human attributes. But how do such people account when an animal whines with pain, runs away in fear, wags its tail in cheerful welcome, offers a paw when an owner is sad, comes to listen to music, or sheds tears of grief? Would aliens see humans the same way as those who believed animals were no more than dumb biological machines? Might they view us how Negro slaves were perceived in the old South, as animals to be picked out of the trees, incapable of higher thought or feeling? Would they treat us with as much insensitivity as humans treat animals in factory farms or research facilities, or as no more than undeveloped brutes? I flashed on a mental image of myself trudging zombie-like from exhaustion or mental manipulation, digging ore out of mines or staggering under a load of alien laundry.

The terror escalated but I couldn't quit. No matter how far or fast we run, we pull our fears behind us like tin cans tied to a dog's tail, the very clatter terrifying us further. I must not run. Waiting wide-eyed for whatever was to come down the steps, dozens of possibilities flashed through my mind, everything from slime beasts to giant arachnids when…

Poof! The spell snapped

The ship was gone.

It was over.

I was breathing hard but the airport searchlight swept past, showing nothing but an empty lot again between me and the cornfield. I'd vanquished my demons. It wasn't that I'd done battle with them. I had only stood my ground, sweat pouring off me when the understanding came of its own accord. What had clicked into place was the recognition that whatever happened, it would never be more than what *could* happen. Do you see? Our greatest terror is that strangeness will consist of horrors beyond the pale, something as terrible and soulless as we can imagine.

But such fear is irrational because *there is no supernatural*. Every possible form, situation, or creature arises the way all bodies and forces of nature arise, in understandable evolutionary steps. Bad things happen, yes—fire, flood, death, profound mistakes, metal ripping through metal in car crashes, planes exploding into buildings, the rape of not just women but men and children, vicious torture, senseless killings, concentration camps, and on and on. Cruel as such things are, these are nonetheless part of the natural world. What triggers mortal dread is *alienness* itself, concentrated fear of the unknown, out-of-control imagination. If we can control ourselves long enough to analyze or familiarize ourselves with it, then chances are that we can handle it. Whatever, or whoever, space aliens were, they would not be from beyond the borders of reality; they would have arisen naturally because nothing can exist outside the wholeness. Dread is a terror of strangeness so great we can't bear it, a feeling Emily Dickinson described as "zero to the bone." But if we can stand still and bear the feeling until it disappears, then the panic begins to melt. It becomes something a composed mind can understand, and manage. Dread is only a feeling, not a promise.

The gedankenexperiment had snapped the head off my terror. I tore off the unseasonable clothes, threw myself into the chaise lounge, and whooped a sigh of relief. I'd done it. I had not only succeeded at facing my fears of aliens; I had grasped an underlying truth that would help me for the rest of my life. My success didn't mean I would never be afraid again. Indeed, if a real spaceship landed, I would be fearful all over again because we are always afraid of what is new— but I would no longer panic. I looked up, savoring the satisfaction of the dazzling night sky, glittering in its majesty, a universe of all possibilities. I waited until my heart stopped pounding and my breath was back to normal. Then, feeling like I could sleep well this night, I went in, brushed my teeth, and went to bed.

I had won.

But don't we know that conquering one layer is usually a signal to the universe that we are now ready to face the next bigger one?

Chapter

26

HORNS OF DILEMMA

Having overcome my terror of aliens, I felt tremendously proud of myself. Yet when I got back on the internet, dang! Reading about abductions still gave me fright. Clearly it was less than before, yet still there. What was it that was so deep that it left me so afraid?

This up-down was wearing me out. In my frustration, I felt increasingly resentful against the government for disrespecting the public's need-to-know. Why should I, as a common citizen, be required to do my own research? No amount of eyewitness stories, evidence, and conspiracy theorizing was ever proof enough to allow the questions about UFOs and aliens to come to rest. Without trustworthy official affirmations, every intelligent argument had a counter-argument that mostly served to muddy the waters. For instance, when the Pentagon released Top Secret papers about Project Mogul, claiming it explained everything about Roswell, many celebrated that the mystery was at last solved. But it was obvious that the Project Mogul glove fit only to those who didn't know how big the Roswell hand really had been. Even respectable news sources such as the *Smithsonian*, *National Geographic*, and *NY Times* insisted the breakup of a balsa wood and aluminum balloon carrying a six-foot-tall dummy could cover an area witnesses described as a "square mile of debris," and "truckloads of debris," including several four-foot-high aliens. For Pete's sake, to write stories like that, you must assume people are so stupid that proper background research isn't needed. But, don't most of us believe that the general public is more stupid than ourselves? Both political sides call the public "sheeple." And in no field are they considered more stupid than those who believe in ufology. Didn't I myself believe this until I did the research and found the evidence outweighing the noise, the nay-saying, and the propaganda?

But here's another dynamic that needs to be understood—*facts alone are insufficient to convince.* What we accept as truth depends less on evidence than on our threshold for acceptance, and/or how fully our level of education allows us to understand the facts, and/or our attitude or willingness to accept it.

For instance, if you only understand and believe in classical Newtonian physics but don't yet understand how quantum physics applies, then you won't believe evidence that ETs exist because Newtonian laws say space travel over vast distances is impossible. Likewise, if you assume that everyone who believes in conspiracy theories is a kook, you won't be open to evidence that says *some* conspiracies really do exist. If you enjoy ridiculing others, you won't accept any evidence as valid because it would mean you have to give up the delicious game of criticism that makes you feel superior. In the latter case, you will certainly be unwilling to accept evidence that makes you look foolishly short-sighted. In a reversal of that, if you are fearful and in denial, then you will resist accepting evidence that aliens exist because you don't want to know. At least not until, like me, you are forced to accept the reality.

Moreover, the mind makes up theories using however much evidence it has at hand. Where years of research and other life experience made it "obvious" to me what happened at Roswell was a government cover-up, to others with less evidence and a different mindset, it's "obvious" that it's only a hoax to get tourist trade. If we close our minds too soon, larger viewpoints can't penetrate.

Unfortunately, even though most people are not educated enough to sit on the ufology jury, each bit of information is left to the courtroom of popular opinion. Without an Institute of Exo-Standards and Technology to define what parameters we can use, we have no equal standards. Without the American Medical Association separating the bogus from the legitimate, we have no ultimate authority on the symptoms of abduction. Without a Safety Commission to ensure fair play between ETs and humans, we had nothing but arguments and more arguments. I dislike bureaucracy as much as anyone, but I would prefer having ufology legitimized rather than trying to figure every dang thing out for myself while a bunch of self-styled critics attack all the evidence.

I felt stymied. Research on the Internet had long ago reached the point of diminishing returns. Same themes, same arguments, just different details, just further interminable stories and endless theories. Some swore by the exo-theories, that aliens came from other planets. Some said they were interdimensional. Jacques Vallee presented good evidence that they're fairies and other creatures of ancient myth. Some said they're our space "brothers" here to help mankind. Some, like Rael and Von Daniken, supported theories that aliens were the master race, our creators. Others said they were angels or demons. Some called them shamanic symbolism, intrapsychic phantoms triggered by our own minds, or hoaxes. Luke, the guy in Iceland who claimed that aliens shared his head, said their mission was one of peace. Gilbert's description fit best with how I understood the universe to work, the enlightened theory. My personal theory was that if we had the big picture, we'd find that somehow all those theories contained some aspect of the truth.

But I didn't have the big picture.

Abductions aside, most perspectives at least leaned toward the picture that ETs were not threats. So, why couldn't I accept that they were benign and that none of it had anything to do with me? I longed for the return of innocence before I had this hydra of endless questions and fears. Hercules killed his hydra by cutting off each head and then cauterizing the stump with torch fire before it could grow back. That's what truth does—it burns the seeds of karma, thus ending the questioning. I thought my hydra of questions was dead after Gilbert's answers and Tom's lies had cauterized my need to know more. But the night Tom predicted the light, all nine heads came back hissing and demanding answers. I felt trapped between craving to know more and being unable to get it, impaled on the horns of a dilemma.

The word dilemma is Greek, meaning, "two premises, both abhorrent or unacceptable." In junior high, we loved to torment each other with gross dilemmas like, "which would you rather do, swim in a river of snot or slide down a 20-foot razor?" *Sophie's Choice* was a horrendous dilemma about a woman forced by Nazis to make a deadly choice. My dilemma was that on the one side, I was in anguish being unable to find answers, yet neither could I let go of the questions. In the *Art of Motorcycle Maintenance*, Phaedrus argues that the solution is to choose neither option but to pass the horns through the middle to a larger world of possibilities. That choice is about transcendence, about going beyond into a larger understanding. That is the choice I would have preferred but I hadn't found a larger understanding. The light Tom predicted was seen-with-my-own-eyes proof that something was happening. Yet, if all other methods had failed, how was I to discover what that was?

Suddenly—unhappily—I had the thought, What if this is an unsolvable problem? I firmly believe that all problems had solutions... but what if the answer was that this problem was too big for me to solve?

***

Tom called me a few days later, pulling me out of the bathtub where I'd been trying to soak out muscle cramps in my back. I groused to him about beginning to think I couldn't solve this problem. He wasn't sympathetic. "Aren't you happy now that you've seen a flying saucer?" he asked.

"No!" I retorted. My once driving goal to find the divine in him had evaporated into hoping I could at least be civil. "It's driving me crazy trying to figure out how you predicted it, and you won't tell me."

"I told you," he said in his half-smug, half-teasing tone, "I'm in on these things."

"Good. If you're in on them, then explain it to me."

"It was a patrol, just like I said."

"I don't believe that, Tom. Even if I did believe it, you said they patrolled at ten and four, but nothing ever shows up."

"You must have been there at the wrong times. They must have passed earlier or later."

"You're lying to me again."

His voice got squeaky with feigned innocence. "Would I lie to you?"

"Of course, you would lie to me. Have you forgotten I caught you red-handed in lies back in Florida?"

"If I lied, it was because you wanted me to."

"What do you mean, I 'wanted' you to?"

"That day in the park, didn't you tell me you wished it was true?" (A mental tickle found it curious that his reference only included the park rather than go all the way to be beginning. Why wouldn't he admit to fabricating the whole story, as well? But, the thought was vague and I wasn't alert enough to catch it at the time.)

"All I said was that I wished it to be true. I didn't invite you to make up stories."

There was a tiny pause. "I wanted to make you happy."

I admit that I was touched by the faint sound of sincerity but it was too little too late. I was too frustrated for it to have any useful effect. "I've told you what makes me happy—truth. Are you aware that a lie is the opposite of truth?"

"I suppose it is," he said. His tone didn't encourage me to trust that he recognized the difference.

"So why not tell me the truth now?" I asked. "The evidence is suggesting this whole thing is irrational."

"What do you mean, irrational?"

"Irrational means that the question has no answer because it is the wrong question. Asking about the Eloysians and Deneb and my supposed involvement with them, there can be no final answer because most likely they aren't real. It's like arguing what kind of cheese the moon is made from. We could argue that question for a hundred years and never come to a conclusion because the moon isn't made from cheese. The argument is based on the wrong question." I sighed just thinking about it. "The other possibility that makes it irrational is that maybe I'm simply not competent enough to figure it out because it is too far over my head. It is outside the range of what is can be determined with the tools available to me."

"They aren't irrational questions. You just have to find out for yourself."

I couldn't believe he'd said that yet again! "Tom Banks!" I sputtered. "When you say that, it makes me want to… to… hang up. Why don't you just confess that you made up this entire tall tale?"

As always, his response lacked any sympathetic understanding for me or the struggle I was going through. "You saw that light, and I told you all I can tell you. The rest is up to you."

I lost it. Nothing frustrated me as much as Tom telling me I had to find the answers to mysteries he himself had generated. "You're the one who created this moon-cheese mystery and when you say that it's up to me to solve it, I…I…"

I was so floored I didn't know how to continue. Our entire history flashed through my mind—how he had teased and stonewalled me while dangling fragments of clues and nonsense in front of me. I'd known all along it would have been smarter to end our dysfunctional relationship but I'd believed that failing to find the good in him meant I'd failed as a human being. Well, obviously, I *had* failed. I'd known him for what, four years? Four years of trying to be respectful, courteous, accepting, ever looking for the deeper aspects trying to find something in him I could love. Today I crossed the line. Today, I didn't even try to use non-accusatory language. I spit the words out in cold fury. "I don't like you, Tom Banks. You are not honest. You and your ambiguities are tiresome and disrespectful and I'm done. My patience is over so hear and understand this—don't call me again. *Ever.*"

Shaking with rage, I slammed the phone into it's cradle.

We know when we are done, and I really was done with him.

With the thought that these questions either had no solution or I wasn't competent to solve them, I was also done with ufology.

It hurt to say that. I believed that all problems had solutions, so why hadn't I been able to solve this?

Maybe I was guilty of functional fixity so I couldn't see more complex alternatives.

Maybe I couldn't see the forest for the trees so I couldn't see answers that were right in front of me.

Maybe I needed more spiritual development to see the larger picture.

Or, maybe I couldn't find the answers with the tools I had to work with.

Whatever the truth, I hadn't been able to make the questions go away. Ufology's mix of legitimate but often distorted facts, real and nonsensical rebuttals, and endless conjectures had slithered around the questions like wraiths, forming and collapsing again and again while never coming into a fixed focus that could stand up and walk into the room. No rebuttal was sufficient to prove UFOs didn't exist yet no evidence was sufficient to bring the issue to rest.

It broke my heart to admit I'd been defeated but reluctantly—very, very reluctantly—I articulated to myself that the need to solve this issue had become an addiction, a stuck place in me, an obsession with no end. That meant that the final, most logical answer was that I must overcome the addiction—I must stop thinking about it. To use Navy Seal language, I had to "get off the X." To stop the itching, stop scratching the bite, isn't that the formula? I would take neither the left horn nor the right horn, not even transcendence, but the fourth choice—denial. I would deliberately stop wrestling with it.

Unless you have Rubik's Cube syndrome, you can't appreciate how distressing it was to admit defeat. The questions burned inside me and craved answers the way a smoker craves to light up. I agonized thinking that I would go to my grave with these questions unanswered.

Yet I made myself stop asking them.

Trying to stop something with willpower often has a backlash the way a strict diet tends to trigger binge eating. But I was smart. Instead of charging into this like waging a war using "won't" power, I leaned into it the way one directs a bicycle not by turning the handlebars but by leaning one's weight. Instead of struggling to resist thoughts about lights in the sky, Tom's tales about the Deneb and Eloysians, aliens, extraterrestrial and interdimensional beings, I practiced gently encouraging my attention to lean toward other things.

Gradually, the emotional circuits and habitual responses began to desensitize. I resisted the impulse to look for lights. I invited myself to stop doing Internet research. When something sparked the analyzing again, I gently shifted my attention to some other problem.

You're sure to ask, "How can you deny the light that made the 90-degree turn? Didn't that really happen?" and "How could he have known unless he really did have insider knowledge?" Indeed, there always seemed to be a "but" lingering somewhere to launch me into a new cycle of questions. But "buts" and "on the other hands" are like the infinite swing y'er partners and do-se-dos in square dancing. Even when there is an allemande left or allemande right, the progress consistently goes nowhere except round and round. Mentally going round and round is a sign of irrationality or insufficient data. The solution is, just stop dancing. It took determination. Stopping was as painful as letting go of a lover. The angst, the longing, the grief over giving up trying to solve the mysteries was so intense I ached from it.

***

Over the next few months, I got good at it. Those who practice mindfulness will understand how it happened. When something triggered a memory about Tom or UFOs or about being a half-breed alien needed to stop a war, I didn't forbid the intellect from doing its thing. I simply allowed the analysis to play in the background like Muzak, heard but not listened to, or like a rerun of a TV courtroom drama playing in another room. The script weighed evidence pro and con, revisited clues and refutations, and arrived at conclusions I'd heard before. In the foreground, I cut 2x4s, set screws, paid bills, spent my emotional energy focused on down-to-Earth issues like pain and fatigue, dealing with workmen, and threatening a rooster with hatchet death if he didn't stop flogging me at unexpected moments. I just didn't mind the arguments. The script needed no attention from me because it was always the same.

In it, the attorney for the prosecution argued that Tom was a hoaxer and I was a fool for ever letting him get a foot in the door.

The Defense argued that the ring of truth indicated that I might have some yet-to-be-understood responsibility in helping aliens. The Prosecution argued that catching Tom in lies negated any ring of truth.

The Defense argued that too many things added up for it to be all nonsense.

The Prosecutor would fold his arms over his chest and say, "Then, prove it."

And so on. Yadda, yadda, yadda. It was all as predictable as a script for a soap opera. There was no need to listen. The arguments were always the same; the end was always the same. With a hint of sneer, the Prosecutor would offer the winning argument. "No planetary intelligence is going to bank on an unknown. If she was needed, aliens would only know that by meeting with her in person, and she had no memory of ever meeting them face-to-face, and no missing time."

Conceding that since there was no evidence of missing time, my mental Judge would bang his gavel decisively and pronounce, "Insufficient evidence! Case dismissed."

I always agreed with the outcome. Even though most abductions happen at night, I'm observant—I trusted I would have noticed something.

Observant. Yeah, right.

Chapter

27

COURTROOM

It was probably summer 2004 when Tom predicted the light that made the right-angled turn. It was probably August when I had the culture shock crisis, then told him to stop calling. That was when I formulated my plan to stop obsessing over the questions. Insulation, basement work, and installing the picket fence happened in September, October, and November. In December, my attention was on getting the glass-front wood stove installed. In January and February, the theme was the pretty stuff—tile, trim, and paint—and in March I was shopping at thrift stores for pictures and other decor. In April of '05, the time ee cummings called "in-just spring," the house finally looked more like a home than a construction site.

That same month, even though the no-frost/safe-to-plant date wouldn't be for another month, the temperatures shot into the 70s for a week. The unseasonable warmth seduced spring into thinking it safe to come out. Then, overnight, as vicious as a Viking raid, the temperatures dropped into the teens. For five days, this hard freeze left spring, "nipped in the bud." It not only killed the tender nibs on the ancient apple tree, it blackened even the hardy crocus, daffodils, redbuds, and forsythias. Memory works in chains of connection so perhaps what triggered a fresh round of courtroom drama that day was the mental image of raiding Vikings, reminding me of Tom's description of the Deneb "swooping down and destroying everything in their path."

While the Prosecutor and defense started arguing this proof versus that lack of proof, I decided to counter the cold with fresh bread and vegetable soup for lunch. The courtroom drama did its thing in the background while in the foreground, I punched and kneaded bread. Waiting for the bread to rise, I cleaned the tops of jars of beans and grains lining the shelves dividing the kitchen from the dining area, made mental lists for the grocery and box stores, and calculated whether I had enough firewood to finish the season. In the background, the arguments were so familiar they were almost companionable, like the snoring of a sleeping dog. I didn't pay any attention. A fire burned in the glass-front stove in the living room. If I couldn't have Florida sunshine, I'd settle for a crackling fire. With all the sheetrock dust and construction debris finally out of the way, with the new paint job adding a finished look, the place felt homey and comfortable. Maybe the sun wasn't shining but new track lights glistened onto new cabinets and a clean, new countertop. Life was good. I took the bread out of the oven, buttered the top, and put it on a rack to cool. Nothing like fresh bread on a cold day. In another ten minutes, the soup would be done. It was perfect timing as the rodent wheel of arguments had reached the point about no missing time.

Missing time. Haven't we all experienced the feeling of 'Where did the time go?' I'd showed up at a dental appointment a day too late. I'd burned every pan in the house at least once after putting something on the stove and then leaving it to do just a "little" computer work, not to become aware again until the smoke alarm went off. I also recall when I was in the sixth grade, I was reading a book ironically titled, *Spaceship on Saddle Mountain.* I'd been so engrossed that it wasn't until another student touched my arm that I realized my name had been called several times.

But these are only common lapses of memory, ordinary confusions, not—as happens to abductees—a slice of time missing from life that neither you nor anyone can account for. In the courtroom drama, the lack of missing time was the main issue, proof positive that aliens had never met me, and therefore proof Tom's story was a fiction. It was the point that always brought a resounding "Case Dismissed!" from the judge. Then the arguing would end. My Rubik's Cube syndrome would reset itself to zero, and my background mental chatter could move on to other topics. Today, while I arranged a bowl and eating utensils on a tray, the Prosecutor said what he always said, "The most important clue is still lacking—she has no missing time."

The defense waggled his finger and said, "But the absence of evidence is not evidence of absence. Ninety percent of abductees have no memory of their encounters. She ranks high enough on the lists of abduction symptoms that we can surmise that she has been abducted."

Dismissively, the Prosecution waved his hand. "That list could just as easily be PTSD, and there's plenty of reason for PTSD other than abduction. But we know that no intelligent species is going to bank on an unknown. Without lost time to indicate that she really did meet with aliens, the rest is merely circumstantial. You have no proof, no memory, of such a meeting, do you?" This should have been where the defense conceded, followed by the Judge banging his gavel and saying, "Insufficient evidence! Case dismissed!"

But what happened next had never been in the script before. Instead of backing down, this time the defense sneered, "What about

Iceland? Wasn't *that* missing time? How do you account for the 24 hours gone missing there?"

Stunned, the Prosecutor, the Judge, and I hold stock-still, breathless. My God. I had forgotten all about Iceland.

Chapter

28

MISSING TIME

"**D**amn the Navy!" The howl came from a window somewhere among the rows of dirty, two-story barracks in the mud and rocks, the cry so anguished it ripped your heart out. But in the dreary Icelandic dusk, his grief did not seem out of place any more than the wail of the wind. It was the signature, the tone, the note typical of the environment. Iceland itself, the land of ice and fire, was captivating, its people and culture fascinating, its language and traditions ancient and honorable. But the NATO Base at Keflavik was the epitome of a military slum, indifferent to the beautiful, the uplifting, the humane; exemplary of despair words like desolate, despondent, depressed. The landscape was so barren that gnarled limbs would have softened it but ceaseless winds forbade even the hardiest of trees to grow anywhere except invisible inside the protection of dead volcanic craters. Pilots said that if you can learn to fly in the erratic Icelandic winds, you can fly anywhere in the world.

You could tick off the fingers of one hand what there was to see. Besides the dirty barracks and Quonset hut admin buildings, strands of electric wire hung limply between poles. Gray, stumbler-sized rocks lay in one's path like broken toys in a disordered house. At least once a day, overcast clouds heaved their load of tears as if they too grieved over that desolate peninsula. The pervasive damp left ever-present mud puddles and dripping eaves.

And then there was the asphalt. The salient feature at Keflavik, the acres of runways were perfect metaphors for the Base whose emotional heart had long ago flatlined. The brass barked, yelled, snapped, lectured, demanded, muttered, insisted, threatened, or droned in a bored monotone, while the swabs grumbled, played pool, gave up, drank too much…or howled out of windows in futile misery.

"One thing I've come to understand in the time I'd been here is that just as individuals can be dysfunctional, so can organizations," an officer told me. He, a psychologist, and I had become friends after discovering that we both practiced TM. We joked about feeling certain we were the only two sane people on the base. Both of us had heard officers say that stress was necessary to keep troops on their toes, ready for combat. But we knew that a stressed soldier isn't "on his toes." He was strung-out, wound-up, and less stable, while, like a cat, a stress-free soldier could go from relaxed to battle readiness in an instant. He and I joined with the Icelandic center to get TM taught on base.

I appreciated hearing his perspective about the organization's dysfunctional aspects. My entry scores had qualified me for Officer's Candidate School but I'd been a year too old. That meant that, beyond the painful trickle-down effects of their decisions, I wasn't privy to what went on "upstairs," as he was. At 29, I was too experienced, too analytical, too intellectual, and too much the hippie-philosopher-poet-rebel to fit in. In a documentary about the military, I heard a recruiter say, "We don't want soldiers who are too intelligent." The reason for not wanting the enlisted to be too smart is the same reason you don't want horses to be too smart. You don't want them making the decisions, you want them to obey yours. You want them to start, stop, and turn at your command without asking why. I'm not saying this is wrong, I'm just saying I didn't fit in. In the wake of my *Maha* experience, morality and spirituality had become primary in my awareness and, even beyond the general hippie rebellion against the wrongs of the "establishment," I'd seen themes of power, abuse, and unnaturalness that drove people nuts. One such unnaturalness was a work schedule I'd long blamed for losing 24 hours of my life. This schedule required working six shifts of scrambled nights, days, and evenings, in five days, with three days off for recovery.

"This schedule is insane," I protested to the officer who explained the routine to me when I first arrived.

"What do you mean?" he snapped, his voice coldly challenging.

I didn't know how to explain the obvious. "It's unnatural, it's stressful," I stammered.

The officer curled his lip. "Stress makes you tough. Get used to it. Anyone who can't take it is a weakling and needs to get weeded out."

In *Journey to the Center of the Earth*, the opening to the bowels of the Earth was in Iceland. I thought Verne's choice was prophetic. From the moment I arrived, seeing a normal sun one last time before the jetliner broke through the clouds to land at Keflavik, it felt like I'd arrived in hell. This man was one of many who was going to ensure that it stayed that way. I stared at him, unable to believe that any grown person could be so dense and uneducated about ordinary human needs. Did he really not know the difference between legitimate challenge and abuse? The people who can tolerate high stress tend not to be the strong but those who have so many layers of strain that they don't even notice when weird stuff happens. They aren't unflappable, they're numb.

Even a minor time shift like Daylight Savings Time causes increased accidents. Frequent time shifts create effects like living in perpetual jet lag. Plus, it causes sleep deprivation. Sleep deprivation is associated with human errors in the Exxon Valdez oil spill off Alaska, the Challenger space shuttle disaster, and the Chernobyl nuclear accident. It's estimated to be a culprit in one-in-six fatal road accidents.

To add to the stress, Iceland had its own special devils: perpetual light or darkness. In the "summer" when the sun goes below the horizon, it leaves ten to twelve hours of monotone dusky twilight before it comes back up again. In winter, the sun comes up at about eleven o'clock in the morning, rises to about a third of the way up the sky, and then, as if disgusted by what it sees, descends into a 3:00 P.M. sunset. The result of this can be hypomania—the craziness one experiences when there is a lack of darkness or too much of it. Hypomania causes such symptoms as elevated or irritable moods and the inability to produce melatonin, one of the body's natural sleep aids.

In my case, the fatigue and confusion were so much the order of the day that, at the time, losing 24 hours seemed plausible.

"Where were you yesterday?" the OD (Officer of the Day) had asked. I can't recall any other morning entering our workstation, but this day left a memory so strong that I recalled it now. I sucked in my breath and tried to recall more.

"Yesterday? What happened yesterday?" I'd asked then, no doubt sounding like a dumb blond.

"Yesterday was the first day of the string," he said. By string, he meant the weekly row of scheduled duty shifts.

"Isn't today the first day?"

"No. Today is the second day."

I blinked and frowned, trying to make sense of what he'd said. Four days off instead of three? How was that possible? I said, "I don't know what to say. I didn't do it on purpose."

He must have seen my confusion for he looked at me over his glasses and waved me on. "Just don't let it happen again." Unauthorized absence was a court-martial offense so, whether it was his kindness or his apathy, it worked in my favor.

I went to my workstation, still trying to figure out what had happened. An extra day off would have felt like a vacation. I had the routine down to a science so how could I have misplaced a day? The last shift of the string put us in bed after midnight so catching up on sleep dominated the first day. Day Two was when I did chores— cleaning, laundry, shopping at the Exchange, writing letters, and such. Day Three was my treasured day of enjoyment, reading, visiting, an occasional day trip. In such a structured routine, where is there room for an accidental extra day off?

Under hypnosis, many abductees discover they made up semi-plausible explanations to account for their missing time. In Iceland, as I stood by the plotting table that day trying to figure out how I could have lost so much time, the explanation I gave myself was that I must have been so exhausted from the crazy schedule that I'd slept through it. I'd even claimed as much in occasional conversations over the years. "I was so tired once I slept around the clock. Isn't that amazing?"

Now, three decades later, staring unseeing at the simmering soup on a gray day in Iowa, I asked myself for the first time, was it even possible to have slept around the clock without being aware of it? The facts argued against it. Most people working that schedule had difficulty sleeping. Many, myself included, sometimes found themselves sitting bolt upright out of a dead sleep, flushed with a cold sweat, having the panicked thought, "Oh God, I'm late for work."

Another argument against sleeping around the clock is that I had come down with what would later be diagnosed as fibromyalgia. One of its symptoms is shallow sleep.

At the very least, wouldn't I have staggered down the hall to the bathroom during that time? Wouldn't that have given me some sense of time passing? Of moving into a new day?

Missing time associated with abductions can last from a few minutes to a few days. Harold Schirmer's duty book showed a half-hour gap. Betty and Barney Hill lost two hours. Betty Andreassons' abduction lasted four hours. Travis Walton was gone for a week. To appear so seamless that I wouldn't have noticed, would have required me to lose between 24 and 36 hours.

Suddenly, Luke's image flashed into mind. I nearly gasped. I hadn't made the connection until now but the meeting with him had to have happened in this timeframe. Was that how aliens knew I was the one needed to help because they had already met me through an abduction? Was this the explanation for why, twice in one lifetime, six thousand kilometers and three decades apart, two different men had asked me to help extraterrestrials bring peace? My head spun. I felt disoriented. For the last five years, I had been looking for an *aha!* when all the pieces would fall together and this mystery would be solved. But what was snapping together was not an aha! It was an oh no! It strongly suggested that my worst fear—abduction by aliens— had actually happened. Missing time is a keynote of abduction and I had just recalled verifiable missing time. Could this be why aliens and abductions had so terrified me, because, even though the conscious mind contained no specific memories, such events in the past had been embedded into blood and bones, sinew and muscle, *unconsciously?*

In the flood of conflicting thoughts and feelings, blood rushed past my ears with such force I could feel it—thu-thump, thu-thump, thu-thump, like a voice, half-haunting, half demanding, Have you? Have you? Have you been abducted by aliens? Have-you? Have you? Have you failed to help other beings because twice you were too pig-headed to understand the message? I struggled to sort and compare dates, times, solid facts.

Soon after arriving in Iceland in springtime, I fell in love with a fellow swab named Jon. He and I were doomed to a star-crossed end when he transferred back to the states in late August. The missing time couldn't have happened while he was there. We worked the same schedule on the same team so if I had gone missing before he left, he would have looked for me. Then, in October, I visited him stateside on leave but it was obvious our relationship was over. While Jon was there, I would not have gone to lunch with Luke, nor for some time after ending the relationship. Then, in November, I transferred to a different duty assignment. That meant that meeting with Luke and missing a day of my life probably happened close together in late October or early November.

As the timeline solidified, I reached out to the counter, to steady myself. In my mind's eye I could almost see Tom shaking his head at me as if to say, *I told you so*. Did this mean his story was true, and that beings were dying on other planets because I'd failed to listen to him? I'd told him to never call me again. Now I realized that he was the only person I could turn to. I struggled to recall what I'd done with the phone. I finally found it in my coat pocket from when I'd gone out to feed the chickens that morning. The world had turned upside down since then. I tapped his number and electronic sounds tapped out what I hoped would be a lifeline. His phone range. Perhaps, hearing how upset I am, he would finally confess that it had all been a hoax. At the very least, he'd mock and make a joke of it and I could end the outrageous thought that I might be a murderer because I'd refused to believe him.

His phone rang again in my ear. He would surely tell me I was upset over a story he'd fabricated out of whole cloth. After he'd laughed at me and we'd gotten the nonsense out of the way about my failing to help Eloysians the same way I'd failed to help Luke's alien in Iceland, then I'd take a shaky deep breath, and say, "There's something else, Tom—I now have reasons to believe I've been abducted. What if they come back for me?"

I'm fully aware that it's a contradiction to feel guilty for not helping while being terrified they might come for me, the same way it had been a contradiction to believe Joy Gilbert's perspective that aliens were benign while I continued to quake in terror of them. Conflicts like these make computers crash. Is it any wonder my head was spinning?

Tom's phone rang a third time. Why didn't he answer? What if, God forbid, he really had told the truth? Was that why his story had haunted me so, because there really had been truth to it?

The fourth ring sounded as empty as a stone dropped into an abyss, followed by Tom's pseudo-cheery voice: *Top of the morning! Leave a message.*

My heart sank. I rasped, "Tom, call me. It's an emergency."

***

Afternoon bled into evening, then night, while I paced the floor, chewed my fingernails, stared out the windows, trying to sort out the real from the silly. After my angry retort to Tom to never call again, had he become so negative that he now refused to call me even in an emergency? I didn't think so. He may have played mind games and been meanly critical but it would be unlike him to be spiteful. There are other reasons for not answering calls. Phones get lost or stolen, left in cars or meeting rooms, or cell towers fail. Could he have gone fishing and forgotten to take his? Had he finally gotten a girlfriend and turned his ringer to "off?" When he said he'd be in danger if the Deneb found him, I assumed that was just another invention of his mind but now, listening to the empty rings, I wondered, was it possible *they* had gotten him? Was his phone ringing in his pocket somewhere on the backside of the Moon, lying lost in Martian dust, or with a dead battery in some holding cell in the rings of Saturn?

I hit end-call, feeling a mix of madness for thinking such thoughts, and near panic. I had no one to turn to for help. If I'd broken my leg, I could call an ambulance. If I'd been hit by a storm, I could call the Red Cross. If a thief had broken into my house, I could call the sheriff. But who could I call about alien abduction? I couldn't go to the emergency room. There are no billing numbers in the *Physician's Diagnostic Manual* for abduction by aliens, and certainly no help for a patient who thought they might be responsible for a war on other planets. I could just imagine how, after listening to my story, the doctor and his nurse would exchange knowing glances. As soon as I left the ER, they'd crack up with "Beam me up, Scotty" jokes. Indeed, if I called any agency, from the sheriff to the USAF to the White House, I would be laughed at, treated as if I were a nutcase, possibly investigated, maybe even jailed as a threat to government security.

I stared out the kitchen window at the lowering skies over the frost-burned fields, the cognitive dissonance surreal. I didn't know how to think intelligently about this. U.S. stats say that about a thousand individuals a month have the courage—or the desperation—to report alien encounters to agencies such as the Mutual UFO Network (MUFON), the Center for UFO Studies, or the National UFO Reporting Center. But the truth is that people are reluctant to report any painful, humiliating event. Experts estimate that ordinary muggings, rape, and domestic violence go under-reported by 300-to-700 percent. If that many victims of common crimes don't report their experiences out of shame, fear of ridicule, and anxiety about social stigma, imagine how much less likely the victim of alien abduction would be to report their experiences in our hostile social milieu where people consider aliens a joke. This is especially true when, like me, they aren't clear about exactly what happened. We can't get medical, academic, societal, or government help except as mental patients. While politicians perfect their hairstyle, have power lunches with deep-pocketed lobbyists, and take "fact-finding" junkets to vacation countries (all while protesting that they know nothing about UFOs), countless citizens have faced what is possibly the most profound shock of all time: meetings with beings totally outside our culture of knowledge, beings no authority or official educational program has prepared them to comprehend. Afterwards, they then can find no official information but only do as I had done, to sift through the squabbling among dubious opinions on the internet or through the mountain of books by independent authors. I felt bitter just thinking about it.

I know all this sounds crazy. It felt crazy. Common sense said there was no sign of immediate danger yet emotionally the menace felt *imminent,* the way it had felt when I feared they might read my mind and come get me when I was afraid to go outside. It didn't make sense but I couldn't shake it off. I didn't eat. I didn't meditate. I didn't even go to bed that night. I sat huddled on the couch, wrapped in a shawl, getting up periodically to put logs on the fire. I'd doze sometimes then jerk awake with an adrenalin rush to look around for bug-eyed beasts prepared to take me away.

***

As it neared morning, the world turned upside down yet again, or maybe, finally, right-side up. Incomprehensibly, the whole thing suddenly became a non-issue. It simply melted away. I went from terror one minute to feeling silly over the whole thing the next. What had just happened?

I didn't know.

At dawn, I finally meditated. Afterward, burned out from the long night, I sat and stared out the meditation room window, waiting for motivation to move me. I needed to take a shower and feed the chickens. Laundry needed doing. The kitchen was still a mess from yesterday's uneaten lunch. The terror was gone but my mind felt muddled. I was no longer afraid but I felt depressed, almost ashamed for what had just happened. It didn't make sense.

For the first time in nearly a week, sunlight crawled out between the clouds, spreading normality across the fields. From 94 million miles away, a ray of golden-yellow light shot through the blinds, sending patterns of light and shadow over the white carpet to touch my bare feet. The effect was like a kind word to someone sitting in rubble after a disaster—poignant and reassuring. I don't know if it was from the fragility of physical and emotional exhaustion, or from gratitude, but tears welled in my eyes. With it came what felt like the first rational thought I'd had since noon the day before when the oh no! had happened—I realized that I'd been on a journey. What was it Tom had said on a day I'd been pestering him to tell me the complete story? Something about my not being able to understand some things until other things had been learned? It hinted that I needed to be brought "up to speed." And wasn't this exactly what had happened? Looking back, I saw that my education in ufology, including the psychological stretches and the culture shocks, looked not only like intellectual learning but steps of personal growth. My mind had been gradually opened. I'd learned scientific facts, gained intellectual understanding, and gained psychological strengths. Had yesterday's revelation come any sooner, it would have been incomprehensible. I wouldn't have had a framework for understanding it. But since ufology was so far outside my normal interests, I would never have gone on this journey voluntarily.

In *Hero of a Thousand Faces*, Joseph Campbell wrote that if the hero resists the journey, then fate forces him into it the way it forced Luke Skywalker to become a Jedi when his home burned and his aunt and uncle were killed. I'd been forced into this path by Tom's crazy story and that vague ring of truth. I resisted but my Rubik's Cube syndrome drove me to seek answers, following a trail of breadcrumbs that led to deeper awakening. In the beginning, certain I would be a myth buster, I'd held the entire UFO community in contempt, believing they were bad scientists guilty of the grossest delusions. Yet I'd found myself drawn in as if by compulsion. Memories surfaced that forced me to reinterpret my past (or to better understand it in a new context) like what happened with Luke and the light that chased us as children. After the twin releases of Joy Gilbert's book and catching Tom in lies, I'd danced nervously around the campfire of my discoveries and boasted that I'd conquered my fears of the dark. I'd told myself that Deneb and Eloysia were figments of a fat man's imagination and that ETs had nothing to do with me. I'd tried to tell myself that the mystery was over and I didn't have to think about it anymore. But the mystery hadn't gone away because I hadn't yet arrived at the beginning.

But where, exactly, had I arrived? Where I was, I realized, was on the other side of the Rubicon—I had crossed a line of sorts, transcending from a lesser to a larger understanding. It is the same place one always arrives, at what Buddhists call beginner's mind, where we look at ourselves as if for the first time only with a larger, more mature understanding. The "beginning" had most likely been in the unconscious long before Iceland. For reasons we don't yet understand, aliens remove or reduce the memories of being taken. Possibly it is to lower stress, possibly it is like a time capsule holding off the memories until the individual is ready to accept it, possibly it is to postpone awareness of it until our culture is ready to awaken collectively. Joy Gilbert entitled her book *A Time to Remember* because when we become enlightened, it feels like we are remembering our fundamental natures—and because the time was coming when many of us would remember our encounters with aliens. In my case, apparently subconscious memories of former encounters had been rising, telegraphing to the surface in the form of the phobia about abduction. I didn't remember actual events, only the fear I'd once felt. Yesterday, that decades-old imprint had arisen so fully that it felt immediate, bringing the fear to the surface where, for several hours it had felt as fresh as if it was happening that very moment. Then, when the buried stress dissolved or released, the fear went away as if it had never existed.

Many times, I'd wondered if I had made a bad choice to get involved with ufology but now I realized that it had been a spiritual journey all along. To become enlightened, we must face our fears and resolve whatever is in the unconscious. The stresses, the old karmas that reside inside us, must either be erased through meditation or therapy or by working through it in daily life. This is how we burn the seeds of karma. Tom's tale served as a doorbell to the unconscious. The ring of truth I'd heard most likely had nothing to do with his story but everything to do with deeply buried memories, pushing me to wake up. The years of research, the working out of understanding about the reality of extraterrestrials, that had all been necessary to provide a foundation got comprehension when the memory of missing time finally surfaced.

How do I know this is likely to be a true analysis? It is because, when one finds truth, doubts cease. The questions get put to rest and the fear goes away. I found myself at the point the Roman Catholic Theologian Monsignor Corrado Baldauchi openly spoke of when he stated that extraterrestrials were "other of God's creatures." "We can no longer think…is it true? Is it not true? Are they truth or are they lies?" I'd made a 180-degree shift from asking "Is it true or not true, to finding myself at home with the understanding, "Yes, it is true."

***

As the future draws us toward it the way a river current draws us toward the falls, our greatest fear is of the unknown. The nearer we get, the more frightening it becomes. But, unlike the falls where it leads us to death and destruction, new futures often mean larger new realities. Having gone over this edge, I felt victorious. I felt like a pioneer, like someone who had just graduated into a larger paradigm, into a universe that now included beings from other worlds, other dimensions. I realized that our fears are what cause us to "see through a glass darkly." On this side of the Rubicon, the questions were no longer fearful. They were curious, eager to know, more like a kid interested in what friends it will bring when a new family moves into the neighborhood. My questions now were, "Who are they?" "Why are they here?" "Is it possible to meet them consciously?" I felt an angst of longing wishing that I could ask questions of Luke or Tom, but Luke was in the distant past and Tom wasn't answering his phone. Yet, even if I found Tom, isn't it likely he would only say yet again, "You have to find out for yourself"?

Isn't it true that we must all find out for ourselves? Isn't this what we humans have always done, to become pioneers? To meet new challenges? To explore, expand, grow, to transcend into new and larger worlds, to face the unknown with courage, curiosity, and hope? To go over the edge of the horizon to find ourselves on the other side and to grow bigger than what we were before?

EPILOGUE
ON THE OTHER SIDE
OF THE RUBICON

I never heard from Tom again, nor was I able to locate him. Had the Deneb gotten him? Common sense would still argue that nothing about his story was true. Still, I'm inclined to think that there has to be more than what appeared on the surface, wouldn't you agree? How, from a thousand miles away, could he have predicted the light that made the 90-degree turn? And, remember how he said things that sometimes even sounded wise such as, "You aren't ready to understand yet," and "Some things have to be learned before other things can be understood." I am quick to admit that I could have been so naïve that I read more into him than actually existed. And, of course, any consideration of who Tom was requires us to ask the question about how much he himself understood. As unconscious as he appeared to be, had he been grilled at Gitmo it's possible that even he couldn't tell us.

I doubt I would have ever come to like him but time and distance at least brought me acceptance and a grudging respect that, in his way, he cared for me. Despite my sincere efforts, I see that I was also impatient, hypocritical, irascible, even sometimes unkind. I think it would have been smarter to have been honest to my feelings and avoided him altogether.

Other questions remain unanswered. Did I miss some hidden opportunity through Tom as I did with Luke? Doubtful. The evidence I found overall indicates that extraterrestrials (ETs) are superior beings with awakened consciousness who would hardly need Earthlings to solve problems for them. My conclusion is that that the ring of truth I heard had been tickling in the unconscious from the memory of abduction, not an indication that Tom's story was true.

My phobic fears disappeared after the revelation. Once I recognized those subconscious memories had caused the terror of aliens, it allowed a swift and dramatic turnaround. I quickly became an enthusiast, devouring books, videos, documentaries, and discussions with other ufologists. I even became an official UFO investigator, and I found clues that supported the probability that not only I but both my sons (whom I will call Mark and William) had been abducted. The first was a journal entry dated November 9, 1973. *I had a horrifying dream last night… about the men from outer space getting William. I woke up feeling real-life grief, and it has nagged me all day. I'm fighting it. I have to fight it or I might be overwhelmed.*

Many abductees report that their experience felt like dreaming. Because most people believe that dreams are only distorted fantasy, this has created doubts for experiencers and witnesses alike. But if you understand that dreams are another dimension of consciousness, it begins to make sense. It is not only possible to be conscious in dreams, it is even possible to direct what happens in them. This is called lucid dreaming. Experiences in lucid dreaming are authentic experiences, just on a different plane of reality. ETs have apparently mastered this state, or mastered the ability to induce it. (I think we can expect that dimensionality will be an area of intense future focus for science.) When I saw "the men from outer space getting William," it had the vivid quality of lucid dreaming. I moved swiftly to protect him and had barely reached out my hand when, as if I had been ejected, I found myself suddenly fully awake. It wasn't like waking up from a nightmare where one instantly recognizes that what just happened was fantasy. It was more like I had stepped sideways from one reality to another, still burning with angst. That sense of reality was what made it so hard to shake off.

Not everyone will understand this subtle clue, but had it been merely a one-off fantasy, I believe that I would have written, "I dreamed that spacemen got William." This is how most people would have written a generic narrative. But I was more specific. I wrote "*the* men" from space got him. The "the" suggests that I was writing about beings I already knew.

I have since learned that abductions often run in families.

I wished I could ask William questions but long before I found the entry, he'd been killed in an accident. My older son is disinterested in such things but, without explaining my reasons for asking, I wrote to him. "I know this will sound like a strange question but have you ever experienced a sense of lost time, found weird marks on your body, or had dreams about aliens?"

He wrote back, "Nope, no lost time, weird marks, or alien dreams. Closest I got was a dream about an amphibious 'monster' with black shiny skin, webbed hands and feet, and big dark eyes."

I gasped. That was a perfect description of a reptilian ET. At the time, my only information about reptilians had come from British researcher David Icke. Icke had made big bucks presenting reptilians as evil shapeshifters, claiming that they feed negative forces to bring disruption. I was horrified. Without telling Mark anything about why I was asking, I wrote back for any further details.

"I don't remember a lot about it other than already mentioned— amphibious, black shiny skin, webbed feet, and big dark eyes. Like a mutated scuba diver. It was probably 5-to-6 ft tall. I don't remember it having any ears or mouth. It was probably about ten feet away from me when I saw it; it was standing there or perhaps moving slowly toward me. Seems like I saw it suddenly and immediately woke up."

From someone who had no interest in or knowledge of the subject, this is a further match of the common descriptions of reptilians.

He reported feeling no fear in his dream and I, likewise, remembered no fear in my own dream until they brought William. My sense was that I knew who they were and I understood what the program was but I still didn't want my child subjected to it because he was too young to understand. Whitley Stieber reported having the same experience when they took his son.

Reptilians look scary and they have scary reputations but dire perspectives should always be considered suspect. Remember this—fear is almost always based on misunderstandings or exaggeration. The darker the picture, the more likely it is to be from prejudiced exaggerations and imaginings rather than truth. (The path to enlightenment requires us to develop inner strengths to conquer our fears.) Conscious abduction experiencer Jim Sparks stated that he had met with reptilians and (after he stopped being a hard-ass and started cooperating with them) he found reasons to respect and even to love them.

ETs are usually described as cold and unfeeling, but I think there is more to it. It might be possible that some of the shorter grays are biological robots but considering that they deal with erratic, potentially violent humans, all types of ETs are probably business-like. When I think of ETs trying to deal with humans, the image that comes to mind is of humans trying to help wild animals. Like animals, we struggle in terror over what we don't understand. Once we overcome our fears, the relationship changes. Whitley Strieber and others report that they ultimately experienced exchanges of deep love. Joy Gilbert described them as not only loving but having a sense of humor. Jim Sparks described even the scary-looking reptilians as sensitive enough that he could feel their sadness over the plight of the earth. In his book, *The Keepers*, he quoted them as saying:

Yes, it is true that we have been in contact with your government and heads of power. It is also true that agreements have been made and kept secret from your people. It is also true that in the past some of your people have lost their lives or have been badly hurt to protect this secret. Our hands had no part in this.

We contacted your leaders because your planet is in grave trouble. Your leaders said the vast majority of your population wasn't ready for this yet, so we made time agreements with your leaders as to when your people would be made aware of our presence. This part of the agreement has not at all been kept.

It was also agreed that in the meantime steps would be taken to correct the environmental conditions with our advice and technology. We say 'advice' because this is your planet, not ours. They also broke this agreement.

"I felt an awful wave of emotion from them," Sparks wrote, "the feeling of abandonment. To feel any emotion from them at all was amazing, but this was overwhelming."

They continued:

Your air, and your water are contaminated. Your forests, jungles, trees, and plant life are dying. There are several breaks in your food chain. You have an overwhelming amount of nuclear and biological weapons, which include nuclear and biological contamination. Your planet is overpopulated. Warning: It is almost to the point of being too late unless your people act. There are better ways of deriving energy and food needs without causing your planet any damage. Those in power are aware of this and have the capability of putting these methods into worldwide use."

Beings with these intelligent attitudes do not seem like monsters. Rather, they sound like beings I want to know. I believe the more we know, the less we will find to fear. Most importantly, the more we develop in consciousness, the more ways we will harmonize with such intelligence.

***

After my awakening, I found myself more afraid of humans than I was of ETs. I feared ridicule from citizens as well as fear of government sanction should anyone learn I was researching ufology. In 2011 or 2012, I finally gathered the courage to talk to a therapist. Terry was tall, blue-eyed, and nearing retirement age. I'd started seeing him on the pretext of anxiety and depression regarding my ex-husband, which was true enough, but hardly important considering the real reason— that I wanted to talk about the ET issues. I'd seen him maybe a half dozen times trying to size him up, to see if I could trust him enough to tell him the truth. Finally, I said it. "You may think I'm crazy, but I have reasons to believe I've been abducted by aliens."

He raised his eyebrows slightly. If I was reading him right, it was more with interest than with disbelief.

"No, I don't think you're crazy," he said. "I've had some experience with this. I am a certified hypnotherapist and I've worked with several people who believed they had been abducted. I've even been a guest speaker for MUFON."

It was my turn for raised eyebrows. In small-town Iowa, was it possible to find someone with skills and experience like this?

"The way I handle this is, I don't try to tell you what I think. We just do the work, have some discussion and perhaps some regression, and just generally give you some support that lets you come to your own conclusions. What makes you believe you've been abducted?"

My mouth was dry and my palms were wet as I hit the highlights about Tom and Luke, and about the day I realized I had missing time.

"Have you ever seen a UFO?"

I nodded and told him about the light that made the 90-degree turn. (I wouldn't recall the one that hung overhead until several years afterward, and I hadn't yet seen the third one.)

"Do you think it could have been a plane or satellite?"

I shook my head. "It didn't have blinking lights and it was going faster than a jet. It couldn't have been a satellite because it made that sudden right turn. The part that makes it the most mysterious is that Tom predicted it over the phone as it happened."

"Could he have seen it from where he was?"

I shook my head again. "He was over a thousand miles away, in Texas."

"Interesting story," he said. "Did you ask him what it was?"

"I did, of course. But the thing is, I always thought of Tom as a… well, I don't know what to call him… a neurotic nobody. He couldn't or wouldn't give straight answers and I never trusted that he knew what he was talking about. I asked him what it was and he said it was a patrol, making sure I was okay." I rolled my eyes. "Obviously, a stupid story."

"How do you know it wasn't a patrol?"

I was surprised he would even ask. "Because the story makes no sense. If it had been a sheriff's deputy driving up in a vehicle, that's a patrol. But space beings flying overhead to check up on someone tens of thousands of feet down? That's absurd, wouldn't you think?"

"So, what would you like from me?"

"Well, now that I know you've had some experience with abduction, I'd really like to try hypnosis."

"Okay, we can do that, but before we do, let me ask some questions."

I nodded.

"What happens if we do regression and you discover that you have not been abducted?"

I said it would be a relief to know.

"And how would you feel if we discover that you have been abducted?"

"Then I'll have confirmation for what is now only intuition and logical deduction."

"Do you feel that if you've been abducted, it will make you someone special?"

"It may be that it gives me special responsibilities, but it wouldn't make me superior to anyone else if that's what you mean."

"What do you mean, 'special responsibilities?'"

"Tom told me a crazy story that they needed me to stop an interplanetary war. I didn't believe it but I still can't shake off the feeling that there's something to it, that I'm supposed to do something."

"You said that you had 24 hours of missing time. Can you tell me about that?"

I told him about missing the day of work in Iceland. "There's other evidence, too. I found a journal from 1973 that refers to an intense dream I had about 'the men from space' having gotten my younger son. I was terribly upset about it. Also, reading that journal reminded me of a scary experience that happened earlier that same year—I thought I was pregnant." ETs are often responsible for interrupted pregnancies but back then, I knew none of that. In the Midwest in 1973, an out-of-wedlock pregnancy was still a matter of whispers, scowls, and scorn. That was before Roe Vs. Wade. When I wasn't struggling to figure out how I could possibly deal with a third child, I fretted over how to go about finding someone to do an abortion. It stuck in memory because it had been so stressful, so traumatic that, to make sure it never happened again, a few months later I got a tubal ligation.

"But with no pre-menstrual warning, my period came. Never, until menopause, did I go for over three days off schedule."

"How do you feel about hypnosis?" Terry asked.

"I want to do it but I doubt if I can be hypnotized."

"Why is that?"

"Because I'm so analytical," I said. "I think I'd keep trying to analyze the process instead of surrendering to it." Like many who had childhood abuse, I was hypervigilant. Also, conditions in Terry's office were not supportive of settling down. The chair was uncomfortable and, with the thin walls, I worried; what if I screamed? I was afraid of embarrassing us both. No surprise that it didn't work. Shortly thereafter, Terry retired. Not long afterward I learned from 23andme that DNA showed that I was unlikely to be hypnotizable. I still regret being unable to find out more but at this late date, it would serve no real purpose except to satisfy curiosity.

***

In 2013, I discovered MUFON, the Mutual UFO Network. MUFON is the largest of several organizations that attempt to deal factually with UFO/ET questions. When I found out they had Field Investigator training, I was eager to take the course. After learning that there was already a local investigator (who happened to be another TMer), I called him.

"I think you're wasting your time, "he said on the phone. "I haven't been assigned a case in over a year." (This surprised me. Besides my own sighting, I'd heard stories of others in the vicinity. I was to learn later that MUFON only investigates cases that are formally reported to it.

"Have you had some experience with ETs?" I asked, eager to think at long last I had someone rational to talk to.

"No," he said, "I've never seen a UFO or been abducted."

"Then how did you get interested?"

"Do you recall the Trent photo," he asked, "the one where you can see the edge of a farmhouse?

"Yeah," I said, thinking it was probably the one taken in McMinnville, Oregon in the 50s, a round-flat-topped style craft. Mrs. Trent had been checking her chickens when she saw it, then her husband snapped two of the best photographs in ufology history. Most UFO photographs are of a blurry object with nothing but sky around it. In these photos the object was not only clear, it had the farmhouse and electric lines in it to give perspective for size and location and to provide details nearly impossible to hoax. No one has disproved its authenticity.

"That's the one," he said. "I saw that photo in a man's magazine—*True* or *Argosy*—when I was seven. I was amazed to think there were people, or beings, from other planets that we'd never met. It fascinated me ever since."

I'll call him Keys. His search since childhood without the reward of direct experience reminded me of the unnamed government agent in the movie E.T. (FYI, a Rotten Tomato's survey ranked E.T. as the greatest science fiction movie ever made. In 1994, it was selected to be preserved in the U.S. National Film Registry.) Early in the movie, we see a man only from the waist down, with keys clipped to his belt, searching for the ET. We don't see his face until the second half when he and Elliot are trying to find the missing ET.

Keys: Elliot, that machine, what does it do?

Elliot: The communicator? Is it still working?

Keys: It's doing 'something'. What?

Elliot: I really shouldn't tell. He came to me, he came to me.

Keys: He came to me too. I've been wishing for this since I was 10 years old, I don't want him to die.

But unlike the warm and promising Peter Coyote, who played Keys in E.T., this Keys was closer in character to that cantankerous critic, Phillip Klass.

He agreed to meet with me at the MIU cafeteria. He was a few years younger than me and, following nature's unkind rule that says aging women only look older while aging men look more distinguished, he was handsome, casually but neatly dressed. Like other long-time TMers, he was clear-eyed and intelligent. It was hard to talk in a cafeteria over the clatter of lunch trays and conversation among hundreds of students. With a ridiculously presumptuous trust that he would understand, I boldly half-shouted Tom's tale that I was a half-and-half alien who needed to stop an interplanetary war and Luke's story about the ETs who shared his mind. Too late, I realized my story was bouncing off a wall of cold skepticism. He fidgeted, then interrupted. "I don't see that this is getting anywhere." Judging by his facial expression and the set of his mouth, he thought I was a kook.

"I try to keep an open mind," he drawled with barely disguised dismissal, "but some people see aliens behind every tree. Those guys [referring to Tom and Luke] were just yanking your chain." He looked at his watch. "I have to leave. Is there anything else?"

Embarrassed prickles burned at the edges of my face. Wasn't this exactly what I thought would happen if I tried to tell anyone my story, that they would just think I was a dingbat? He hadn't even heard the part where I discovered that I'd probably been abducted, but my guess was, he wouldn't believe that either.

Struggling for dignity, I blathered what was to me the pièce de résistance. "It wasn't that I believed Tom's story but that there was this ring of truth." But it was obvious that he wasn't hearing any ring of truth about my story, only silliness. He fidgeted, glanced at the exit, and glanced at me again. "You still haven't given me any actual information," he said.

As happens when we find ourselves disapproved of, I suddenly couldn't make complete sentences. "The one thing that kept me from believing...well, you see, I ranked pretty high on the PAS [Post

Abduction Scale] …but as you and I already agreed on the phone, those symptoms are too general to be proof of anything…and, well, what was real 'proof' was missing time, and one day I remembered I did have missing time. That was the day of work I missed when I met with Luke, the guy in Iceland who said he was sharing his mind with an ET and…"

His eyes didn't exactly roll, but close. His eyebrows flicked upward as if with long-suffering disbelief, and almost shrugged. He stood up. "I don't think there's anything I can do to help you," he said.

Help me? Did he think I was here as a MUFON client? "It isn't my story I need help with," I blurted. "I just need to pick your brain about MUFON, about what you do, about your experiences as a field investigator."

"I'll be happy to give you that. But like I said, I have another appointment."

He made it sound like he had a lineup of waiting dignitaries. My guess was that it was an excuse to extract himself from someone he saw as a nutcase.

"Could you come to my house where I have the computer to take notes?"

"I can do that."

"Before you go," I said, grasping at straws. "What did you make of my story?"

He looked down at me. "You want the truth?"

I nodded, almost certain that I wouldn't like what he was going to say.

He shrugged. "Fifty-fifty," he said, turning and walking away, leaving me sliding into an emotional pit where I was going to drown in his scorn.

Was this karmic payback? I'd never treated Tom with as much dismissive disdain as Keys had shown towards me but was this how Tom felt when I'd been suspicious of almost everything he said? Had he felt this belittled? If so, I was very, very sorry.

***

Besides chaffing over being only half-believed, I hadn't realized how deeply I'd been longing for an *Oppa*, a brother, a sidekick, a knowledgeable go-to guy who had answers, to solve cases together. But I'd ignored all the clues about him until they flashed through my internal lens the way a drowning person sees their life flash before their eyes. Even on the telephone, he'd been skeptical, more ready to find fault than feel compassion. The psychological twists and turns of my story had been of no interest to him. He was a just-the-facts-ma'am type. He wanted dates, times, footprints, radioactivity: hard data.

Regardless that he found me ridiculous, as the first live human that I'd engaged with outside of a therapeutic office, I hungered to learn more.

"What does a MUFON field investigator do?" I asked when he came to my house days later.

Grinning, he cocked a foot over his knee and put one hand on his ankle, hanging his other arm over the sofa like he owned the room. His self-assuredness rankled.

"An investigator talks to people who claim to have seen something abnormal," he said. "We're trained to listen to their story and look for evidence using forensic techniques. Then we use precise terms to do formal reporting accordingly."

Keys seemed less like a listener and more like a sarcastic cop, but his interest in ufology appeared genuine.

"How does one get to be an investigator?"

"MUFON gives you a manual. I found it to be quite thorough.

Then, if you pass the test, they make you an investigator."

"Are you allowed to talk about any of your cases?" I asked.

"Sure," he said, "I just can't disclose identifying information. The most interesting case I had was a cattle mutilation in southeast South Dakota in the Mennonite territory."

"South Dakota is a long way from Fairfield. Why did they send you there?"

"I was the closest available investigator that day," he said.

His told the story in precise details. "About 200 yards from the farmhouse—a ranch style place, maybe three bedrooms—there were two burn rings. These were about nine inches thick on either side of a circle about twelve feet in diameter where all the vegetation had died. Past this, another 50 to 80 yards away, there was a dead bull. You could see it had been dropped out of the sky. It had fallen across a barbed wire fence with the head on one side and the tail on the other, with the fence mashed straight down. The ground around it was dry and hard so I couldn't see any footprints, but if you're familiar with these things you know that even when there's snow or mud, there are no footprints anyway, not even an animal's. There was nothing on the ground except some saliva—all the blood had been drained out of him before they dropped him." Keys' intellectual scrutiny was pin-prick sharp.

He was just getting warmed up. In his enthusiasm, he unwound his leg and leaned forward, elbows on his knees. "Now here's the part that really dramatizes the situation," he chuckled. "Before I got there, the farmer had called in the vet. According to the farmer, the vet was really spooked. The guy just started backing up saying, 'Whoever did that had really sharp instruments.' And then he left. Didn't want any part of it. Then the farmer called MUFON. That was how I got involved. When I got there..." Keys paused, looking at me through squinting eyes, looking uncertain. "I don't know how squeamish you are..."

Having read about cattle mutilations, I suspected his hesitation was because the explanation was going to include unsettling, gory details. When I first read about the mutilation of cattle, horses, sheep, and goats, even occasional dogs, rabbits, elk, and deer, I had indeed been unsettled. It included precise and bloodless surgical removal of the genitals, eyes, ears, lips, and sometimes the heart and other internal organs.

"It's all right," I said, wanting to hear the story no matter how awful it was. "Continue, please."

Now that he had the go-ahead to speak, the words came out as if he'd been dying to tell someone. "The bull's lips had been cut off so you could see all its teeth. It was missing one ear and an eyeball. The testicles were gone and the skin on the penis was pulled back all the way to the stomach—all this without a cut mark anywhere. The anus had been cored out almost a foot deep in a perfect funnel shape."

Keys shook his head in the slow way people do when trying to digest disturbing events. "I'd read about it many times, but to see it, it really hit home." I understood what he meant. The "hit home" had happened to me many times during my ufology explorations, particularly the big culture shock when I fully realized, *they are here.* Reality has the power to be sobering.

He was silent for a few seconds like he was reliving the moment. Then almost to himself, he said, "The farmer hadn't heard a thing, no noise at all."

"Did anyone attribute it to UFOs?" I asked. In in the documentary, *A Strange Harvest,* Colorado Deputy Sheriff Millwall told investigator Linda Moulton Howe, "whenever you see those fiery orange balls [in the sky] then you are going to have animal mutilation." Evidence of UFOs has been found near some mutilations such as indentations into the ground that look like landing pads, exhaust marks, and sometimes radioactivity. American counterintelligence had told Howe, "We've made it clear—we don't want UFOs and animal mutilations connected in the public mind. Now lay off!" She didn't comply, meaning that today good data is available to researchers. Even so, animal cases are still not understood.

In answer to my question, Keys nodded. "It's been suggested that ETs use blood as a food source and there had been sightings a day or two before. Also, someone claimed to have seen an unmarked black military-style helicopter hovering low over another person's house. Those helicopters are often associated with UFOs, though I'm fairly certain those are US military."

Reports of mutilations go back as far as the 1700s. The first in modern times was on a horse in Colorado in 1967, with the rest following the same pattern. In the beginning, they happened primarily in the Western U.S. Over time, the range increased to 40 U.S. states, South American countries, and Great Britain. The British animals are usually sheep, with the added feature of a triangular cut over the head. The bull Keys investigated was typical. Appearing to have been dropped from such a height that it left an impact crater; the carcass was entirely bloodless. All the blood had been drained out of it before it was dropped. Most of the bones were broken from the fall. Just as in the horse's case, pathologist reports often find the brain and internal organs missing—with no cut for surgical entry. Where the heart had been removed, the pericardium—the casing around the heart—is in perfect condition, with no cuts at all. Where even skilled human surgery leaves imperfect lines, tears, knife marks, or signs of sawing motions, the wounds in mutilations appear cauterized by intense heat.

It was insulting to intelligence that, after finding the first horse, the Condon people claimed these abnormalities resulted from blow flies, cult activity, or savaging by predators. Anyone who has ever come across an animal brought down by predators knows they don't leave bloodless precision cuts. Predators rip skin, muscles, and internal organs, creating a ragged mess of blood, hair, muscle, and bones. Despite the offer of free lunch in the winter when starvation is a constant threat, predators won't touch mutilated victims. Cultists would have had no better instruments than a vet. And blowflies? Don't be ridiculous.

Keys shifted his position again, crossing his arms across his chest in what I interpreted as a self-defensive posture, not against me but the disturbing memory. "The farmers told me they'd bought armor-piercing rifle shells. I told them it wouldn't be wise to shoot at aliens."

Mirthlessly, we both chuckled, both aware of what the other was thinking, that we were in the grip of a great mystery. "I'd read about mutilations before," Keys said. "When you see a photo, you think, this is interesting, but when you see it for yourself…"

He trailed off, shaking his head slowly.

Once again, I saw who Keys was. My kind of story just would not cut it in his world. He wanted solid facts that lined up or, like in this story, gory details.

To escape the weight hanging in the room, I asked, "How many MUFON investigations have you done?"

"Oh, maybe a couple of dozen," he said. "They were all interesting, though not all of them were legitimate. I've seen a couple of crop circles and I've talked to others who have seen them. One was the President of the Iowa Corn Growers Association at the time. He said it was an oval about 90 by 60 feet. It happened in full-grown corn with tassels still in them. What was interesting was that all the stalks pointed toward the center, going between the rows, except the very outer rim where the stalks pushed outward. The plants were all still alive, still growing. None were damaged or broken.

"Here's another kicker. The guy said, 'The temperature was 90 degrees. I knew that if anyone was out playing pranks, they almost certainly would have some beer with them. But there was no trash, beer cans, or cigarette butts. I couldn't even find a footprint.'"

"As someone with such a public job title, he certainly wouldn't make up a story like that," I said.

"You're right there," Keys said, grinning. "I couldn't have asked for a better witness. But that wasn't even the best case. One of the best was a farmer that gave a presentation to MUFON on a crop circle done on a field of dry soybeans."

"Dry? You mean after they turned yellow?" I'd lived in Iowa long enough to know that dried soybeans are as fragile as spun glass.

"Yeah, yellow. When he found it, all the stalks were going in the same direction with none of them broken. He did business with Land O'Lakes—you know, the butter people?"

I nodded.

"He called them in to look at it. A dried soybean stalk snaps off easily but there wasn't any path at all into this crop circle. They had to break stalks to get out there to even examine it." The lack of paths meant that neither humans nor animals could have created that circle.

"There's more," Keys said. "The Land O'Lakes people did something unusual—they dug down and found that not only were all the stalks bent, but the tap roots as well. Tap roots should go straight down and in no other direction, but they were also bent. By human standards, it's just beyond the pale."

"It sounds like you do believe that some things are outside the norm," I said. "My impression of you over lunch was that you were more of a debunker than an investigator."

With no hint of apology, he grinned. "I admit I'm quick to judge, but skepticism is the natural quality of a clear mind. Maharishi said that faith is born from experience, but blind faith is born of ignorance. My job in life is to find the truth about everything."

It was something I might have said myself. It restored a little faith in him.

"So, overall, what do you believe?" I asked. "I mean, about UFOs and such."

"I really don't know what to think," he said. I've been investigating UFOs my whole life and all I find are a lot of conflicting stories. Some say the ETs are evil beings, others say they are highly developed beings here to help save the Earth—and everything in between."

I nodded. That was pretty much my experience. Of all disciplines of knowledge, the UFO/ET field must be the muddiest, with more conflicting stories and unresolved mysteries than exist even in religion.

"Have you met people who claim to have been abducted?"

"Oh, yeah. Several. Most of them are just nuts," he said.

I winced for the poor souls subjected to his scrutiny. "How can you tell the difference between the 'nuts' and the ones you believe to be legitimate?"

"The real ones want answers," he said. "Like here in Fairfield a year or two ago, I investigated a couple. They were smokers but who didn't want to smell up the house, so they'd open their garage door to sit and smoke and enjoy the evening. One night they saw four lights, round-shaped, all the same size, all in a row, 'like a string of pearls,' that's how they described them. They said it zigzagged, then shot straight up into the air like a meteor going backward. I talked to them separately and got the same story, and the awe and fear of the unknown in their voices was clear. They couldn't fit it into anything they have ever seen or known to exist, and they wanted answers." (Here was more evidence of the *tone* that characterized the reports I'd read.)

"The most interesting story happened when I was at an informal cookout with some MUFON members," he continued. "Someone brought some women who weren't members, and those women impressed me more than I'd ever been impressed with anybody involved with an abduction. It was a grandmother, her daughter, and a granddaughter. The grandmother was had sighting experiences, back in the 70s. She even brought an old, yellowed calendar with her to show us the dates she'd seen UFOs. She said it started when one night she got up to get a glass of water, looked out the kitchen window, and saw a strange light over the shed. 'A funny-looking thing,' she called it—round, with a glass bubble on top. In it, she met a being she called 'the Doctor' because he wore a white smock of some kind. She said she felt like she was in a dream, and the next thing she knows it was morning and she had no memory of going to bed.

"She was really backwoods," Keys said. "She used words like *chimbly* for chimney, and *wender* for window, uneducated like that, but not an ounce of guile I could detect. She told us about photos they had of a circle burned in the snow where a saucer had landed. When spring thaw came, she described how the grass under it stayed dead.

He chuckled and shook his head the way one does when marveling at something. "I really wanted to ask her a lot of questions but it was a party, not an investigation, so I just listened."

After a moment's silence, he said, "The daughter was a truck driver. She was as poorly educated as her mother, married to a classic hillbilly drunk who beat her, and she had no recollection of any experience at all.

"But where the two older women were grizzled and uneducated, the granddaughter, who couldn't have been more than twenty, was especially attractive, really eloquent. She had both memories of experiences and marks…" Keys touched alternate palms with index fingers… "triangle indentations and other marks. She was so different that I just kept thinking, 'Did those aliens do some tweaking in there?' But she had no memories of it. In the general population, most people don't know they've been abducted. It takes hypnosis to bring it out."

"I've read that 95 percent of sightings turn out to be something explainable. Has this been your experience in investigating them?"

"Pretty much," he said. "Something increasingly common is Chinese lanterns. You know what these are?"

I nodded. They were large paper bulbs with candles or some other light source inside that makes them rise into the air.

"I'd say this accounts for maybe a third of the calls we get now. Another common call we get is about iridium telecommunications satellites. Most satellites go in a west-to-east orbit but these iridium satellites go north-to-south and they have big solar panels. At certain points the sun reflects off some sections, sending a beam down to the Earth."

I decided against telling him about a UFO I'd seen recently while attending one of the monthly Art Walks in Fairfield with a friend, who saw it, too. It sped up the sky in a straight line from southeast to northwest, then blinked out. That was not the direction of any satellite orbit.

He continued. "Some things are a true mystery, but when I find ordinary answers, a percentage of people don't want to hear it—they want to cling to spaceships."

***

After passing the MUFON test in October 2013, I did a few interesting but unimportant investigations. These included a post office official who saw a light making high speed maneuvers at five in the morning. In another case, a woman described a hovering, transparent-appearing ship. My most interesting case was unofficial and was an example of Key's statement that some people see aliens behind every tree.

A Fairfield woman I'll call Mary told me I should check out the "UFO landing site" at a local park at the edge of town. Mary met me at the entrance then showed me two, nearly perfect, reddish brown circles, one about 70 feet across, the other about 30 feet.

"Do you want to know what I see?" Mary asked.

Preferring to be objective at this stage, I said, "Thanks, but I'd like to look for myself." Still, she persisted, telling me that locals "with intuitive abilities" claimed that ETs had made the circles. After investigating, my intuition said the opposite. Keys supported my opinion. When I emailed him about it later, he wrote, "I'd say their reactions are more from a romance about UFOs and aliens."

My perspective was that "nearly perfect" wasn't enough. Had an ET craft created them, the edges should have been crisp, not raggedy, like they were in this case. Also, the brown areas were not burned grass but some kind of twiggy vegetation. Theoretically, such scraggly stuff might be what would grow back if the ground was recovering from radiation but I wanted to talk to park officials before I concluded.

The Park CEO laughed. "Every time there is a drought, we get this UFO business," he said. "At one time, concrete waste treatment tanks were standing over those circles. After removing the tanks, the only vegetation that grows on that hard-packed ground turns that burned color when it dries out."

I was proud that I'd been objective enough to solve the case. But when I told Mary, she said, "Don't tell anyone about that. Let people believe."

A similar thing happened when I told this story at a MUFON meeting with the public. I told it with pride in my investigative skills but they attacked me for being "overly skeptical." Apparently, for every person who mistakenly dismisses UFOs as non-existent, there will be romantics who believe even when there is evidence to the contrary.

But what good does it do to criticize each other? We are all in this together, everyone from the scientists to the dingbats, all of us trying the best we can to understand this many-sided mystery.

***

After the first few years of research into ufology, my method was not so much to focus on fence-post style "proofs" in individual cases as it was to search for and try to understand the big picture. The big picture "clicked" into a coherent wholeness with two important pieces of information.

The first key solved the mystery of the cover-ups. By external appearances, it looks like the government has been responsible for UFO secrecy for the last 75 years. If that was true, it would have made the government an enemy of the people. However, the key evidence demonstrates that it isn't the government itself that is the culprit. If we "follow the money" using the testimonies from the *The Disclosure Project*, it indicates that the source of withholding is the military-industrial complex (MIC). The MIC gained power and profits by back-engineering ET technology then dispersing it into the economy though normal channels. In his exit speech in 1961, former President Dwight D. Eisenhower warned us about this. "In this the councils of government, we must guard against the acquisition of unwarranted influence, whether sought or unsought, by the military–industrial complex. The potential for the disastrous rise of misplaced power exists, and will persist."

The *Disclosure Project* contains the testimony of nearly a thousand people who worked in or otherwise witnessed what is happening in the MIC. I was dismayed to learn that by reverse-engineering ET technology, and by illegally using the nation's security classification system to ensure silence, the MIC has been building spacecraft that apparently can do anything that ET craft can. Ben Rich, the second CEO of Lockheed's Skunkworks, is often quoted as saying, "We already have the means to travel among the stars, but these technologies are locked up in black projects, and it would take an act of God to ever get them out to benefit humanity." I'm sure this will stretch your credulity as much as it did mine, but read (or watch) *Unacknowledged* to get it from the mouths of others.

Due to intense compartmentalization and the misuse of our secrecy classification system, cover-ups have happened without the awareness of most of our elected leaders. They are told it is "above your need to know." Even the President can't get information about UFOs/UAPs. This behind-the-scenes is what some people call the "deep state." When I learned of it, it made me sick but that story is too dark for this book. What's important to understand is that, as much as government can be trusted on any topic, our elected officials can be trusted when they say they know nothing (little play on words there) about UFOs/UAPs.

***

The second key insight I found is that ETs are "people," just like us. The essential difference between humans and animals is that animals can't become fully enlightened, but humans can. Likewise, even though ETs look different (and, in some cases, may look like animals) they are spiritual beings who, the same as humans, have the ability to become enlightened, i.e., fully developed to the highest potential of consciousness, all the way to higher states (dimensions) of consciousness. Not all ETs are enlightened but they are nonetheless much more highly evolved than humans. We need to accept that we have a responsibility to catch up. The more we develop our human potential, the more we will understand who they are and what they do.

Some readers will cry for "proof" of what I write but this is a memoir. My job is tell you what I found. In the Western hemisphere we typically insist on "proof" because we believe that reality is something that exists *outside* of ourselves, and we believe that science can cut through the fog of ignorance to uncover this supposed reality. As far back as a century ago, however, quantum physicists discovered that what lies at the basis of the physical world is *consciousness*. Max Planck said, "I regard consciousness as fundamental. I regard matter as derivative from consciousness... Everything we talk about, everything that we regard as existing, expostulates consciousness."

Many people demand "proof" of UFOs and ETs, but what they demand is what I call fence-post reality. Concrete things exist on the fence-post Newtonian level but neither consciousness nor ETs can be understood from that viewpoint. That view is too small, too fixed.

For instance, anyone with an awakened consciousness finds that knowledge exists that is both larger and fuller than what the intellect or science can fully grasp. Studies demonstrate the benefits of expanded consciousness but the only meaningful *proof* of this larger framework is direct experience. This is not to degrade Newtonian physics nor to degrade the value of proof. It is only to say that proof is a thing of the intellect, merely a dry and limited aspect of one method of knowledge, dependent on the senses, mathematics, and what one is willing to accept as proof. It is not the end-all be-all of life. Likewise, demanding proof of the existence of ETs is like school children demanding to understand adult perspectives. Children can rote-learn information about adulthood but until their biochemistry changes into an adult form, they cannot understand the reality. If we are to understand beings from other planets or other dimensions, *then we must rise to those dimensions.* We must ask better questions. To know how to ask better questions, we must awaken our own consciousness. (Research says the easiest, safest, and most effective method to awaken consciousness is Transcendental Meditation. WWW.TM.org)

***

I no longer think I am a dingbat, though I know some will see me that way. In the end, you will have to find out for yourself but the big-picture evidence I've seen is that ETs are benign. Our own history has been filled with war, greed, and lust for power so it is only natural that we expect that other beings would be here to dominate and take what we have. But their consciousness is more like bigger siblings who take care of their less developed family members. We tend to dislike and fear the unknown but the changes they would bring would be to our benefit. With advanced knowledge they could show us how to eliminate starvation and poverty, improve agriculture, develop free energy, and save the planet from our human-made climate crises. If they were here to take over our planet, wouldn't you think they would have done so many years before we developed the technology to shoot down their crafts? Wise people avoid such primitive emotions as fear, anger, and violence. I consider it tragic that it is the Pentagon that is introducing the existence of ETs. The job of the Pentagon is war, meaning they can be expected to focus on the worst possible slant, and I suspect that even the Pentagon is being manipulated by the MIC. Those who should be informing the public about the existence of our interplanetary and interdimensional neighbors should be the anthropologists, psychologists, sociologists, philosophers, and professional diplomats who can help us get past the fear of strangeness to ease us into peaceful coexistence.

I don't always know what to make of Steven Greer but I fully believe in his motto, *One Universe, One People*. We—and *they*—are all in this together. I also believe what Greer teachers, that each of us, in our own way, using whatever talents we have, have a responsibility to become diplomats. A diplomat is someone more ready to be welcoming than hostile, more ready to call for peace rather than war, more willing to cooperate than to be divisive. A diplomat is willing to endure strangeness until it becomes familiar, and is willing to be a go-between the new and the old. A diplomat is willing to forgive those who have brought abuse in our more ignorant past, willing to see beyond those trying to make ETs appear like threats in the present, while maintaining the calm and courage to work for peace for the future. It isn't what is on the news that matters—it is who we are in our hearts that determines the future. Choose what is highest. Do what you know to be right.

Globally, this is possibly the most momentous time in Earth's history. It is a time of awakening on multiple levels. Awakening to ETs is sign of our transcendence into a vastly larger paradigm of reality. Shouldn't the appropriate attitude toward this adventure not be one of fear but cautious curiosity, the way someone crossing a river on rocks is careful where he puts his feet while remaining interested in exploring what lies ahead? Are you ready to meet them? Are you developed enough to step into this new future? Doesn't it make you feel eager to see how much more there is yet to discover?

The End

ACKNOWLEDGEMENTS

A writer never succeeds alone—it absolutely takes a village to create a book. Here are a few from my village, without whom this book could not have been written.

Jared Morrison In a lull of confidence, I gave up and sold my UFO books on eBay to Jared, an investigation reviewer from Huntington, West Virginia. As a form of provenance for his new library, he asked me to send a letter stating who I was and why I had gotten into ufology. As the story was too complicated for a letter, I had to finish the book. Thanks for the motivation, Jared.

Tom Banks With mixed feelings of resentment and gratitude, I thank Tom (not his real name, of course). Messengers come in all forms, even if we can't make sense of them at the time.

Unity of Sebring What a joy. The Bible says, "You shall know them by their love," and indeed, I knew them by their love at Unity. Reverend Andy, Joanne, Mr. Butler, and most of the people I knew then have passed on to the next reality but they were strongholds of love and inspiration then, and remain so in my heart to this day.

Glen Singley, a fellow explorer of this grand mystery who saved me from many errors. Everyone who writes a book should have such a friend.

Paula Hardin EDD, MMP, teacher of *A Course in Love*, and author of *What Are You Doing with the Rest of Your Life*. Without her precious support and encouragement, this book would never have been finished.

Rick Archer The host of *Buddha at the Gas Pump*, Thank you for taking time out of your busy schedule to read and advise me on this book.

Peter Gold, Psy.D. Peter listened to all my crazy ideas and encouraged me to keep writing. He's not responsible for the crazy ideas but he gets credit that I persisted.

Jim B. of Pittsburg, Kansas, was the first to teach me that communication didn't have to be win or lose.

Dayna Dunbar, co-author of *Awake: The Legend of Akara*, and Julia **Nadine Padawar,** were among the first to associate awakened consciousness with ETs in fiction. Thanks for your lovely book and for your advice and encouragement.

Malcolm. Thank you. To have found a thread in that mountain of words was impressive.

Suzanne Stryker, energy healer at Revealwisdom.com, for propelling me into finishing this book.

The **Transcendental Meditation program**, without which, had I survived at all, I would have ended up as a bartender.

Other authors and researchers I depended on countless researchers and authors who had the courage to write in times when ridicule was even more common than it is now, and far more dangerous. Special thanks to Joy Gilbert, author of *A Time to Remember*, and Jim Sparks, author of *The Keepers*. They are among my heroes.

**Telling the truth in a time of universal deceit is a
revolutionary act.** – George Orwell

J. Allen Hynek

Timothy Good

John E. Mack MD

Whitley Strieber

David M. Jacobs

Bud Hopkins

John G. Fuller

Jacques Vallee

Edward J. Ruppelt

Steven M. Greer, MD

Tom Carey,

& Don Schmitt

Donald Keyhoe

Stanton Freidman

William J. Byrnes

Richard J. Boyland Ph.D.

Randy Koppang

David M. Jacobs, Ph.d.

Dan Sherman

Erick Von Daniken

Robert Sheaffer

Richard M. Dolan

Bob Lazar

Jim Marrs

Linda Moulton Howe

Kathleen Marden

Stephen Basset

Patty Grier

Erick Hansen

Ron James

Leonard Stringfield

Dr. James McDonald

George Adamski

ABOUT THE AUTHOR

Glenda Pliler is a graduate of Maharishi International University and a former MUFON Field Investigator. She now lives in a retirement home in Florida where she facilitates a UFO/UAP club for seniors and is working on her next book.